Under Construction
THE BODY IN SPANISH NOVELS

Under Construction
THE BODY IN SPANISH NOVELS

Elizabeth A. Scarlett

UNIVERSITY PRESS OF VIRGINIA

Charlottesville and London

This is a title in the series
Feminist Issues: Practice, Politics, Theory

The University Press of Virginia
Copyright © 1994 by the Rector and Visitors
of the University of Virginia

First published 1994

Library of Congress Cataloging-in-Publication Data

Scarlett, Elizabeth A.
  Under construction : the body in Spanish novels / Elizabeth A.
Scarlett
    p. cm.
  Includes bibliographical references and index.
  ISBN 0–8139–1532–5
    1. Spanish fiction—Women authors—History and criticism.
2. Spanish fiction—20th century—History and criticism. 3. Spanish
fiction—19th century—History and criticism. 4. Catalan fiction—
Women authors—History and criticism. 5. Pardo Bazán, Emilia,
condesa de, 1852–1921—Criticism and interpretation. 6. Chacel,
Rosa, 1898– —Criticism and interpretation. 7. Rodoreda, Mercè,
1908– —Criticism and interpretation. 8. Mind and body in
literature. 9. Body, Human, in literature. 10. Women in
literature. I. Title.
PQ6055.S26 1994
863'.620936—dc20   94–21028
                                                          cip

Printed in the United States of America

For my parents
and in memory of my grandmother
Rita Lavinia Hogan

Contents

Contents

Acknowledgments

T HE BODY OF this text developed in many phases, some of sudden growth and others of relative dormancy. In the early stages the guidance and inspiration of Luis Fernández Cifuentes and Susan Rubin Suleiman were essential. Noël Valis stepped in to provide further advice and signal new directions. As the work continued to take shape, my colleagues and editors at the University of Virginia were helpful and supportive—especially Donald Shaw, Alison Weber, Alison Booth, and Javier Herrero, all of whom generously commented on parts or all of the manuscript.

Many ideas incorporated into this book have resulted directly or indirectly from discussions with friends over the past few years. Joseph Schraibman edified me each step of the way with the multiple perspectives of a humorist and a realist. Laura E. Pérez was as much an accomplice as an interlocutor, and Bernal Herrera's irreverent temerity led me to challenge old assumptions. Emilie Bergmann, Carol Maier, Carlos Jerez-Farrán, and Jaume Martí-Olivella shared with me their enthusiasm and insights concerning the writers I chose to study.

It would have been difficult to sustain the effort required to finish this book without the kindness of my friends. My warm thanks to Roya Marefat, Martha Tappen and Gregory Laden, Maryam Saedvhafa, Paul Brodwin, Ivy Arbulú, Jorge Secada, Craig Jennings, Tsomato Kono, Diana Guemárez, Ajay Mohan, and Eduardo Espina. The hours spent talking with and listening to students have also fostered my desire to contribute to the study of embodiment in literature. I am especially thankful for a few crucial conversations on the Lawn with Kristen Nickel and for the light that was always on (indicating a door soon to be opened) at Alyce Cook's. No one has been more helpful than one of the subjects of this study, Antonio Muñoz Molina, who listened and agreed or disagreed with equal candor. And I owe more than gratitude, in the aftermath of it all, to David E. Wagner.

My thanks to Joanne Allen for smoothing remaining roughnesses from the manuscript with admirable skill. I am also indebted to David Haberly, whose computer expertise saved large pieces of the manuscript from electronic limbo. Samuel Amell granted permission to include a revision of a previously published piece: the first section of chapter 2 originally appeared as "Rosa Chacel, José Ortega y Gasset, and Bodily Discourse" in *España Contemporánea* 5 (spring 1992): 21–39.

Note on Language

I use Spanish words or phrases where they convey what needs to be said more richly than their English equivalents, and I supply definitions for the non-Spanish speaker unless there are reliable cognates. I also attempt as far as possible to explain terms that relate to specific Spanish literary movements or events in order to make them comprehensible to the uninitiated without taxing those already knowledgeable in the field.

Under Construction

THE BODY IN SPANISH NOVELS

Introduction

Pain comes from the darkness. And we call it wisdom.
It is pain.

                    —Randall Jarrell

IN THE WESTERN LITERARY TRADITION, no question has been more
fundamental or more consistently debated than the relation between the Ideal and the Real, or the spiritual and the material. Often
the opposing sides of this dichotomy are represented as mind and
body. The Christian context from St. Paul onward pits the lowly
drives of the body, its enslavement to physical conditions and mor-
tality, against the intangible superiority of the spirit, while the post-
Freudian, post-Nietzschean age posits the mind, with its internalized
discipline, as a shackle upon the fulfillment of carnal desires. In
representations of women the body often overshadows the mind, so
that women become incarnations of the physical. Moreover—as
Simone de Beauvoir observed—in a male-oriented culture, Woman is
associated with all things noncultural. In recent years the human
body has been a point of reference for a large corpus of literary and
cultural criticism and theory. This new materialism has the advantage
of being grounded in our most immediate experience of reality. At the
same time, it does not suffer the limitations of being an entirely
materialist perspective, for much of this writing follows the example of Michel Foucault in viewing the body as both a biological and
a political-historical construct. Feminist analysis has also followed
Beauvoir's practice in treating the body, not as a thing, but as a
"situation," thereby unraveling the binary opposition that placed the
body on a lower rung.[1] Political anatomy, the analysis of the interactions between power configurations from without and the desiring

subject located in the individual body, replaces the narrower poetics of the body that in the past has been a part of humanities discourse. Another benefit of this critical current is that it seldom equates *human* with *male,* for this area of study puts gender difference constantly in play, forming the basis for some of the most provocative findings.

During the time spent composing this text I had to squirrel myself away for long periods and apologize for abandoning the social get-togethers I otherwise enjoy. Tired of telling people I was busy writing, I looked for a new synonym each time. The physical nature of most of these writing euphemisms—concerning the need to put pen to paper, to turn on the Mac, and so on—drove home for me the centrality of writing as material manifestation of thought, as the most nearly perfect union of physical and mental spheres. This helped to illuminate what underlies the current fascination with the way the body finds representation or becomes inscribed in literature. Since writing itself makes one conscious of the intersections between body and mind, embodiment in fiction (the degree to which characters inhabit textual bodies and the sensations attributed to them) is always an essential constituent of meaning. Even its relative absence in a "disembodied" text is equally telling. The solitude my apologies afforded me made me aware of another intersection between physicality and textuality, especially since, as fate or the vicissitudes of my affective life would have it, I lived alone. Sitting down to write does more than isolate a person: it forces one to be alone with that most intractable significant other, the physical self. What I may have planned as an evening with me, myself, and I turned into me, my body, and the body of my text. In time, the books I consulted piled up around us like old friends. Alone but somehow accompanied by the growing profusion of bodies in these texts, I found the solitude of writing more enjoyable.

Modern Spanish literature is fertile terrain for the exploration of the body as textual marker. As Fanny Rubio has stated of this canon, "All characters in novels, from *La Celestina* onward, are the result of a tension between their roles as characters and their bodies in a direct relationship with the world."[2] Before beginning to read the criticism that has sprung up surrounding this canon, I had a seemingly spontaneous interest in depictions of the body, and particularly of the female body, found in Spanish novels I had read in college. Perhaps this interest was sparked in me because, like the authors in question, I come from a Roman Catholic (though Irish-American rather than Spanish) heritage. Like the writers I analyze, especially the female ones, I have had to wrestle with a tradition that alternately exalts and excludes women, one that relies upon embodiment more unabashedly and more problematically than any other religion I can think of. It starts, of course, with the centrality of the Virgin and Mother combined in one body. Now the parish church of my childhood in Brooklyn has modernized its décor with brighter lights and an austere wood carving of Christ on the Cross above the midpoint of the altar. But back when I attended the parish grammar school, my schoolmates and I would sit inside a dark and cavernous structure where the main icon was a softly lit Murillo Virgin, her flowing gown exposing only her head, hands, and one foot (crushing a horn symbolizing the Devil). It now strikes me as no surprise that one day, after what seemed like hours of prayer, my classmate Christine Monteleone became convinced that she had seen Mary's hand move and did everything an eight-year-old girl could do to publicize her personal miracle. We all grew up with this sense of a personal miracle, incorporating it into our own bodily perceptions. If on the one hand it made us feel somehow special, on the other hand it meant that something mysterious and beyond our control inhabited us. Later I found it impossible to reconcile the many contradictions regarding women in Catholicism with what I knew to be true about my physical self and, above all, with my hopes and dreams. I left the church, but I knew that I could not erase what it had ingrained in me. When a contemporary American novelist of Catholic background, Mary Gordon, states her wish to write to explore female desire and "what it's like to live in a female body," I recognize at once the impulse behind my curiosity regarding embodiment in the Spanish novel and, in turn, the motivation behind the women writers I found inscribing the female form in new ways.[3]

Scholars and critics find great satisfaction in revealing a topic previously hidden from view so that it strikes the reader with the immediate impact of something that always needed illumination. However, given the profound relevance of physical inscription to Spanish fiction, several Hispanists have published pioneering studies in fields contiguous to mine: Paul Julian Smith's *Body Hispanic* (1989) fruitfully pairs writers of Spain and Latin America with specific theorists; Malcolm Read's *Visions of Exile* (1990) explores the body as subject in Golden Age literature and language; Nina Molinaro's *Foucault, Feminism, and Power: Reading Esther Tusquets* (1991) reveals Lacanian and Foucauldian threads in the work of this contemporary novelist; Mary Gossy's *Untold Story: Women and Theory in Golden Age Texts* (1989) backs up surprising conclusions on subversive subtexts in *La Celestina* with the weight of bodily writing; and a germinal article by Elizabeth Ordóñez, "Inscribing Difference: 'L'Écriture Féminine' and New Narrative by Women," suggests the primacy of a new mythology of the female body in recent novels by Spanish women. Having learned from their distinct approaches, I have fashioned my own mode of analysis and brought it to bear upon a series of notable Spanish novels that chart a definite progression in the evolution of physical inscription from roughly one hundred years ago to the present. In the process, I have found that a particular kind of literary history emerges from examining common strands and new developments over time and among various authors, both male and female. The chapters of political anatomy extracted from the chosen works coalesce into a history of the mind-body connection in the Spanish novel from realism of the late nineteenth century to the present, albeit passing over some very significant works because of the selective nature of the study. In selecting the novels, I have been guided by an interest in new developments in casting the body as protagonist against social subjection. These developments often, though not always, coincide with a special place in the Hispanic canon. For example, it is no accident that both *Memorias de Leticia Valle* and *La familia de Pascual Duarte* protagonize the body in astonishing new ways and that both are seen as crucial texts of Spanish postwar fiction, the first in exile, the second under the Franco regime. Often the innovation in political anatomy is a main aspect that sets the work apart from the rest.

The evolution of embodiment has gone through periods of relative dormancy, and this accounts for some of the more conspicuous omissions of literary movements or individual authors. This manner of passing from one text to another in search of an ideological or stylistic current has already proven useful in valuable studies of about the same literary period: Jo Labanyi does an admirable job of tracing demythification in *Myth and History in the Spanish Contemporary Novel* (1989), as does Silvia Burunat in examining the technique of interior monologue in *El monólogo interior como forma narrativa en la novela española* (1980).

Hence, physical inscription served as a barometer for examining a group of factors at work in the writing of novels: narrative strategies, social and psychological configurations, and, not least of all, gender differences in perspective. While I do not subscribe to set definitions of *feminine writing* or even of *feminine sensibility,* I find that the *corporeísta* approach reveals significant tendencies in constructing the body with words; these tendencies prevail in one gender or the other, and often one gender responds to its representation by the other. In a study of English and French narratives, Peter Brooks helps to define the crisscross of meanings between bodies and the texts they inhabit: "Along with the semioticization of the body goes what we might call the somatization of the story: the implicit claim that the body is a key sign in narrative and a central nexus of narrative meanings."[4] Like Brooks, I have often found the erotic body to be the most highly charged, the one inclined to speak for the text and move the story along. However, Brooks concentrates on the myth of privacy arising from the European Enlightenment and its subsequent undoing by literary voyeurism. For Spanish literature the concept of *pudor* (a blend of modesty and shame) is more essential than that of privacy (for which there is no exact Spanish equivalent), especially regarding the female body. If one combines this with the relative lack of consequence that the Spanish Enlightenment left in its wake, one begins to see why the Spanish body, though equally semioticized, and its accompanying story, though equally somaticized, will be quite different from what Brooks revealed concerning the literatures of Spain's neighbors. The more enduring sway of Catholicism as dominant ideology, or as the normative one against which new strains take shape, accounts for much of the distinctiveness. Nevertheless, it is important not to take Catholicism, whether as ideology or institution, as a monolithic structure, but as a shifting configuration of knowledge and power. The texts themselves should work to trace some of the transformations.

An analysis along these lines of selected major women writers of

Spain from Emilia Pardo Bazán to the present raises questions that need to be addressed (and answers some of them). While it is true that many modern women writers of great merit have yet to be admitted to the canon, I found that existing criticism of even the canonical ones, such as Emilia Pardo Bazán, Rosa Chacel, and Mercè Rodoreda, had yet to take note of the difference, often relating to the female body and its inscription in the text, that makes reading these authors especially meaningful for me and other contemporary readers. Furthermore, these differences constitute innovations in the practice of embodiment, for, as I hope to demonstrate, elements of them cross over into men's writing, probably not as a result of conventional literary influence but as a response to the very transformations in gender roles that women's voices have helped to set in motion.

A number of valuable monographic studies of some of these novelists furnished points of departure for the present study, as did four books recently published in the field of feminist Hispanist literary criticism: Elizabeth Ordóñez's *Voices of Their Own* (1991), Geraldine C. Nichols's *Des/cifrar la diferencia* (1992), and collections edited by Joan L. Brown (*Women Writers of Contemporary Spain*, 1991) and Noël Valis and Carol Maier (*In the Feminine Mode*, 1990).[5] As the study progressed chronologically into even less explored critical terrain, I found that male authors ceased to form a background against which the vividness of the mind-body configurations in the work of female authors could be measured. Now male peers entered the focus alongside the more contemporary women writers, such as Carmen Martín Gaite, Adelaida García Morales, and Soledad Puértolas. It became evident that although some marked gender tendencies persisted, a rapprochement was developing in the construction of the body across genders, a point that is addressed here in chapters 4 and 5, on the novel during and after dictatorship. Both genders now tend to vitalize and protagonize the body as experience, or *vivencia,* to bring the forces of social subjection to the very surface of the text, and to illustrate the interconnectedness of textual bodies.

The writing of Emilia Pardo Bazán, an openly feminist novelist and essayist of the late nineteenth century, constituted the natural place to begin in the quest for bodies that produce meaning in a style that continues into the present. Her novel of sexual awakening,

Insolación, was also the logical text to bring into focus, representing as it does a *Fear of Flying* in a discreetly bourgeois realist context. After Pardo Bazán, the next novelist I found to embody the struggle of female subjectivity encased in the female body was Rosa Chacel, whose productive conflicts are traced from her vanguardist period, represented by *Estación: Ida y vuelta,* through *Teresa, Memorias de Leticia Valle, La sinrazón,* and the first dialogic novel of her memoirlike trilogy, *Barrio de Maravillas.* From Chacel we go to another writer known mainly for her work in exile, the Catalan Mercè Rodoreda. Her first three postwar novels are *novelas de protagonista,* following the interior monologue of an otherwise self-effacing narrator who is suddenly invested with the power of speech as if by means of some refreshing outburst. *La Plaça de Diamant, El carrer de les Camèlies,* and *Jardí vora el mar* lead to her cross-generational novel *Mirall trencat.* They employ similar codes in the reconquest and remythification of inner feminine space. Chapter 4, on novels written during the dictatorship of Franco, gives equal weight to Camilo José Cela's *La familia de Pascual Duarte,* Carmen Martín Gaite's *Entre visillos,* and Luis Martín-Santos's *Tiempo de silencio.* The fact of writing under subjection to authoritarian rule appears to draw male and female novelists closer in their protagonization of bodies under restraint. Finally, in discussing "new novelists" of the past decade I have found ample cause to pair male and female novelists according to their preferences for escape and conspiracy plots. My focus is on Adelaida García Morales's *El silencio de las sirenas* read alongside Julio Llamazares's *Luna de lobos* and on Soledad Puértolas's *Queda la noche* alongside Antonio Muñoz Molina's *Beltenebros.* The theoretical writings of Gilles Deleuze and Félix Guattari provided the most adequate analogies for the distinctly postmodern bodies and the ways in which they wander, escape, and mutate in these four engrossing novels. All told, these chapters in political anatomy encompass one hundred years, from 1889 to 1989.

Regarding the three precontemporary female authors—Emilia Pardo Bazán, Rosa Chacel, and Mercè Rodoreda—at least three points of intersection between feminine physicality and textuality began to stand out in most of the novels I chose to study. One is the prevalence of the body-as-text, in which bodily markings or movements take on the significance of writing, or the body appears to "speak" textually, as if in dialogue with the narrator or with other characters. Related to this is an empowerment of the female body, through which the body becomes a speaking subject or is imbued with a vitality or creative capacity that often draws upon maternal metaphors. Maternality also appears as a determinant in representations of mature love of every kind, developing a meaningful parallel to the popular romance, or *novela rosa*. The body-as-text contrasts with the gap often constituted by the figure Woman in writing by men. The third, often consequential, phenomenon is a dissolution of mind/body dualism, a dichotomy that pervades patriarchal discourse from Plato through the patriarchs of the early Catholic Church and beyond, ubiquitously privileging the intangible over the material. The writers studied here tend to break through the barrier separating mind and body and to dissolve it, revealing it as at bottom a fiction itself. To this aim, they use the body as another form of language, as a communicative organ that can function on the levels of signifier and signified, much as Terry Eagleton has found the Christian liturgy to do.[6] Where women writers are concerned, instead of the mystical body of Christ, it is the female form that assumes a central role. This has led Patricia M. Spacks to suggest, referring to women writing in English, that their ultimate goal was the restoration of a female divinity that was denied in patriarchal culture.[7] The tendency of male writers, on the other hand, is also to imbue the female form with a more than material significance, but by means of a parcelization of the whole and an ensuing fetishization of components that estranges parts from the totality and body from psyche.[8] This fragmentation of the figure of Woman is distinctly avoided or parodied in writing by women.

The harnessing of bodily sexual energy that places the human body at the service of continuously shifting power structures—a channeling rather than a total repression—has been traced by Foucault to roots in the eighteenth century, when sex became "a 'police' matter—in the full and strict sense given the term at the time: not the repression of disorder, but an ordered maximization of collective and individual forces." The policing was carried out through "useful and public discourses" that continued to evolve during the nineteenth century—medicine, psychiatry, criminology, and others. "Were these anything more," Foucault asks, "than means employed to absorb, for the benefit of a genitally centered sexuality, all the fruitless pleasures?"[9]

Another type of discourse, Foucault might have added, although it proclaims itself to be a moral and often religious authority rather than a scientific and secular one, is the precept manual. These codes of feminine behavior articulated by precept manuals had been present in Spanish culture from the time of Luis de León's *La perfecta casada* (1583), but they assumed special importance and became more systematized in the latter part of the nineteenth century. At that time new editions of the old favorites abounded alongside new manuals such as *Guía de señoritas en el gran mundo*.[10] The Spanish woman novelist of modernity thus responds to these explicit forces of socialization and sexualization. Although she is instructed by preceptors such as Severo Catalina that she "must not know a lot, but rather be familiar with many things,"[11] when she turns to authorship she is measured alongside masculine paradigms such as narrative mastery. If she is to deal with the theme of adultery—without which the nineteenth-century novel would be bereft of a story, according to Tony Tanner[12]—she must also contend with "the sexual ignorance and passivity [required of her] in counterpoint to masculine knowledge and activity."[13] With mind and body held firmly in check, the reconquest of female inner space is often etched upon the female body as the central signifier. As Luce Irigaray has suggested, women's sexuality defies pinpointing but rather is symbolized by the plurality of lips (both sexual and communicative organs) and the diffusion of erogenous zones throughout the body.[14] The female body offers women writers a virtually limitless area for the production of meaning. Ultimately, male writers have followed an analogous inclination to write with and on their bodies in a more vital way, more aware of the body as the situation of consciousness rather than as the cell of the soul.

1.

The Body-as-Text in Emilia Pardo Bazán's *Insolación*

T HE "ROOM OF ONE'S OWN" that Virginia Woolf saw as essential to the flourishing of a woman's literary career lay out of reach for the vast majority of Spanish women of the nineteenth century. Widespread illiteracy reached epidemic proportions in the female population, and the Napoleonic Code, imposed in Spain in 1804 and continuing unweakened except for a brief respite from 1868 to 1875, placed married women in a permanent legal infancy. Meanwhile, feminism burgeoned in countries where industrialization and Protestantism coincided. The dominant culture of Spain lacked both a tradition of free thought and a strong industrial base, except in parts of Catalonia and the Basque country.[1] Only women of very high social status who were encouraged from childhood to go a different route— as illustrated by Javier Herrero in his biography of Cecilia Böhl de Faber (1796–1877)—could beat the odds against a woman's gaining access to the forum of literature, carving out a space of their own where none had existed before.[2] Böhl used the pen name Fernán Caballero to publish novels that bridge the gap between romantic *costumbrismo,* a movement that emphasized local custom and "color," and modern realism with a hefty dose of traditional moral didacticism.

In contrast, Emilia Pardo Bazán (1851–1921) took up writing with an explicitly feminist agenda. Her essays demonstrate a more unequivocal championing of feminist causes than do her novels. Among other contributions, she translated John Stuart Mill's *Subjec-*

tion of Women (1869) and became the first chaired professor, or *catedrática*, in a Spanish university in 1916. As she did for literary naturalism in *La cuestión palpitante* (1882), Pardo Bazán endeavored to make feminism palatable to the Spanish reading public in a predominantly hostile atmosphere where feminism was viewed "as another heretical legacy of the French Revolution: a hybrid monster unleashed by the enemies of the faith and of Spain with the intention of destroying Spanish national, social, and family life."[3] Her aims allied her with the broader movement toward the Europeanization of Spain, which was gaining momentum among her peers, and for inspiration in lieu of female feminist precursors she could trace her progressivism back to Padre Feijoo (1676–1764), a forebear of Spanish Enlightenment, about whom Pardo Bazán wrote a prizewinning poem and essay in 1876 (the year her first child was born).

While reading for a survey course on Spanish literature twelve years ago, I found that in Pardo Bazán's *Insolación* (1889) humor and irony, and a seemingly happy ending, enveloped a subtle, subversive subtext dealing with the heroine's dwelling inside a female body. I agreed with the novelist's most enthusiastic critics in regrading the work as a "small masterpiece," but for reasons other than those already articulated,[4] for I was responding primarily to this subtext rather than to the decorousness and grace for which the book is traditionally recommended. There was something unique in its treatment of a lived-in female body, or what I will call the female body as *vivencia*, as experience. Given the pervasive harnessing of women's physical energies for the purposes of reproduction, it is natural that the pursuit of pleasure for its own sake in this novel leads at first to a negatively charged significance of the body, or the body-turned-against-itself. The refreshing differences I perceived in the inscription of the female body had to do with the way this struggle in the protagonist's inner space turns the body into a main character and with the way the resolution, or lack of one, has the effect of saving the heroine from the fate of the "fallen angel," a fate that was common in novels by the two other paragons of the nineteenth-century realist novel, Pardo Bazán's longtime lover Benito Pérez Galdós and her friend-turned-rejected-suitor-turned-enemy Leopoldo Alas (Clarín).

With Sandra Gilbert and Susan Gubar's notion of an "anxiety of female authorship" in the nineteenth century, the meaning of the body-against-itself broadens. Since the source of anxiety of author-ship emanates from gender identification, it follows that for a large part of the work the protagonist's body should be represented as a vulnerability and that when the sexual instinct—Pardo Bazán's natu-ralist translation of *desire*—located in her body awakens, it should speak at first in a code of pain, fever, nausea, violence, suffocation, paralysis, and sensual overload. Spatial representations in the novel repeat the bodily code of discomfort through a sense of confinement and inescapable heat. The sun acts as a mediator of desire, connecting inner bodily space and outer stimuli; the protagonist's shifting atti-tudes toward desire chart her progress toward abandoning social norms. The close tie that exists between Asís as transgressing female lover and Pardo Bazán as transgressing female writer is constantly reinforced in both the narratorial voice and the content of the work.

In the language of contemporary French feminism, which in turn is based upon Jacques Lacan's revisionist interpretations of Freudian psychoanalysis, the "law of the Father" reigns over the Symbolic realm, a stage we enter early in life when we realize our separateness from the Mother, who previously was viewed as being in harmonious and perfect union with us. Once we have made this realization, our only access to the lost perfect state is by the substitution of signifiers for what is now perceived as missing. Language then becomes the medium through which our semiotic drive courses in its never-ending quest, and the figure of the Father takes on importance as an inter-mediary in social intercourse.[5]

So strong is the law of the Father in the work of Emilia Pardo Bazán that the mother-daughter dyad never achieves preeminence; the protagonist has a daughter who is mentioned fleetingly and for this reason seems conspicuously cast aside. This may be one reason why, as Ordóñez points out, contemporary women writers in Spain look, not to past writers, but to foreign counterparts for a sense of community.[6] Perhaps the baggage with which Pardo Bazán must struggle is too great, for she is often found explaining things to, assuaging, and cajoling the Father, as evidenced in her epistolary efforts to persuade her traditionalist friend Menéndez y Pelayo of the wholesomeness of her literary intentions.[7]

What immediately concerns the protagonist Asís Taboada, a widowed marquess in her early thirties who hails from Vigo, Galicia, and resides part of the year in Madrid, is the reaction of her confessor, Father Urdax. His opprobrium will surely be unleashed upon her when she begins to recount to him the previous day's adventures. Whether she has done anything immoral yet or whether her conduct while accompanying a gentleman she had just met at a friend's house to a local festival has been merely unseemly depends upon how one reads some highly ambiguous and elusive passages. Maurice Hemingway finds her first foray blameless, while Donald Shaw recounts that the lady has "seriously compromised herself."[8] This is exactly the undecidable quality cultivated as a hedge against the Father's law. Despite the warnings of her conscience, Asís will continue to see her new acquaintance and soon will spend the night with him. After her brief, unsuccessful attempt at escaping the situation by returning to Galicia, the couple suddenly decides to marry, and the novel abruptly ends.

As she anticipates, her own tale will be filled with circumlocutions, palliatives, ellipses, disclaimers, excuses, and explanatory notes, literary devices to which both she and the author must resort if they are to avoid the wrath of the Father. Urdax is allied with a broader, male-dominated power constellation; when the narrative is not following Asís mentally composing the confession she plans to make to him, it follows the narrator speaking to a group of "señores"—gentlemen and *perhaps* ladies.[9] The confessional mode into which the novel deftly slips places a guilty heroine answering to male authority in a way that is not at all random. Foucault has articulated the power relation inherent by definition in the confession: "One confesses—or one is forced to confess. . . . The confession is a ritual of discourse in which the speaking subject is also the subject of the statement; it is also a ritual that unfolds within a power relationship, for one does not confess without the presence (or virtual presence) of a partner who is not simply the interlocutor but the authority who requires the confession, prescribes and appreciates it, and intervenes in order to judge, punish, forgive, console, and reconcile."[10]

The imagined confession takes up about a third of the novel. Whether this confession, or a similar one, is ever actually uttered by the heroine is not disclosed, for by the end of the story she has succeeded in releasing the hold of the Father's law over her mind and body to the extent that this is no longer a concern. For the duration of the narrator's recording of Asís's planned confession, however, the logocentric gentleman is ever present in the mind of Asís the narrator, and that presence is closely associated with her physical suffering:

> Intentólo en efecto [rezar]; mas si por un lado era soporífera la operación, por otro agravaba las inquietudes y resquemores íntimos de la señora. Bonito se pondría el padre Urdax cuando tocasen a confesarse de aquella cosa inaudita y estupenda. . . . ¿Qué circunloquios serían más adecuados para atenuar la primera impresión de espanto y la primera filípica? ¡Sí, sí, circunloquios al padre Urdax! ¡El, que lo preguntaba todo derecho y claro, sin pararse en vergüenzas ni en reticencias!

> [She did in fact try to pray; but if on the one hand the enterprise made her sleepy, on the other it aggravated the lady's personal doubts and worries. Wouldn't Father Urdax have a fit when the time came to confess that outrageous and spectacular thing. . . . What manner of circumlocutions would be the most adequate for lessening the first frightful impression and the first invective? Yes, indeed, circumlocutions for Father Urdax! He, who asked everything straightforwardly and clearly, without pausing for embarrassment or hesitation!][11]

The hedges Asís plans to use to mitigate the Father's wrath are similar to the devices the third-person narrator will use in the remaining two-thirds of the text to distance herself from the protagonist's actions, which is to say, when the narrator is not playing Asís's accomplice. The narration of the latter part of the novel approximates the protagonist's "inner" thoughts somewhat less closely through the use of *style indirect libre,* which style occurs whenever the perspective slips almost imperceptibly from an external one to one that copies the character's inner thoughts, without switching from third-person to first-person narration. Hemingway has dealt convincingly with the elusiveness of this second narrator and with the reactions his or her refusal to unambiguously state value judgments elicited among prominent writers and critics of the time; Leopoldo Alas, the old friend turned enemy, who was instrumental in preventing Pardo Bazán's entry into the Real Academia de la Lengua, expressed particular exasperation and disgust.[12] More radical interpretations of the narrator's unmistakable ambivalence toward the opposition of civilization to barbarism and his or her failure to adorn the love affair with the trappings of romantic love are overlooked by Hemingway in favor of two motivations he finds ubiquitous in the author's work: a concern with the tension between romanticism and realism and the goal of portraying human relationships "as ultimately mysterious."[13] While these are undeniable products of the narratorial mode, the political aspect of Pardo Bazán as a writing woman clamors for attention in these obvious examples of conflict with the norms of logocentric and patriarchal narrative authority. In this respect, Tolliver has cited Bakhtin's concept of the hybrid construction, a narrative structure composed of two opposing semantic and axiological belief systems, in an enlightening explanation for the hedges, ambiguities, disclaimers, and ellipses of narration in *Insolación*.[14]

Through moral constraints and the physical suffering the reader assumes to have something to do with her feelings of guilt, Asís's body at the outset is as surely under the Father's control as her consciousness. The more it breaks free, the more problematic it becomes to Asís's mind, which has internalized the Father's law. In this manner, one of the most time-honored of binary oppositions of patriarchal culture, mind/body dualism, is established in the text because of the author's partial adherence to "scientific" naturalism. According to this French offshoot of nineteenth-century positivism, evidently a literary version of the "useful and public discourses" deployed to regulate sexuality, "race, milieu, et moment" are main determinants of human behavior. For this very reason, Pardo Bazán cannot be an uncritical disciple of it; she verbalizes some of her points of contention in *La cuestión palpitante* (1883), while others appear only as they spontaneously occur in her fiction. The body enters the naturalist formula mainly through the first term, *race*, encompassing drives and instincts that flow "in the blood," in addition to the outward physical appearance, or phenotype, of the individual. Readers would not find *Insolación* to be such an engaging narrative of sexual awakening, however, if Pardo Bazán had not gone further than the setting down of the binary opposition of barbaric body to civilized mind, to its ultimate ironizing, subversion, and dissolution. Robert Scari has catalogued the humorous devices that lead to this effect and help to camouflage the lack of an explicit and unflinching moral condemnation of the lovers' premarital affair.[15] The laugh of the Medusa rings audibly in the pervasiveness of humor of various forms, all of which contribute to the defusing and overturning of the predictable messages of dominant discourse.

The reader enters Asís's consciousness just as she reaches wakefulness. Both are greeted with images of throbbing pain, excruciatingly described: drills and red-hot tongs are boring into her temples, and needles stab her scalp. It seems like a scene taken from the Inquisition, or from an Edgar Allan Poe re-creation of the Inquisition. Only later, when the cause for this pain becomes clear, do we realize that its source is far more quotidian. But then it is the excess of the pain, if we consider the incident from which it has resulted, that is striking. For clearly, Asís suffers too much, and in an overly determined way, for this to be an ordinary hangover. The sensual bombardment that characterizes this short novel as a whole likens it to the Victorian sensation novel, known for its performative dimension, or its ability to produce similar states in the reader, and for feminizing nervous distress.[16] The pairing of mental awakening and bodily pain establishes from the very outset the founding of Asís's character "on the indissoluble unity of body and soul."[17] That this pain afflicts areas surrounding the brain signals the conflict between mind and instinct (localized diffusely in the body through the concept of "blood," which comes to signify race). Pardo Bazán's poetics of pain draws on metonymical relationships between parts of the body and their moral functions. Asís's cheeks burn, and her mouth is also affected: its bitterness and aridity almost impede her speech as she mumbles the first utterance to her maid, asking her to soften the arrow of light that has assaulted her eyes. Her punishment fits the crime, and her suffering corresponds neatly to the logic of an eye for an eye, in that each bodily part affected had its role in her transgression of the previous day. The sins of having spoken, seen, and thought evil are translated directly into physical ills. With wry hyperbole, the narrator compares Asís to St. Lorenzo, martyred on the grill. The language of the body becomes textualized as the lived-in body charts Asís's actions and their consequences. Likewise, the text is embodied as it is coopted into following her quest, conscious or otherwise, for sensual pleasure.

The elements of exposure, illness, and intensity of light and heat, all sememes of the one-word title, become a code through which the body speaks throughout much of the work. It is not so much the external phenomenon of a sunburst that is being conveyed (a possible meaning of the title), but its effects on various parts of the body and, inevitably, on Asís's mind, which in this way comes to be viewed as inseparable from her vulnerable body. Her body appears mainly in fragmented form in reaction to pain, as each separate symptom or source of discomfort emerges, and is not represented as a cohesive whole until later in the text, when it assumes an active role. This articulation of the body answers, in symmetrical opposition, to the synecdoche male writers have tended to employ, textually isolating and fetishizing each part of the female form as an object viewed from the outside. Rather than focusing on the sensations each part makes known to the subject or to the totality of body and mind, the mode of representation still predominant among male authors of the time portrays each feminine attribute in a highly stylized manner specific to a particular male-defined aesthetic of femininity.[18]

Gilbert and Gubar describe the tradition of discomfort and dis-ease imagery in writing by nineteenth-century British and American women as symptomatic of their dis-ease with the male-dominated endeavor of writing.[19] If, as Harold Bloom writes of poets, an author (male by default) in the act of literary creation is on some level answering to and seeking to oust a father figure in the guise of preexisting authors,[20] might not the Freudian family drama have a different configuration in the case of women writers, and might this not find expression in the resulting texts? Gilbert and Gubar postulate convincingly—on the basis of close readings of Mary Shelley, the Brontë sisters, George Eliot, Emily Dickinson, and others—that the nineteenth-century woman writer was confronted by something still more formidable than the basic anxiety of influence that challenged male writers. For her there was also the lack of female precursors, persuading her that she herself could not become a literary precursor. In some French feminism we find something similar expressed in the idea that women are deprived of the "phallus," the ultimate socio-linguistic signifier, and hence exist outside of culture, language, and writing.

Furthermore, the dearth of women writers in the nineteenth

century stands in contrast to the predominance of women repre-sented in fiction as main characters, often lending their names to the novels that contain them. In Spain this asymmetry was all the more pronounced. On the one hand, novels such as *Pepita Jiménez, La Regenta, Fortunata y Jacinta,* and *La desheredada* display a concern for characterizing the female protagonist in increasing psychological and material detail, in keeping with the aims of fictional realism. Yet among Pardo Bazán's contemporaries, most of those empowered with authorship were male, and female precursors were few and far between. Before Pardo Bazán, the canon admitted few others be-sides Rosalía de Castro, Gertrudis Gómez de Avellaneda, Fernán Caballero (Cecilia Böhl de Faber), St. Teresa, and María de Zayas. Even in Pardo Bazán's wake, women novelists did not hasten to appear on the scene, and the anomalousness of those who did was reflected in a tongue-in-cheek advice column in the 1940s humor magazine *La Codorniz:*

> *Curiosa.—Logroño*
> ¿Las escritoras suelen ser simpáticas y atractivas, o no?
> Hay de todo. Pero en la mayor parte de los casos muchas escritoras han empezado a escribir simplemente porque no encontraban a nadie con quien hablar.

> [Women writers are usually pleasant and attractive, or aren't they?
> —*Curious in Logroño*
> There are all sorts. But in most cases many of them began to write simply because they couldn't find anyone to talk to.][21]

Spanish women writers indeed found few others with whom to "speak" on a textual level, and they were isolated from others of their gender if they defined themselves as writers. The concentration of Asís's pain, in the initial pages, in her head functions metonymically to unite her complaints with the constraints placed upon the mind of a woman with the desire to write. The double bind of lacking female precursors and abundant representation of women thereby inten-sifies the Father's law and creates a specifically feminine "anxiety of authorship," making a woman writer wary of becoming entrapped in the mirror of fiction. Since she has received the cultural message that the only place literature holds for women is as characters imagined by men, her persistence in writing may lead to fears of ceasing to exist, because she has written but cannot "be an author." This last conclusion may be extreme with reference to the intrepid countess who wrote *Insolación*, but Gilbert and Gubar do succeed in finding a prevalence of certain images, which they then relate to the situation of the nineteenth-century woman author: texts abound in silencing, submersion, and containment. In relation to the female body, the imagery often presents itself in scenes of aphasia, unconsciousness, and disease (or dis-ease), which are often followed by flight, solitude, or smokescreens by means of which the author herself appears to vanish. Many of these images and devices show up in *Insolación*.

Asís's amorous transgressions draw her unmistakably close to Pardo Bazán as transgressing female writer. This may be what causes the narrator to seek increasingly to distance him- or herself from the protagonist as the latter grows more willing to ignore the precepts that had held her in check.[22] It may be argued that of all the characters authored by Pardo Bazán, Asís most closely resembles her creator in the incidents of biography, except, of course, for her being portrayed as neither an extraordinary intellect nor an author or even a *literata*. In addition, the incident is based loosely upon the novelist's relationship with José Lázaro Galdiano, to whom the book is dedicated.[23] This enables the transference of the "female author syndrome," so that it occurs more strongly (i.e., more readably) here than in her other works, although *Los pazos de Ulloa* (1886) and *La madre naturaleza* (1887) also present interesting subtexts having to do with female authorship.

As Gilbert and Gubar note, afflictions that incapacitate the mental faculties of female characters in works by women hold a privileged place: "Aphasia and amnesia—two illnesses which symbolically represent (and parody) the sort of intellectual incapacity patriarchal culture has traditionally required of women—appear and reappear in women's writings in frankly stated or disguised forms."[24]

Pardo Bazán battled the stifling patriarchal world that would silence her literary accomplishments: her husband finally left her over his discontent with her literary activities, and her ultimate aim of gaining entry to the Real Academia was stymied by male colleagues and rivals.[25] Asís, in turn, feels instruments of torture at work on her head and drifts in and out of consciousness at the fair. She is referred to alternately as "in a swoon or deceased," "spiritless," and in "syncope" (64, 96, 91). Her ability to reason is simultaneously questioned, as she feels herself to be "annihilated, in the most complete state of idiocy," "not in my right mind," and acting "like a fool" (95, 97, 99). Visual impairment is mentioned several times as another symptom of her distress (66, 67). An inability to speak clearly plagues her throughout the story, as she becomes hoarse or stutters in numerous situations with her male companion and during the morning-after episode. Affliction of the intellect also plagues Asís when she avers that she is incapable of relating her story satisfactorily (addressing her self-deprecating statements to Father Urdax), for lack of either verbal dexterity (41) or memory (96).

The motifs of nausea or seasickness and of suffocation or entrapment are still other forms of the dis-ease and disease that appear to be overdetermined by the femininity of character and author. These two kinds of imagery are surpassed only by heat as unifying elements in the poetics of the feminine mental and physical predicament in *Insolación*. The word *mareo* can refer to an entire spectrum of symptoms, from intoxication to nausea or seasickness. Asís avails herself of its nonspecificity to cloud the true nature and cause of her malaise. The reader infers, however, that her symptoms have much to do with her remaining in the company of an attractive and flirtatious man she does not know very well and finding herself in a throng of lower-class revelers at a festival that should be off-limits to a lady of her social standing. She applies the word *mareo* to the first dizziness, ostensibly caused by exposure to the sun, likening it to "a liquor that goes to one's head" (66), and also to the more vivid seasickness that takes hold when she feels herself adrift on a sea of human bodies:

> Al punto que nos metimos entre aquel bureo se me puso en la
> cabeza que me había caído en el mar: mar caliente, que hervía a bor-
> botones, y en el cual flotaba yo dentro de un botecillo chico como
> una cáscara de nuez: golpe va y golpe viene, ola arriba y ola abajo.
> ¡Sí, era el mar, no cabía duda! ¡El mar, con toda la angustia y des-
> consuelo del mareo que empieza!

> [The instant we mixed in with the revelry I became convinced that I
> had fallen into the sea: a boiling hot sea in which I floated inside of
> a tiny bottle like a nutshell: blow after blow, one wave after another.

Yes, it was surely the sea! The sea, with all the anguish and despair
of seasickness setting in!] (84)

In addition to seasickness, nausea, dizziness, and tipsiness, another meaning of *mareo* can be motion sickness, an important meaning when we consider that the protagonist's body, propelled by desire, is in effect traversing a labyrinth consisting of social norms and
mores toward a destination unknown to it. The female body in
motion acts out what Pardo Bazán would call its acquired shame
through this illness, but no degree of motion sickness, not even when
it results in unconsciousness, can halt its propulsion.

The illusion of being lost at sea, and hence at the mercy of the
elements, is bolstered as the story continues and serves to underline
the helplessness of woman in male-dominated society, once again
running parallel to the predicament of the woman writer.[26] As the
mareo worsens, Asís increasingly refers to a sensation of weightlessness: "I didn't even notice the weight of my body" (89). In this
context of weakness and illness, the sensation does not bring gratify-
ing freedom from natural laws, but a reinforcement of her body's
insignificance and defenselessness: "If I were pushed with one finger, I
would fall down and bounce like a ball" (89). All of this occurs
tellingly after she has taken hold of her companion's arm for support
and glimpsed a revolver in his pocket, an effort on his part to reassure
her of safety. This only redoubles her dis-ease and puts her on guard,
for she has as much to fear from this stranger as she does from the
crowd. To say that it is the phallic quality of the revolver that reminds
Asís of her powerlessness would seem banal to some, far-fetched to
others. However, here and elsewhere in the novel Pardo Bazán plays
half-humorously with phallic imagery to accent her heroine's sense of
vulnerability. Ultimately, Asís succumbs to the maternal illusion of
being surrounded and rocked by the sea; when she sits with Pacheco
beside the Manzanares River, she sees round her the waves of her
native Vigo and winds up shouting for the boat to stop, then fainting.
An anecdote planted earlier in the narrative relates that Alexandre
Dumas once ceremoniously offered a glass of water as a donation to
the trickling Manzanares. Even the reader unfamiliar with Madrid
can then appreciate the amusing incongruity of Asís's suffering a
fainting spell brought on by such a body of water. Furthermore,

suspicion regarding the real cause of her ebbing strength continues to grow. As we learn from a quick flashback, this healthy, fun-loving woman has reached her early thirties without ever satisfying her sensual desires, and now that the possibility of doing so hovers as close as the gleaming revolver, the flaring of crude sexual instinct from within her body threatens to floor her and then succeeds. Out of interest in reclaiming feminine desire, Pardo Bazán couches in delicately humorous terms what she, as a naturalist, should only portray as the most animalistic of passions.

Still more incongruous, and therefore noticeably overdetermined by the subtext of the female-body-turned-against-itself, is the reappearance of torture imagery as Asís sits on the riverbank: "It was as though they were pulling out my stomach and insides with a hook in order to tear them out of my mouth" (91). Pérez Galdós, for example, reserves torture imagery of penetration such as this for Mauricia la Dura undergoing delirium tremens. The use of the third-person plural, an amorphous *they,* is reminiscent of the "legion of enemies" who try to extract her brains on the morning after (34). However humorously these similes are handled in the text, they emphasize the solitude of the female protagonist in her plight, the plurality and nebulosity of the agents of social subjection, and the vital importance of what is at stake. In these and nearly all of the torture images of *Insolación* there is penetration and violation of an inner bodily space, a space that is filled with some of the protagonist's essential organs, whether they be cerebral, digestive, or reproductive in function. The heightening and dramatization of discomfort into a scene of inquisitorial torment contrasts with the mundane or absurd incidents that appear in the story as their immediate provocation: a tame river, a four-legged woman in a sideshow, Asís's own distorted reflection in a funhouse mirror, the consumption of a heavy, hodgepodge lunch.

The seasickness motif will not subside until one final connection emerges. When Asís's first-person narration concludes and the "impersonal" one begins, one of the few retrospections of the text indicates that she lost her mother as a child (aligning her with the vast collection of motherless or orphaned heroines in novels by women from the Brontës to Carmen Martín Gaite) and was raised by her father. The same retrospection also relates that her first romantic interest was a naval officer with whom she corresponded. She broke off relations with the young man when a distant uncle courted and married her. The ensuing marriage is described as benignly affectionate, if lacking in passion; the womanly desire in Asís's body enters a remission of sorts as her avuncular husband keeps her safely within the family fold and she becomes a mother herself. But when her much older husband leaves her a "serene" (but not merry) widow, the affliction of desire is destined to flare up anew, and it carries the embedded nautical motif. The recurrence of seasickness suggests that her marriage never quite succeeded in erasing the memory of "the slender shadow with a white cap and golden anchors" (101).

The heat that oppresses Asís's body begins for the reader with her burning face and body on the morning after, which the narrator likens with irony to a martyrdom scene: "Both bed and body of the guilty one were burning, like St. Lorenzo on the grill" (38). In the plot it goes back to the beginning of her Sunday outing with Pacheco, when she innocently inserts a flower in his lapel and catches a whiff of his heady cologne, provoking in her face "an extraordinary heat" that Pacheco observes as a blush (59). Heat reaches an unbearable crescendo in the dream sequence that has Asís fleeing her lover by train across a parched Castile, her brain fairly simmering, her pleas for water met with offers of dry sherry, and her eyes bursting from their sockets like those of "cats being scalded" (183).

The personification of the agent of desire, suffering, and awakening as the sun god completes the progress toward an exclusively Thetic, Father-dominated stage begun in Pardo Bazán's earlier novels. In the rural environment of *La madre naturaleza* it is a vaguely personified mother nature behind the scenes that attracts two unknowingly incestuous lovers to each other. This label was seen as unsatisfactory by Gabriel Pardo de la Lage, who thought a better name for an entity that caused such tragedy would have been *stepmother*. In *Insolación* we are another step removed from the paradisiacal, rural union of mother and child—Asís grew up motherless, and in the urban landscape of Madrid there is no mother nature, but a ravaging male sun god, whom she and her lover finally greet as their patron deity.[27] Considered in the framework of the semiotic versus the Thetic or the Symbolic state, the urban setting of *Insolación* is clearly more related to the latter, and the Father's law thus emerges as more monolithic in its opposition to the female character. In *La madre naturaleza* there is still evidence of the "free play of drives" characteristic of the semiotic stage viewed in the representation of nature, even though the Father's law, in the form of social tabu against incest, curtails the wild, unbridled situation.

One of Lacan's most resonant writings, for Hispanists as well as feminists, is his analysis of the figure of St. Teresa's ecstasy as sculpted by Bernini. Irigaray also has incorporated this figure into her writings.[28] Lacan's placement of mystics in the schema of relations between the sexes can be applied to males as well, yet he finds in St. Teresa a powerful image of the inexpressible quality of feminine *jouissance* and of its relation to authoritative knowledge: "The male divinity is supported by (and perhaps even dependent on) the pleasure which woman experiences, but cannot express."[29] Feminine *jouissance* is correspondingly elusive in *Insolación*. Much is made of desire (in Lacan's terms, the gap that opens up between demand and need) through the harsh textual events previously described; and indeed for Lacan woman's desire is infinite, fixed as it is upon completion through union with some absolute *Autre*, or Other.

With an overwhelmingly male constellation of figures (the sun god, Father Urdax, the husband's ghost) mediating desire and suffering, only Asís's body is left to speak, in isolated instances, on behalf of the erotic and semiotic drives. Pleasure as well as pain is written upon her textual body. Most commonly this occurs merely as a relief from the discomforts of heat, suffocation, *mareo,* and the like. Relief keeps the body and its sensations ever present in the text and thus engages the reader's sensory imagination continuously in the way of the Victorian sensation novel. In the opening, morning-after passage, pleasant sensations alternate with relapses in rapid succession: her "nice and hot, well-prepared" infusion only causes more waves of nausea when it reaches her lips. Afterwards, she begins to feel a bit better when she lies down "curled up in a shell of cloth," and the association of maternity (in this case, a fetal position) with bodily well-being and pleasure appears for the first time in what will be a recurring cycle in the work. The pleasure principle alternates with bodily discomfort but never equals it in intensity. For there is no explicit moment of *jouissance* or bliss to balance the torment of sunbeaten senses—a curious thing in a novel that has been taken for a very light-hearted, even frivolous, one.[30]

Cleansing also becomes closely associated with relief and well-being. At first only the refreshing effect of water against Asís's face can bring about a respite from headache: "after this, she felt her thoughts become clearer and the tip of the drill withdrew little by little from her brain" (39). Later, bathing takes on the significance of moral cleansing, with the narrator explicitly exposing Asís's self-deception: "With each hygienic operation and each part of her body left clean as a gloss, Asís believed she saw the mark of the day before's immorality disappear, and, unwittingly confusing the physical with the moral, while grooming she thought she regenerated herself" (104).

The young woman slips into her ordinary-looking zinc bathtub, and a passage follows that has been labeled plagiarism by one critic.[31] Zola's *L'Assommoir* (1877) refers to an adulterous lover, Gervaise, who scrubs her hands and shoulders after each tryst as if to remove the moral stigma, and Pardo Bazán uses the essentials of the scene in Asís's toilette above. In its integration, however, it is reworked in a way that significantly differentiates it from Zola, making the charge of plagiarism inappropriate. In the first place, the correspondence between physical and moral cleansing is already a literary universal, as evidenced by Shakespeare's Lady Macbeth. In *Insolación* there is an earnestness of tone, as the narrator continues her gentle mocking of Asís, and an insistence upon material detail that reveals the action as ridiculous from a narratorial viewpoint:

> En el agua clara iban a quedarse la vergüenza, la sofoquina y las in-conveniencias de la aventura. . . . ¡Allí estaban escritas con letras de polvo! Polvo doblemente vil, el polvo de la innoble feria! ¡Y cuidado que era pegajoso y espeso! ¡Si había penetrado al través de las me-dias, de la ropa interior, y en toda su piel lo veía depositado la dama!

> [The shame, discomfort, and improprieties of the affair would be left behind in the clear water. . . . There they were, written in letters of dust! Dust that was doubly vile, dust from the ignoble fair! And watch out, for it was sticky and thick! It had gotten through to the inside of her stockings, her underwear, and the lady saw it deposited all over her skin!] (104–5)

In *L'Assommoir*, when Gervaise is disgusted with herself at the outset of her affair with Lantier, she succinctly washes her hands, wets a dishrag, and goes about scrubbing her shoulders "as if to rub them off."[32] What lies latent in Zola's text, and what Pardo Bazán develops in her passage with gentle mockery, is the female body as a text that records its transgressions. This is where the primary "writing" of *Insolación* takes place—in letters of dust on the subject's very skin, cutting through the secondary, cultural trappings of clothing. Asís's body comes to bear the marks of the incompleteness of its social subjection. The fundamental unity of body and mind is clear in that only Asís, because of her disconcertion, can read the writing on her body. Then, she is careful to erase her bodily text, as its contents are potentially incriminating.[33]

Still, critics scold Pardo Bazán as though she were an unscrupulous schoolgirl for what is actually an intertextual reference to Zola that adds semiotic value to the "borrowed" material. In so doing they discard the pious tone reserved for male authors. Adding insult to incrimination, Robert E. Osborne offers Pardo Bazán's supposed real-life obsession with personal neatness as an explanation. When she names scores of articles for feminine use that scarcely appear elsewhere in Spanish literature—the *antuca* she mentions (56) is an obscure and specialized item, a sort of parasol—she is following a realist tendency to record the material, and especially the visual, details of everyday life. The difference is that she does so from a female viewpoint, capturing a nearly lost quotidian language that includes words borrowed from other languages that more *castizo* authors avoid, concerned with keeping Spanish pure of foreign influences (the *antuca* derives from *en tout cas*). Just as the realists intended to arrive at the essential by means of the material, Pardo Bazán suggests the severity of feminine codes of conduct with such concrete details as the "bristled glove, softened with almond paste and honey," used to scrub the neck, and the constricting corset, which must be removed when Asís faints. The proliferation of these feminine artifacts serves not so much to provide additional objects for use in visualizing the commodified heroine (as in Galdós and Clarín) as to detail the complicated process of transforming oneself into a socially presentable woman.

While decorum circumvents a textual arrival at full-fledged bliss, ecstasy, *gozo*, or *jouissance* in *Insolación*, there are moments of joy, or *regocijo*, expressed in physical terms. These moments appear when, in the first days of her acquaintance with Pacheco, Asís walks in the open air and responds to the pleasurable effects of the sun and atmosphere before these become overwhelmingly powerful. Specifically, her body responds actively to these sensations, and speaks to "herself" (her consciousness, her soul), across the chasm of the mind/body split:

> Ganas me entraron de correr y brincar como a los quince, y hasta se me figuraba que en mis tiempos de chiquilla no había sentido nunca tal exceso de vitalidad, tales impulsos de hacer extravagancias, de arrancar ramas de árbol y de chapuzarme en el pilón presidido por aquella buena señora de los leones. . . . Nada menos que estas tonterías me estaba pidiendo el cuerpo a mí.

> [I suddenly felt the urge to run and jump like when I was fifteen, and it even seemed to me that as a little girl I had never experienced such an excess of vitality, such impulses to do extravagant things, to pull out tree branches and to splash about in the fountain presided over by that good lady with her lions. . . . My body was asking me for nothing less than this sort of foolishness.] (52)[34]

Likewise, at the start of the St. Isidro Festival, she finds physical pleasure unexpectedly taking hold, although she purposely checks her impulses and maintains propriety against the effects of alcohol: "All I experienced was a most pleasant liveliness, with my tongue loosened, my senses enhanced, my spirit aflutter, and my heart contented" (81). Her body is vocal once more when a theater date is suggested by a friend: "No: what my body asks of me is exercise" (122). The *cuerpo que pide,* or requesting body, would be hard to encounter in the writings of male authors of the day. As Smith and others have noted, the "commodity fetishism" played upon in works by Galdós sees the female body for its external accoutrements only.[35] In *La de Bringas,* for example, there is insistence on clothing and fashion in a way that makes them continuous or synonymous with the body, and blazonlike renderings of the bodily parts. Lou Charnon-Deutsch accounts for this materialist objectification by the influence of serialized novels, illustrated reviews, and other popular literature of mass consumption that recycled old female stereotypes by bringing dress and mannerisms up to date.[36]

In *Insolación* the body exists independently as a desiring subject in its own right. As extensions of the protagonist's inhabited body, four distinct types of space emerge in the course of the novel: the aristocratic domestic interior, the urban thoroughfare, the popular carnival or inn (on the fringes of urban settlement and society), and, finally, the oneiric (here, a train compartment). Except for the last one, all are socially shared in a direct way. All firmly connect with motifs of helplessness and entrapment they elicit in the heroine, causing her body to respond to their influence. Breathlessness or suffocation becomes associated with Asís's suffering from the first passage, where it accompanies her realizations of guilt (38). She loses her breath as a result of hurrying to prepare herself for further encounters with Pacheco, when she feels like a shipwreck victim while alone in her house with Pacheco, when she enters the alcove where she is to dine with Pacheco in a restaurant on the outskirts of Madrid, and when she awakens from her nightmare concerning leaving Madrid.

Loss of breath reminds her urgently and physically that she has lost all control. The heroine fluctuates between a feeling of being cast adrift on the sea and one of being confined and slowly asphyxiated. On the level of spatial representation this dichotomy emerges as the twin poles of exposure and enclosure or entrapment. To a certain extent, the spatial constructions of *Insolación* work as extensions of bodily space; the same forces that propel or repel Asís's body "from within" are equally at work on the mimetic stages of landscape and man-made interiors. In general there is a tendency toward internality: when she is outside, she is continually driven inside by the elements. The narrative style heightens this internal movement, commencing in the first person and hence enclosed within the heroine's consciousness. Even when the narrator changes to the more omniscient third person, Asís's inner "happenings" are always on the very surface of the text. She at times forsakes the safety of interiors in favor of gusts of fresh air, which often provide pleasure or relief. In this respect, the most general spatial tendency in the work can be construed as one that abhors stagnation and finds complete comfort in no single spot. Even though the exteriors prove hostile environments for a variety of reasons, refuge can turn into entrapment, and she must then escape it as well.

At the Duchess of Sahagún's salon, in the passage in which the mind/body split is articulated and placed in a Spanish context by Gabriel Pardo, there is a conspicuous lack of description of the interior and a disembodiment of Asís that coincides with the stressing of transcendent mind as divorced from the body and its base instincts. Asís's contentious friend Gabriel Pardo happens to be lecturing those present about how in Spain the mind is no match for the body. As he tries to convince the socialites that they are little better than savages, Asís's body is uncharacteristically silent. The introduction of her future lover Pacheco brings on no physical reaction in Asís, but rather a "cold curiosity." The absence of physical inscription coincides with an interior filled with a concentration of her peers listening to a harangue that privileges the mind over the body and implies that Spaniards as a race let the latter get out of hand.

It is not until the following day, on the way to Mass, that the amenity of her outdoor surroundings makes Asís want to run and jump. Outdoor settings serve as enabling conditions of either explicit pleasure or explicit discomfort, keeping the heroine's physical affective state on the surface throughout the work. This is reinforced and determined by the omnipresence of the sun as mediator of desire. Thus, there are instances of the outdoors acting as a refreshment on Asís's senses: "The calm of night and the open air produced the effect of a cold shower on me" (95). These are balanced by instances of oppression in the form of heat, crowds, and the *piropos* of loitering men (customary acclaim for passing women intended to bolster the speaker's consideration among other men). The sidewalks of Madrid are not a place where a woman of her rank can walk unmolested, and when men turn their attention to her she is forced to quicken her pace; rarely in male-authored literature is there an indication of the subtle factors that add up to women's basic lack of liberty on city streets. She resorts to flight in this and other instances that jeopardize her personal safety or social standing.

The interiors afford intimacy in scenes that include Pacheco and shelter her from the excessive heat of the direct sun, but a number of descriptions evidence a sense of entrapment, especially when the heroine is alone or with other women in the house. Her maiden aunts' house, which inspires the most excruciating boredom and a bout of yawning, stands for an entire way of life that cannot satisfy her, no matter how saintly and secure it is. An amusing vignette describes the embarrassing situation of two ladies caught in traffic, so that their carriages force them to face each other, yet they are not sufficiently acquainted to converse and can only smile at each other as they await the end of the awkward encounter (106). The furnishing of her own apartment in Madrid internalizes the labyrinthine entrapment that awaits her on the outside as female character: "Everything intermingled, placed in whatever way created the most obstacles to people passing through, forming an archipelago that could not be navigated without practice" (114). In addition, a masculine figure humorously presides over the maze: "Only the porcelain bulldog, sitting like a sphinx, watched the couple on the sofa with an alarming persistence, displaying an appropriate alertness, as if he were a guard stationed there by the spirit of the respectable deceased marquis" (115).

In the kaleidoscopic landscape of the St. Isidro Fair disparate figures or scenes come one after another into Asís's view. It represents a carnivalesque break with daily life and the usual urban setting, a place outside of social norms where the newly formed couple can take pleasure in "slumming" and in each other's company with relative freedom from the gaze of others of their social circle. In addition to the amusements, the carnival space evidently poses risks to Asís's self-control; excesses of food and drink, exposure to the sun and to Pacheco's attraction, and contact with the lower classes, particularly with marginalized women, threaten her sense of autonomy and her moral behavior. The novel's last utterances consist of Pacheco's joking impersonation of the gypsy fortuneteller at the fair who predicted their ultimate, happy union.

This final crossing of gender boundaries strengthens another feminine subtext activated in the text through the carnival sequence: that of *brujería,* or witchcraft, linked with marginalized women. It begins with Gabriel Pardo's pompous condemnation of the St. Isidro Festival as an *aquelarre,* a witches' sabbath or Walpurgisnacht. The description of the fair itself reinforces what might have seemed an offhand remark. Three gypsy women in succession besiege the couple at their restaurant table. The first one launches into a detailed reading of Asís's palm, predicting good luck in love and an important letter. Besides the letters of shame on her skin and Pacheco's initials on his wallet (which incriminate Asís in the mind of Gabriel Pardo when he glimpses it in her apartment), Asís's palm represents the only significant text that is "read" in the course of the narrative. The final parody of a palm reading executed by Pacheco thus closes the novel with the recurring image of bodily writing. In addition, the mystery of occult practices interweaves itself in this way with the couple's love for each other. This adds to the mystery surrounding human relationships that the novel leaves unresolved;[37] true to the forecasted *aquelarre,* the witchcraft emanates from a feminine source and etches itself on the textual female body.

When the third gypsy in the St. Isidro restaurant is told to depart, she lets loose a string of curses against the waitress. Asís describes all the gypsy *brujas* in animalistic terms: their claws, their serpentine foreheads, how they fight like tigresses or Amazons. In so doing she tries to hold on firmly to the ethnic (Asís would say racial) and class privilege that separates her from these women. Although she perceives them as bestial, their witchcraft does have the power of writing Asís's future for her. Their undefinable characters, inhumanly portrayed bodies, and compelling powers hark back to medieval texts such as the *Celestina,* in which feminine subtexts of witchcraft, prostitution, and virginity restoration, all connected to women's bodies, have a key role in the production of meaning because they are perceived by the reader as intolerable gaps.[38]

As the carnival passage continues, Asís's conception of her own body does not remain altogether divorced from the female witches and monsters she encounters. Immediately after looking at a four-legged woman in a freak show tent, she feels more nauseated than ever. She seeks her own image in a wavy mirror but finds herself reflected in "grotesquely deformed lines" (87). Furthermore, she begins to display her own extrasensory powers, for example, when she senses Pacheco's presence with her eyes closed, although she takes pains to explain it away as a common experience (92), and when she and Pardo feel each other's thoughts through the contact of their arms, "as if via magnetic force" (123). The stereotype of "women's intuition," when exaggerated, is reminiscent of the historical, suspected connection between powerful women and the occult, an area that lies outside of authoritative, logocentric knowledge. Asís has reason to feel haunted by the more marginalized women she encounters at the fair, for they are very close to distortions of her own image.

This is why Asís cannot endure the sight of her reflection in a distorting funhouse mirror, having just viewed female "freaks" on display in a sideshow. Carnivalesque themes often force a confrontation with a danger or harsh truth that lies below the surface of merriment. Pardo Bazán takes advantage of this function to dramatize the fear of social disapproval that normally keeps women like Asís in check. Naturally, *Insolación* gives the last word, and the undecidable ending of the text, to the witch (or parody of one). But for readers the story does not end here.

In the absence of the balanced extremes of fire and ice metaphors comparable to those Gilbert and Gubar find prominent in *Jane Eyre*, *Insolación* careens toward the flames, but the flames of what? As we have seen, heat is variously associated throughout the book with punishment and guilt (not unlike El Burlador's final punishment in the original version of Don Juan), as well as with incipient passion. Once the sun god receives his homage, however, he greets the lovers as a beneficent patron. The shifts in significance betray an ambivalent attitude toward sensuality, which is not surprising in one of the first novels that deals straightforwardly with female erotism and neither punishes nor entirely condemns a woman for a premarital affair.

The insistent alternation between pain and pleasure draws the work closer to St. Teresa's *Libro de la vida*, particularly in the light of Smith's relation of her ecstasy to Kristeva's semiotic state. Smith asserts that the mystic state as revealed by St. Teresa's writings fluctuates between exaltation and despair. Aside from this, there are many coincidences on various levels in *Insolación* and the *Vida;* Pardo Bazán was continuing a feminine dialogue, consciously or not—it is likely that she had in mind another mystic-influenced heroine, Clarín's Ana Ozores—with one of her rare Spanish precursors. Both texts begin with a confession made to a "father" (their confessors). Both are sprinkled with statements of humility that apologize for the subject's inability to express herself or to behave properly. Irigaray signals the expression of women's desire in a public forum as an important contribution of mystical writing, and *Insolación* does nothing if not articulate this desire over and over, using various conceits, including the nautical or seasickness metaphors. The *Vida* also relies heavily on this kind of imagery.[39] Both protagonists describe penetra-

tion of an inner space. In St. Teresa's case it is a blissful mystical vision
tinged with a burning sensation. For Asís it is a most unpleasant
daydream of torture based on actual physical pain. Perhaps Asís does
feel a more pleasant kind of penetration as well, but who can say?
Certainly not the narrator.

On the level of stylistics, there is also a clear resemblance to St.
Teresa's text in the frequency of "paradox, ellipsis, and discontinuity" and other seeming aberrations. Smith opines that these wind up
breaking the bonds of male rhetoric, charging that adherence to male
literary conventions afforded an insufficient medium for female subjectivity, at least in a Golden Age context.[40] Pardo Bazán's situation is
of course different: as a secular author not directly related to any
mystical tradition and an aristocrat whose material wealth shields
her from the most basic discriminations (she has managed to educate
herself), she participates on the same level as male novelists and
engages with them in friendships, rivalries, and amorous liaisons.
However, the texture of *Insolación* is defined by its use of ellipsis,
which is executed so perceptibly that Genette's concept of paralipsis,
when what is omitted from narration becomes the center of attention
for that very reason, is more appropriate.

All novelists of the time were faced with the need to circumvent
occurrences in their plots that would violate decorum. As a result, the
gaps in their texts take on importance, for the consequences of these
scenes for the rest of the story are such that the reader is forced to fill
in the gaps. Without whatever Emma Bovary does inside her carriage
with drawn blinds, for example, the rest of the novel makes little
sense. Even though the text does not take us into the compartment,
the effect is the same, and all the more compelling for having this
sense of mystery, being "where the garment gapes."[41] In *Tristana*,
having already introduced the story of Paolo and Francesca de Rimini
as an intertext, Galdós can state with a wink that Tristana and
Horacio "strolled no more after that day."[42] Pardo Bazán was indeed
criticized for not withdrawing sufficiently from the parts where her
story line becomes improper. José Maria de Pereda called *Insolación*
immoral for showing the pair of lovers in concubinage visible to the
reader and for including meticulous details about the way they com-
mit sin.[43]

Even when the narration does recede from the scene of the crime, the ornateness of the narratorial "doorways" to these boudoir scenes calls attention to them. The disclaimers offered by the narrator also turn back on themselves in irony, since imagination, and not truth, forces the telling of the tale: "It is painful to have to admit and set down certain things; however, honesty militates against leaving them out of the narration" (117). The feigned obligation to tell historical truth (one of Cervantes's favorite tricks) leaves the author less accountable for having invented, embellished, and published a story of premarital transgression that goes unpunished. This same passage, while keeping its "discreet reticence," lingers very conspicuously in the street outside; where most novelists accelerate, Pardo Bazán decelerates narrative time, describing the tedium of horses and coachmen falling asleep at the curb below and daylight disappearing little by little from the sky.

Whereas discontinuity is apparent among female Golden Age writers, in Pardo Bazán there is narrative intermittence or fluctuation. As Stephen Gilman and Gonzalo Sobejano have noted in different ways, a major transformation of "imported" naturalism was wrought by Spanish novelists, who reflected or retold their plots through a Cervantine mirror of irony and perspectivism.[44] This narration that calls attention to itself often utilizes a fluctuating perspective that is at times omniscient, at times so linked to third-person indirect style that it cannot know information that falls outside of the character's consciousness. Gilman, for example, finds that this is enriching to the reading experience in *Fortunata y Jacinta*. He sees an increasing rapprochement between Galdós as narrator and Fortunata. In Valera, on the other hand, Smith finds that narrative intermittence is handled less effectively, with a resulting obtrusiveness.[45] Hence, fluctuation in general is not exclusive to Pardo Bazán ("Pardo had picked up a newspaper, I believe it was *La Epoca*" [185]). However, in *Insolación,* the context of fluctuation makes it overdetermined by the struggle between the Father's law and feminine desire. Narrator at times turns against heroine, at times works as her accomplice, and the twin subjectivities exhibit the "law" articulated with irony by the otherwise hypocritical character Gabriel Pardo: that Woman is a perpetual pendulum swinging between desire and acquired shame. The amused, theatrical narrator often feels obliged to censure the heroine condescendingly for the benefit of gentlemen readers:

Asís, en la penumbra del dormitorio, entre el silencio, componía mentalmente el relato que sigue, donde claro está que no había de colocarse en el peor lugar, sino paliar el caso: aunque, señores, ello admitía bien pocos paliativos.

No afirmamos que, aun dialogando con su conciencia propia, fuese la marquesa viuda de Andrade perfectamente sincera.

[Asís, in the half-light of her bedroom, in silence, mentally composed the tale that follows, in which she certainly did not want to be displayed in a negative light, but preferred to attenuate the circumstances: although, gentlemen, it allowed for very little attenuation.

We cannot assert that, even in dialogue with her own conscience, the widowed Marquess of Andrade was perfectly honest.] (40, 100)

As doubt is cast on Asís as narrator, the third-person narrator also claims ignorance about certain key facts: Was Asís really crying? To whom did "the idea" of marriage first occur? An abdication of authority, and thereby of accountability, stems from the refusal to narrate these details, in a way that differs from the more generalized uses of Cervantine narrative fluctuation in male Spanish realists.[46] The overall effect is to confirm the subjectivity of all possible points of view by upholding feminine flexibility against the Father's law.

The resounding declaration made by Asís to the effect that women should be allowed to respond to and comment on the appearances of the men they find handsome throws into relief a contradiction for the contemporary reader. For, indeed, what Asís refers to explicitly in this passage and others concerning Pacheco's attraction is his clothing, grooming, accent, and manners—all of which are tied to culture—when supposedly the offensive aspect of women engaging in *piropos* about men would be their sensuality. Instead, the remarks are usually located one step from the physical: "the favorable impression the Andalusian's personal finery made upon me" (53), "the unstudied elegance of his dress" (111). The "commodity fetishism" noted by Smith (and Marxian critics before him) in *La de Bringas* has a similar effect here, establishing the mannequinlike figure of Pacheco, who is what he wears; the invisibility of the (male) body; and the consequent masquerade of relations between the sexes.

When the references are not so removed, racial characteristics supply the chief code for expressing the Andalusian's appearance. His meridional qualities are insisted upon to the point of setting up a racial difference that complements sexual difference and seems to make Asís's sensual delight in him possible:

> No dejaba de llamarme la atención la mezcla de razas que creía ver en ella [la cara]. Con un pelo negrísimo y una tez quemada del sol, casaban mal aquel bigote dorado y aquellos ojos azules.

> ¿Cuándo se verá en ningún inglés un corte de labios sutil, y una sien hundida, y un cuello delgado y airoso como el de Pacheco?

> Su rostro, descompuesto por la cólera, perdiendo su expresión indo-lente, mejoraba infinito: se acentuaban sus enjutas facciones, tem-blaba el bigote dorado, resplandecían los blancos dientes y los azules ojos, se oscurecían como el agua del Mediterráneo cuando amaga tempestad.

> [I couldn't help noticing the mixture of races I perceived in his face. The jet-black hair and sunburned complexion clashed with that golden moustache and blue eyes.

> Is there an Englishman who can boast of the finely etched lips, sculpted temples, and graceful, slender neck Pacheco has?

> His face, transfixed by rage, losing its indolent expression, improved immeasurably: his lean features were accentuated, the golden moustache trembled, his white teeth glinted, and his blue eyes darkened like the Mediterranean when a storm threatens.] (60, 60, 177)

The factor of race is essential in the argument of biological determin-ism versus sociomoral influences that enters the novel in the conver-sation at the salon where Asís and Pacheco meet, and where Gabriel Pardo holds forth on a number of issues. The recorded dialogue makes the rest of the narrative a naturalist experiment that will prove or disprove one side but insists upon maintaining ambiguity.[47] Gabriel Pardo affirms that Spaniards have African blood coursing through their veins, presumably making them more susceptible to the biological imperatives (41). At the same time, the external forces of nature (sun and heat) are at their most unbridled in Spain, and even more so, one assumes, in Andalusia, leaving Spaniards still more vulnerable to the instincts localized in the body by way of blood. The racial mythology utilized here encodes and shapes bodily discourse. Its comforting effect upon both aristocrats and bourgeois, who looked to the physical for signifiers indicating their belonging to a certain social caste, has been observed by Foucault: "There was a transposition into different forms of the methods employed by the nobility for making and maintaining its caste distinction; for the aristocracy had also asserted the special character of its body, but this was in the form of *blood,* that is, in the form of the antiquity of its ancestry and of the value of its alliances; the bourgeoisie on the contrary looked to its progeny and the health of its organism when it laid claim to a specific body."[48]

What Gabriel Pardo denies is that gender has anything to do with an individual's giving in to baser nature, a position he reaffirms later when he condemns the double standard of morality in sexual behavior applied to women and men in Spanish society: "There are no men, there are no women, there is only humanity, and humanity is *like that*" (204). Pardo's point of view is subverted, however, when he reveals an utterly hypocritical subscription to the double standard in practice. On a textual level, at least, racial difference and gender difference appear linked, as enabling conditions for desire. Pacheco's body is marked in this respect and is harmonized with the natural forces (sun and sea) of his homeland. He too becomes a target for marginalization, which likens his body to the female body, for Pacheco, though male, is a target for the anti-Southern prejudices of Castilians and other Spaniards on account of his features, even if Asís's reactions are quite favorable. As in the nineteenth-century litany of women's body parts, only reference to his facial features, his "silken black hair," and, occasionally his slender hands and neck appear in the text.

When Asís peeks at the skin below the collar of Pacheco's shirt, she finds it to be much lighter in color than she had expected (62). The male body remains a mystery to be glimpsed only furtively in *Insolación,* and her inclination anticipates Roland Barthes's comparison of literary pleasure emanating from intermittence to the seductive flash of skin beneath a garment: "Is not the most erotic portion of the body *where the garment gapes?*"[49] The misplaced signifier of Pacheco's wallet, inscribed with his initials—"one of those unclasped billfolds of English leather, with two entwined initials in silver, an obviously masculine possession" (121)—is immediately recognized by another male, Pardo, as staking the former's claim in Asís's abode. Masculine articles of clothing identify their owner unmistakably, but Pacheco himself is not so unequivocally masculine; he fluctuates in the text between the maternal caretaker of a weakened Asís and, from a feminine viewpoint, a Don Juan figure. The former is another aspect of the gender blurring and role reversals that frequently rise to the surface of *Insolación*. It is as if no other satisfactory model for the true love that must be depicted can be found other than motherly affection, and one is reminded of the prevalence of incest in Pardo Bazán's other novels as well as in this one (Gabriel Pardo's love for his cousin and Asís's marriage to her uncle): "Pacheco held me in silence and with exquisite care, like a sick child" (91); "I was dying for affection, just like a little girl . . . I wanted to be pitied!" (93); "Pacheco rocked her back and forth as one soothes a child" (152). Of course a note of pathos and irony is not lacking from these descriptions, which portray the full-grown aristocrat, a mother herself, as a helpless child. Still, the maternal encoding of mature heterosexual love, often aligned with sea imagery, which acts as a reservoir for both maternal and erotic drives, manifests itself constantly in the works of Pardo Bazán and other women authors.

A transposition of the Don Juan legend also gives shape to the love affair between the heroine and Pacheco. The salon passage in which they are introduced to each other ends with a hint at Pacheco's similarity to the Sevillan *burlador*, or deceiver of women (Pacheco is from nearby Cádiz), including his turbulent relationship with his father and his philandering: "The only thing he had been good at up until then was upsetting women" (51). Upon hearing this the protagonist deems him "a fine example of the Spanish race," setting the tone for the subsuming of his physical representation into the category of race. While he tends more toward the rake than the villain, the parallel is drawn clearly and reinforced, for no other archetypal character has been made to stand so universally for Spanish manhood. Later he admits that he has had hundreds of girlfriends and has even killed a man, yet for Asís (his Doña Inés) he has but the tenderest of sentiments. He cannot be the full-fledged diabolical antihero of drama and poetry; his transposition into the novel and particularly the requirements of the configuration worked up in *Insolación* call for a mitigation of his darker side.

The resemblance to Zorrilla's *Don Juan Tenorio* (1844) is playfully strengthened by his possessing "a lovely kind of romantic sadness" (153), and echoes of the Tenorio are heard in his amatory declarations: "What is it that you have in this mouth, and in these eyes, and in your whole being, that makes me feel this way?" (144). Gabriel Pardo looks down on Pacheco as "an idle cell in the social organism." Foucault finds that Don Juan's very appeal, which has endured for three centuries, is this: his refusal to submit to a productive sexual code, to forsake the fruitless pleasures. More than a mere libertine, he is a sociosexual outlaw, a pervert: "Underneath the great violator of the rules of marriage . . . another personage can be glimpsed: the individual driven, in spite of himself, by the somber madness of sex."[50]

Pardo Bazán was impressed with Galdós's *Fortunata y Jacinta*, published in 1886 and 1887, which also affixes itself to the Don Juan tradition, in the person of Juanito Santa Cruz. Several aspects of *Insolación* noted by Sobejano and González-Arias respond to the innovations of Galdós's monumental novel: the meticulous linguistic imitation of dialogue between lovers (which approximates baby talk in both novels) and of street, gypsy, and *chulo* slang, as well as the novelization of a modern Don Juan figure. To say merely that *Insolación* (in contrast to *Fortunata y Jacinta*) offers a novelized and softened Don Juan legend from a female point of view would be to oversimplify. As Julia Kristeva has observed, the moralistic condemnation of Don Juan implicit or explicit in all texts where he appears shows that he is always viewed through the victim's eyes—the narrator is the seduced woman.[51] Considered with this in view, condemnation of Don Juan behavior is conspicuously mild in *Insolación*. Asís half-affectionately, half-censuringly calls Pacheco a rogue and wonders whether he might be capable of deceiving her (67). The book is mainly concerned with answering one of the three questions Kristeva finds raised by the Don Juan tradition: "What attracts women to him, to a source of unhappiness and rejection?" Galdós's work has more to do with Kristeva's remaining questions: "What makes Don Juan tick? . . . What assembles around Don Juan these men who imagine themselves, who wish themselves, who conduct themselves *as if* they were he?"[52]

Pardo Bazán's answer to what it is about Don Juan that seduces women is not simple or direct. We have seen how desire, and its attendant punishment, is displaced throughout the work, emanating from the natural elements, from Asís's own body, and now from a man cloaked in Southern charm and impeccable attire who bears a resemblance to the archetypal masked man of literature. Their mutual affection shows traces of motherly care, much the same as the relationship between Juanito Santa Cruz and Jacinta. But here the one who "burns" for her sins is not Don Juan but Doña Inés, and the two are united in their being fugitives from the Father's law (Pacheco's father is displeased with him and would have him become a politician against his will; as Kristeva notes regarding nearly all depictions of Don Juan, his mother is never mentioned). The particular transposition of Don Juan Tenorio in *Insolación* shows Asís as the desiring subject not only of her lover but of his power. She feels a surprising inclination to trade places with him, to be permitted his exploits and moral relativism: "Asís felt a stinging curiosity together with unprovoked anger" (146). In another passage Asís puts her hand upon his chest to feel the mysteriously autonomous and varying activity of his vital organ when aroused by her tenderness: "Beneath the lady's palm, Pacheco's heart, like a spirit obeying a spell, erupted in the most violent dance such an organ can execute" (151). The symbolic power of the phallus is thinly veiled beneath the Don Juan persona of Pacheco. The dynamics of Asís's attraction to Pacheco confirm Kristeva's suspicion: "Could the seducer be the phallus itself? The temporary mastership, the timed power, the exhaustion leading to pure loss? The movement itself of erection and detumescence, phantasmally to infinity?"[53]

The resolution of this yearning to trade places with the Don Juan figure finds Asís listening to her own vital organ and enacting a reversal of the cited hand-over-heart sequence with Pacheco. But what is to be felt there is the entanglement of conflicting sensations within the sensationalized body of Asís, not the power concentrated in the heart of Don Juan:

Y a Asís se le revelaba entonces el amor. Poco a poco, sin conciencia de sus actos, acercaba la mano de Diego a su pecho, ansiosa de apretarla contra el corazón y de calmar así el ahogo suave que le oprimía. . . . Sus pupilas se humedecieron, su respiración se apresuró, y corrió por sus vértebras misterioso escalofrío, corriente de aire agitado por las alas del ideal.

[And then love made itself known to Asís. Slowly, unknowingly, she drew Diego's hand toward her chest, yearning to squeeze it against her heart and thus calm the faint breathlessness that afflicted her. . . . Her pupils moistened, her breath quickened, and along her spine ran a mysterious tingling, a gust swept up by the wings of the ideal.] (189–90)

This final revelation, in which Asís's body speaks its longing and finally convinces her mind, bridges the mind/body split and brings about a hasty conclusion of the plot and the conflicts that set it in motion. There is still, however, no sense of power within that body, no excited beating. The romantic love that has been signified by heat, electricity, pain, and a score of other signifiers remains undecidable. The lovers' decision to marry, referred to euphemistically as *la idea,* no doubt replying in part to Fortunata's *idea blanca,* perpetuates what Lacan calls the "fantasy of reciprocity between the sexes" and allows Asís to reenter the exchange economy, in which her body may be subjected and productive again. As it appears in the text, *la idea* has the ring of euphemism. Yet a euphemism, is generally used to stand for another signifier that is taboo; here, however, it is the conclusion dictated by convention. For this and many other reasons, a sense of unreality hovers over the conclusion. No effort is made to correct its *postizo* (false) quality, and the result is an open text that incites rather than calms the reader's doubts: Don Juan can only enjoy a conquest without possession, and Woman's quest for completion with an absolute Other shows no sign of being fulfilled. For Tolliver, the ending shows Asís's concern with saving face, but at the same time the narrator excites the reader's suspicions with the ironic reference to "something sublime that did not exist" in her lover's eyes. As Spacks observes of eighteenth- and nineteenth-century women writers in general, marriage and family are upheld as avenues to happiness on the surface, with only "subterranean challenges" to their validity.[54] The actual affair on which the story is loosely based did not in fact end in marriage, but blossomed into a long professional relationship, with Galdiano helping Pardo Bazán to direct *La España Moderna.*[55]

Stephen Gilman singles out Fortunata as Galdós's heroine par excellence. He defines her character development as relying very little upon physical detail: her bodily features are never "possessed in memory." She is not seen directly, but "in terms of the overwhelming impression she makes, first on Juanito and then on herself." Gilman holds, on the other hand, that she is a pure presence and that the (presumably male) reader enters her consciousness "in a way we can never know women of flesh and blood—our mothers, our sisters, and our wives."[56] His analysis points to the fundamental gap at the core of Galdós's heroines: they are feminine only in that Woman has come to be the primary signifier for late-nineteenth-century realism. The irreducible, undecidable nature of the figure Woman allows the female character to be a more-than-person. What Tanner writes of the gaps that constitute Emma Bovary applies in good measure to Galdós's heroines: "We have the music of Flaubert's text, and from it and within it we hear and infer the 'motif' of Emma Bovary. But if we search harder and harder for that motif . . . we lose all sense of a founder or 'original' and 'originating person.' "[57]

Whereas Gilman argues that Fortunata transcends the dichotomy of body and mind (to become a "vessel of creative passion"), it could also be argued that the body/mind split is maintained in such a way that a whole person never emerges. For this reason, the difficulty of finding a *vivencia* of the female body in Galdós leaves little room for the kinds of conflicts I have found to be at work in Pardo Bazán's "bodily text." A fascinating passage relevant to this question is "Las Micaelas por dentro," from *Fortunata y Jacinta*. To judge from Mauricia's Napoleonic face, the "manly" inmates, and Fortunata's robustness, one could be visiting a reform school for transvestites instead of a convent sheltering wayward women. In fact, one could well imagine Pedro Almodóvar directing another remake and casting Bibi Anderson in the title role. At any rate, the convent reform school seems to demonstrate that in the absence of men, Galdós's female characters quite naturally take over their role, because their connection to flesh-and-blood women was tenuous in the first place.

Although Pardo Bazán chose to incorporate some of the innovations in dialogue of *Fortunata y Jacinta,* adding to imitation of popular speech the possibilities inherent in a carnival atmosphere, it probably also supplied her with the negative inspiration to pursue her own representation of feminine psychology. Leopoldo Alas, of course, is another matter. Gilman remarks that Galdós lacks the "sensual recollections and libidinal longings that fill the pages of *La Regenta.*"[58] *La Regenta* (1884–85) is indeed sprinkled with the kind of "bodily" markers that abound in *Insolación.* Ana's "nostalgia for her mother's lap" harmonizes perfectly with the tradition of female-authored motherless heroines and the often maternal influence on depictions of mature desire. Clarín looks at the question of honor from the standpoint of its consequences for women, although he consigns Ana to the usual fate of the fallen woman. In addition, fever or heat is used to signify a broad range of emotional reactions: the death of Ana's father, her reading of St. John of the Cross, and the pleasure of being held by Alvaro.[59] Ana also suffers from suffocation, dizziness, and fainting. She feels an affinity for St. Teresa and mysticism in general. But perhaps the greatest difference in the way "the feminine" is conceived of in these two works is that there is no accomplice/censuring narrator—one who acknowledges transgressions and distortions as readily and ironically as the narrator of *Insolación*—in *La Regenta.* Thus, Ana's inner world is another aspect of a chaotic though stagnant provincial world. The narration is not a continuous stream of bodily sensations inciting conscientious objections on the narrator's part.

While more psychologically viable than Galdós heroines, Ana has the second but more essential role of playing a part in the larger mythic substratum of *La Regenta*—on the literary level where honor plays, Don Juan and the mystics interact and clash, and the heroine's body is a battleground. In addition, Ana is portrayed more often from without than from within, as an object of male desire, as when she disrobes and unconsciously strikes an odalisque pose on her bed. Like the odalisque of genre painting, her representation is by and large made for male consumption and casts the reader, whether male or female, as male voyeur.[60]

The inward focus of *Insolación* makes the *vivencia* of the female body of Pardo Bazán's milieu and moment accessible to the reader and also recreates its movement through a variety of social spaces. The panoply of sensations and symptoms to which Asís falls prey brings to mind the hysterization of women, cited by Foucault as one of "the four great strategies [of sexualization] that were deployed in the nineteenth century."[61] There is more at work here than Pardo Bazán loading her heroine with the psychosomatic symptoms that were widely associated with nineteenth-century women of leisure, coming to be regarded as a feminine form of *mal du siècle*. Through insistence upon the internalization of the Father's law practiced by the protagonist—her confessional engagement with Father Urdax, her blaming of herself—and through narration in free indirect style—the oscillation that includes censuring of Asís's actions—*Insolación* does not trap the heroine in a frame labeling her as a hysteric, but reproduces instead the conflict brought on by her pursuit of desire in a patriarchal setting. This in itself—the imperative of a love that satisfies physically as well as emotionally—was revolutionary for the time.[62] The clashing ideologies involved in this conflict include the sexual but do not stop there, as analysis of the carnival and country-inn passages reveals. The Father's law and the feminine semiotic drive develop their own discourses in this short novel, and their skirmishing is facilitated by bodily and spatial codes.

Asís's body is presented as a historical and highly political construct, in addition to being modeled upon a basic biological entity. For this reason, I have chosen to treat its representation in *Insolación* as a chapter of female political anatomy. The particular, historical variety of female subjection at work in the world of Pardo Bazán finds expression in the text, as the protagonist's social situation causes her body to react to the power exercised over it like one of Foucault's soldiers: "Power relations have an immediate hold upon it [the body]; they invest it, mark it, train it, torture it, force it to carry out tasks, to perform ceremonies, to emit signs." Asís's requesting body and the literally physical inscriptions upon it enter into dialogue eloquently with the internalized forces of subjection. The end of these political influences is to render the body a useful force, which is to say, productive and subjected.[63] Hence, the goal is not possession but the exercising of an influence, which ensures an ongoing skirmish rather than complete conquest of the body's forces. In fact, the resolution of the heroine's marriage, which promises to keep her desires in check and productive, is called into question before it even takes place, putting the accent on the ongoing battle.

Similarly, Asís's body is turned into the battleground upon which the Father's law fights a newer ideology of what Luce Irigaray calls "(re)productive earth-mother-nature." The erotic impulse associated with the latter and originating in the semiotic stage of development can be seen both in the lovers' "instinct" and in what fuels narrative and reader and moves them through the text, whereas the narrator's occasional reproaches and the powerful constellation of mainly male figures who stand in the way of desire are concessions made to the former. Undefinable, undecidable, and irreducible to any side of a binary opposition, the female body belongs to Jane Gallop's category of the "remainders" in literature. Thus, the mind/body split is exploded by infinite feminine desire, signified within and without by heat. This is only one of a series of binary oppositions—North/South, educated/uneducated (or rich/poor), male/female, Spain/Europe—on which the novel hinges and which it ultimately undoes. The insistence upon desire, its ravages and punishments, achieves something similar to the excesses of the Marquis de Sade, who, according to Gallop, used images of brutality to show that "the body always exceeds the mind's order."[64]

For this reason, it is not sufficient to cull feminist viewpoints from the text in the form of ideological bits and pieces we might then attribute to the author (e.g., the critique of the double standard), even though Pardo Bazán was an important early feminist.[65] To begin with, the question of a mouthpiece for the author among the main characters of *Insolación* is problematized by the ironization of nearly all viewpoints.[66] In addition, the denigration of lower-class women would contradict any broadly feminist agenda in the work. To assert Pardo Bazán's favoring of a feminist cause by assessing plot occurrences as stacking up in its support also fails to go the extra but necessary distance. It is on the level of the text, with its coincidences, paradoxes, ellipses, and echoes, that life is breathed into the female body as historical, cultural, biological, and political construct. This novel constitutes, to my knowledge, the first Spanish text in which the inscription of this body reaches the level of protagonization.

2.

Rosa Chacel

AS EXAMINATION OF EMILIA PARDO BAZÁN'S *Insolación* under-lines, the female body as textual marker in her work provides interpretive possibilities involving a heroine and an author under the stress of a male-oriented milieu. Ultimately this body is reclaimed as *vivencia,* as the territory of female experience rather than of male consumption. As we move ahead chronologically to Rosa Chacel (1898–1994), the position of the woman writer vis-à-vis literary movements such as modernism and the avant-garde demands atten-tion. One might suppose at the outset that human progress would make this more contemporary environment a more hospitable one for the woman writer; representations of the female body should reflect greater freedom and recognition of Woman as subject rather than object. However, this cannot be taken for granted in place of studying literary politics of the time, since the increased complexity of society may have negative effects that outweigh the benefit of general progress toward the liberation of women. Recent criticism of Felipe Trigo, for example, has revealed convincingly that the pos-sibility of writing the *novela erótica* does not automatically include a more enlightened treatment of sexuality; familiar gender stereotypes resurge, only in more explicit language.[1]

It is also worth considering that greater freedom for women in society at large may at times be reflected in literature in the form of a contrary reaction rather than solidarity.[2] By the end of the second decade of this century, feminism had acquired something of a foothold in the urban Spanish milieu. Activists such as Clara Campoamor and organizations such as the ANME (Asociación Nacional de Mujeres Españolas), UME (Unión de Mujeres Españolas), and JUF (Junta Universitaria Femenina) gave feminism a higher profile, and women no longer needed special prior permission to enroll in universities. In 1915 the Residencia Femenina opened in Madrid, giving female students a place to live and study alongside their male colleagues of the Residencia de Estudiantes. Spanish women did not obtain the right to vote until 1931, eleven years after their counterparts in the United States. In the works of a novelist like Chacel, who grew up at a time when women were beginning to gain some influence in a cultural forum still overwhelmingly male-dominated, representations of the female body again present a useful vehicle for examining relationships between gender, sexuality, and literary politics.

A 1991 interview found Chacel in Madrid, working on the third volume of her diary, to be entitled *Alcancía. Estación Termini.*[3] Her last novel, *Ciencias naturales,* the third in her trilogy of novels in dialogue, was published in 1988. Neglected in the annals of contemporary literature for much of her life, she was rediscovered by a new generation of writers, such as Ana María Moix and Clara Janés, in the 1970s. She found a wider readership in the 1980s and was awarded the Premio Nacional de las Letras in 1987. Still, for a writer of her stature, there is a sense of injustice in her not having received the Cervantes Prize and not having been inducted into the Real Academia de la Lengua.

Chacel's birthdate and some of her friendships and acquaintances place her within the Generación del '27 in Spain. Discussions of the literary production of this group, however, uniformly overlook her, and this neglect crosses over into university courses, in which critical categorization influences which works are covered in classes devoted to chronological periods or movements, perpetuating an undeserved oblivion. One argument against the use of the term *generation* (among many possible ones)[4] for classifying writers of the not so distant past is the inevitably occurring marginalization of contemporaneous writers who did not move in quite the same social circles.[5] (Another writer marginalized by this critical construct, as well as for political reasons, is León Felipe, whose wanderings kept him out of touch with developments in Spain but who perhaps merits inclusion in the canon.) Thus the *generación de la amistad* (friendship), as it has been called,[6] can also function as a *generación del amiguismo* ("friendism," or reliance upon personal connections) when it is used as an exclusive critical construct, placing some writers in the spotlight and others in the shadows as a function of their relation to the central, most powerful cultural figures (mentors or patrons) who called the generation into being.

Chacel's gender in all likelihood played a part in her being sidelined in discussions of the literary scene of her youth, especially since at least one of the group's protectors, Juan Ramón Jiménez, may be assumed to have opposed active roles for *literatas*.[7] Other of her life circumstances, such as her original background in the visual arts at the San Bernardo Academy of Madrid (rather than the Residencia de Estudiantes, home to most of the male writers), her working mainly in fiction rather than in poetry, the extensive periods she spent in Rome and Berlin before the Civil War, her self-imposed postwar exile in Buenos Aires, Río de Janeiro, and New York (1940–74), and the scarcity of Spanish editions of her books until the early 1970s, must have also played a part in her remaining isolated in comparison with the contemporaneous writers who are most widely read and studied today. Some of these factors—life in exile and the difficulty of being published in Spain during Franco's rule—have also resulted in the delayed recognition of her peers, especially those who wrote fiction and who had not produced the better part of their work prior to the war. The uprootedness (and penury) she experienced for nearly three decades, in common with other exiled contemporaries, such as her friends Francisco Ayala and Luis Cernuda, is perhaps what prompted Juan Gil-Albert to call her "la rosa sin rosal" (the rose without a rosebush) in a poem of homage.[8]

The avant-garde prose of those writing concurrently with Chacel's early, pre–Civil War career has not fared well among most critics and readers. Creative and critically acute rereadings of this experimental fiction by Gustavo Pérez Firmat and Robert Spires are shining exceptions to this neglect, but they fail to deal substantively with Chacel.[9] Evidently something in the way these prose writers experimented with form makes their work less compelling than the equally experimental Spanish "new novel" of the 1960s and 1970s. It has been suggested that an exaggerated narratorial presence and focus on the means of representation rather than on what is represented detract from such writers of the "third generation" as Ramón Gómez de la Serna, Benjamín Jarnés, and Antonio Espina. Other new writers, such as Guillermo de la Torre, perceived better what ought not to be done rather than what should be done. Only the older Ramón del Valle-Inclán was able to confront the myriad imperatives for the novel arising in the first few decades of this century and substitute something new—theatricality—for what had been lost in the process of dehumanization (an extreme distancing of art from human experience).[10] Chacel's early work is also salvageable from the label of dehumanization in its most negative sense, thanks in large measure to the gender tensions that surface within her texts.

Although Chacel may have found herself in the margins in several respects, she did at least count upon the mentorship of José Ortega y Gasset.[11] She came of literary age while his guidance, through the *Revista de Occidente,* was of major importance among budding writers. Chacel's novels, in particular the early ones, demonstrate a thorough knowledge of Ortega's prescriptions for the novel contained in *Ideas sobre la novela, Meditaciones del Quijote,* and *La deshumanización del arte.* Her reception of Ortega is always highly charged, whether negatively or positively, and this enlivens the dialogic levels of her novels. She wrote *Teresa* at his explicit suggestion in order to contribute to the series Vidas extraordinarias del siglo XIX, which he was to publish.

Shirley Mangini, Janet Pérez, and others who have written on Chacel state unproblematically that she put Ortega's views on the novel and on psychology into practice verbatim in her work, producing a "novelization" of Orteguian philosophy.[12] However, an analysis of form and of outcroppings of the human form in her work explodes this paradigm of Rosa the obedient pupil passively receiving the master's wisdom and spinning it all, Arachne-like (imitating one of her favorite mythological figures), into fiction. Chacel was an avid reader of Freudian psychoanalysis,[13] and her intertextual relation with her mentor seems to have benefited from the inevitable conflict with the Father's law as represented by Ortega.

In exploring Chacel's writing on the female body and her tangling with the Father's law, I will consider *Estación. Ida y vuelta* for its formal innovations and physical imagery. In *Teresa,* at her mentor's urging, Chacel is sent back to the romantic era and must write her way out of the mirror of a powerless female character. Nineteenth-century Woman is herein uncannily reimagined from the inside outward in a way that recalls the physical discomfort of *Insolación*. The influence asserted by Ortega having become unbearable in the writing of *Teresa*, Chacel rebels and has her young pupil conquer the schoolmaster in *Memorias de Leticia Valle*, which I will read for its markers of physicality and textuality and alongside *Portrait of the Artist as a Young Man* in order to outline gender-influenced differences in producing the Bildungsroman. I will also look to Freud's *Dora: An Analysis of a Case of Hysteria* for what it has to add about archetypal father-daughter seduction, which Chacel's third novel teases into a triangle and subverts to female advantage. In Chacel's later novels I will examine the recurring return to the female form in the guise of dancers, sculptures, and mothers, particularly in *La sinrazón*.

In a 1983 interview Chacel spoke out mordantly against some strains of feminist criticism.[14] I agree with her statement that no definable feminine style of writing exists and that there should be no such thing as a feminine literature considered always apart from the masculine kind (in view of what tends to happen in separate-but-equal arrangements). However, while becoming immersed in literature by women I have observed that certain phenomena—which my study attempts to bring into focus—seem overdetermined by the biological and cultural fact that the writer is female. While it would not have been impossible for a male author to write any of the novels selected (some Pierre Menard with an uncanny talent for reinventing his entire past and present in the act of writing), for the reasons outlined in my study, which often have to do with intersections of textuality and physicality, I find it highly unlikely. In addition, I feel that as readers we are entitled to make use of the author function in supplying the meaning for a given text. It cannot help but interest us that Chacel writes as a woman or, for that matter, that Camilo José Cela writes as a man.[15] If, as Chacel states, "my work is entirely a striptease; I am me, stark naked,"[16] then much of what the reader sees will have to do with gender.

In Chacel's extensive *oeuvre*, the body-as-text reads in different ways. There is the vanguardist Chacel who writes of a disgust with conventional femininity and in so doing uses the female body, or more specifically, its fetishized parts, to take aim at the status quo. There are the strong but troubled female personalities who view their bodies as unfortunate signs of membership in their gender but who also find pleasure and power in the permeability of boundaries (of a self and body that are entwined) between themselves and others. Other bodies are frozen by the male gaze—into art, symbols of maternity, or currency to be exchanged. The perspective is a shifting one, but an undercurrent that reinvests the body as a whole and as a sum of its parts with a surprising power unites these novels.

Estación. Ida y vuelta: Chacel, Ortega y Gasset, and Bodily Discourse

Criticism has emphasized the role of José Ortega y Gasset (1883–1955), for better or for worse, in shaping Spanish fiction writers of the 1920s and 1930s vanguard. Ortega's powerful position as the owner of means of publication, as well as the maturity, authority, and connections he possessed in a less tangible way, cast him as a paternal figure who interacted with each writer in a way analogous to the archetype of father and son. Since the familial and economic configurations of patriarchal society at large are mirrored in the sphere of literary creation, it is important to consider this relationship when analyzing literary production of the time. As is repeatedly the case in the cycle of literary tradition and renovation, when such a dyad is formed, the younger partner, in addition to being influenced, is likely to rebel in some way; the conflict itself fosters the imagination. In the case of Ortega and Chacel, the bond becomes father-daughter, and the factor of sexual difference enters the picture. It can be expected to condition the kinds of tutelage, apprenticeship, and rebellion that will arise. Not surprisingly, markers of sexual difference show up in Chacel's early fiction, and many have to do with her handling of the female body as a trope. Thus far, Chacel's reception of Ortega's aesthetics has been characterized as passive. Here I shall focus on the discourse concerning the body in the works of Ortega and Chacel, problematizing the notion of a passive reception on Chacel's part. At the same time, I shall call attention no less than previous scholars have done to the strong and productive relationship between the two writers.

Most of the fiction produced in an avant-garde vein in the third and fourth decades of the twentieth century, when the second wave of modernism came of age in Spain, has aged poorly and now seems dated, and it was harshly criticized in postwar decades as dehumanized in a negative sense, that is, as forsaking social consciousness.[17] As it is customary to observe, poetry was the dominant genre and constituted the major focus of literary attention. The ingenious *greguerías* of Ramón Gómez de la Serna do not necessarily combine to make a memorable novel (his formula for the *greguería* is a metaphor plus a pun). Francisco Ayala is congratulated for all but disowning his novice avant-garde attempts.[18] The lyrical novels of Gabriel Miró, Pérez de Ayala's "poematic novels," and the deformation of reality found in Ramón del Valle-Inclán's later works, while of undisputed importance, do not entirely break with tradition in the way of full-fledged avant-gardes, the sort defined in manifestos and typified by the dada and surrealist movements in France.[19] These modernists or Noventayochistas (writers such as Miguel de Unamuno and Ramón del Valle-Inclán, whose lives and writings were indelibly marked by Spain's defeat by the United States in 1898, which meant loss of its remaining colonies), leaned more toward *renovación* than toward *ruptura* in their innovations.

One of the few authentically avant-garde efforts that at once both challenges and rewards the reader and still merits reading for reasons other than the archeological is Rosa Chacel's *Estación. Ida y vuelta* (1930). Nor has this work met with misfortune in the eyes of its author: Chacel professed satisfaction with her brief first novel decades after it was written, and she continues to see it as the key to all her subsequent creations;[20] moreover, she used its triangular conflict as the embryo of her major opus, *La sinrazón* (1960). *Estación* represents a unique confrontation of the Spanish woman writer and a primarily male, incipient avant-garde tradition, for which Ortega was spokesman. As such, it can be read with delectation today. In addition, as all the more recent scholarship on the book declares, reading it is essential for an understanding of the Spanish avant-garde.[21]

Estación was written in 1925–26, the final two years Chacel spent in Italy with her husband, artist Timoteo Pérez Rubio, on a grant he had received from the Roman Fine Arts Academy. The first chapter was published in 1927 in *Revista de Occidente,* and Julio

Gómez de la Serna (brother of Ramón) published the work in its entirety at Editorial Ulises in 1930, after Ortega's series Nova Novorum, which was to publish it initially, had ceased to exist.[22] Before writing it, Chacel had read Joyce, Proust, Freud, Dostoevsky, and the Noventayochistas. To these she added essays that gradually made their way from Spain, authored by a man to whom she would soon refer as her *maestro* (teacher, master), José Ortega y Gasset. They would not meet until 1930, after her return to Spain, but it is evident from her first writings onward that both Ortega's general philosophy and his aesthetics of a new art had a profound and personal effect on her.

Chacel herself states that her aim was to make Orteguian philosophy the plot or protagonist of her first novel.[23] In fact little "happens" to the consciousness whose thoughts populate the text, but this does not mean that the work lacks a plot or characters.[24] Incidents in his life are perceived as vaguely as the passing of seasons and come to mind in seemingly involuntary fashion, in the Proustian-Joycean manner of interior monologue. Loosely connected recollections of a first, nameless love, who at times appears fused with the narrator, succeed each other.[25] Breaks in the already tenuous thread follow as the narrator appears fused with the author, who usurps the narrative voice and meditates metafictively on philosophy and the very writing of novels. These digressions alternate again with the original protagonist, who is now in love with someone who has a name (Julia). He travels to France and finally returns to the first *novia* after being notified by telegram that she is pregnant with their child. An interesting consequence of the narrative disregard for outward occurrences is that even astute studies of the novel disagree about the most basic plot events; Gil Casado, for example, holds that the first love is identical to Julia.[26]

Ana Rodríguez Fischer outlines some of the Orteguian ideas that make their presence known: the narrator's *razón vital*, the rational sense intrinsic to the individual that guides her or him along unpredictable pathways in life, is in a continual process of exposition (however, the existentialist quality that results has been effectively likened elsewhere to Unamuno);[27] the interiority of the protagonist never dissolves, although he is presented as absorbed in his surrounding circumstances; life (and the novel) is a pathway determined by the choice and realization of a personal destiny. Rodríguez Fischer also finds that formally the novel is compatible with Ortega's literary aesthetics as expressed in *Ideas sobre la novela* because of the aforementioned interior monologue, perspectivism, and narration of events taking place within the imagined soul rather than outside of it.[28] Shirley Mangini describes more ways that Ortega's description of the avant-garde became a dictum for Chacel in the writing of the novel: her avoidance of concretizing characters and her creation of a Doppelgänger effect to achieve ambiguity in the character's interpersonal relations, making his interior climate the only certainty for the reader. Furthermore, Mangini traces connections to some other currents in contemporaneous Spanish literature: the prevalence of *greguerías* much like those concocted by Gómez de la Serna (yet different in content, as we shall see) and the influence of "pure poetry" as aspired to by the poets of the 1927 group in the "irrational metaphors," which often personify objects or include elements of violence.

Her study also points to a question of guidance (one that I shall develop further here). Ortega's prescribing the art to come—which was paradoxical, since the very function of this new art was to be iconoclastic—as well as analyzing it as it was produced interacted with Chacel's possibly problematic status as a woman writer of the avant-garde. This prompts Mangini to speculate that "Chacel identified so intensely with her male contemporaries that she found it necessary to employ a male character as the mouthpiece for her ideas."[29] Yet there is ample evidence in the text to suggest that the repressed figure of Woman refuses to vanish; as we shall see, the seasons and stations of *Estación* are precisely those of a female body. In order to reflect more fully upon these and other substantial issues in the novel, it will be necessary to reconstruct as best we can some gender differences revealed in literary politics of the time.

The Spanish avant-gardes that arose in the 1920s and 1930s, including some of the poets of the Generación del '27, were important for Ortega as a cultural critic inasmuch as they represented subsets of the *arte nuevo* he had called into being. Ortega sought to describe and analyze what many of his contemporaries preferred to dismiss or eschew, and in so doing he crossed a generational boundary to become a champion for Spain's novice *literatos*. He also installed himself as a father figure among these young artists. It was a time he viewed as a dominion of the young. He perceived himself as unfortunate for having been young while his elders held sway, and now as he entered middle age the pendulum had swung back again.[30] By acting as protector for new writers (as well as editor and publisher through the *Revista de Occidente* and Espasa-Calpe), Ortega was able to live their *mocedades* vicariously, much like Juan Ramón Jiménez, who preceded him in this role. The love-hate relationships that grew out of Jiménez's paternal attitude are more striking and well documented.[31] The fact that Ortega's relationships never became tainted with vituperation attests to his strong identification with the young people of the time; indeed, he blamed the disorder he saw in the Europe of 1927 on the generation to which his elders belonged.[32] To Ortega's drive to prescribe a new art for the young we can also ascribe a desire to provide direction for Spain, and in turn for Europe.[33]

Renato Poggioli proposes *deformation* rather than *dehumanization* as a term that is at once more encompassing and more specific in describing the avant-garde that was arising under Ortega's gaze. When Poggioli criticizes Arnold Toynbee for construing the avant-garde's abandonment of Western tradition as spiritual breakdown (Ortega would have objected as well, but for other reasons), he takes into account a parameter that was not stated in *La deshumanización del arte* but was destined to be exemplified by it, namely, the capacity of avant-garde culture to generate its own traditions: "But his [Toynbee's] greatest error is the inability to realize that the reaction of modernism to tradition is one more bond, *sui generis,* to that very tradition. Avant-garde deformation, for all that the artists who practice it define it as antitraditional and anticonventional, also becomes a tradition and a stylistic convention. . . . The deformation is determined by a stylistic drive, which inaugurates a new order as it denies the ancient order."[34]

With the publication of *La deshumanización del arte* and *Ideas sobre la novela* in 1925, Ortega set down two manuals on the proper means of practicing iconoclasm. The former, geared mainly, though not exclusively, to the visual and aural arts, supplied an epithet, *deshumanizado* (dehumanized), that would be used broadly later in criticizing literature influenced by the latter book. This subsequent derogation of a term that Ortega had taken pains to cast in a positive light may be partially at the root of Poggioli's preference for the notion of deformation. At any rate, my aim in questioning the anti-traditional nature of Ortega's impact on literature is not to undermine the iconoclasm of the avant-garde movement as a whole, which may be better undermined, as we shall see, by exposing the role it assigns to the female body. Instead, in looking at any fledgling writer of the time who was influenced by Ortega, one should step back and observe how he or she has found some way, consciously or not, to rebel against the master. In the case of Rosa Chacel, the additional circumstance of gender difference shows up clearly in her writing, even if she denies the importance of this factor in conversation.[35] Her ability to survive in the environment in question may have been contingent upon her denial of gender significance. Thus, although Chacel's stated intention in writing *Estación. Ida y vuelta* is to compose a novel in which Orteguian philosophy plays the main character, and although most critics have accepted it without reservation as the "novelization" of Orteguian philosophy and of his ideas about the novel in general, I believe that an examination of the text itself, and particularly its intersections of textuality and physicality, reveals that the matter is not so simple.

As Luis Fernández Cifuentes has noted, *Ideas sobre la novela* is grounded in a rigid separation of the elements author, reader, and character or plot.[36] Precisely as the differentiation is established in the essay, it is deemed a necessary feature of better and contemporary novels. Through the use of first-person singular and plural pronouns, Ortega identifies himself with the role of reader only—and specifically, not a mediocre one.[37] As a reader of Chacel I am immediately put on guard by this, since one of my first and most lasting impressions of Chacel as a novelist is that she is a very "writerly" writer.[38] Words, texture, lyricism (not to be confused with sentimentality)—preoccupations of writers like Gabriel Miró, who drew scathing criticism from Ortega—are important constitutive elements in her work. For as much as Ortega claims nontranscendence to be a goal the novelist need not be ashamed of, and no matter how much he prefers that the novel not be put at the service of commitments other than literary ones (i.e., political or social ones), his nonidentification with the author leaves him little to say about writing itself. Instead, he concludes by putting the novel at the service of something equally extraliterary, namely, amateur psychological study. As the lesson of naturalism demonstrates, in order for the novelist to function as a social scientist, scientific objectivity and isolation from the subject being studied must be assumed (even if they are eventually blurred, as *Insolación* makes manifest). Ortega is careful to qualify his preferred subject matter as imagined psyches and does not call the writer a scientist. Yet he holds that when a novel from the past seems trite to the reader of today, "it is because the reader is himself a better psychologist than the author."[39]

Even on this basic level of reader-author-character (or plot) separateness, the novelization of Ortega by Chacel becomes suspect. The "spiritual" autobiography that precedes the story proper of *Estación* forces the reader to consider the author's self-projected image as part and parcel of the reading experience. I use the word *image* in appreciation of Chacel's consciousness of what has come to be known as the Foucauldian "author function." It is as if Chacel, knowing that whatever information the reader may have about an author's life will inevitably influence reception of his or her book, chose to control that image, to provide the reader with exactly the author function relevant to reading the work. As several critics have observed, this autobiographical, or confessional, mode, while occurring frequently in the work of male authors, is almost a universal in women's writing.[40] Here it constitutes the most immediately visible divergence of *Estación* from Orteguian dogma. And the emergence of disparities between the novel and *Ideas sobre la novela* only begins here. It is true that some of the disparities might have arisen from the tension between *Ideas* and *La deshumanización del arte* themselves, for the two texts should not be assumed to be harmonious. For example, it would be difficult to write the provincial novel Ortega describes and still produce a dehumanized work of art. However, the nature of most of these differences seems rooted in the active process of Chacel's assimilation, a process complicated by her own cultural definition as female.

Care must be taken in the first place in assuming that a philosophy expressed in a certain essay may be embodied in a literary work. Either or both of these entities may be bent in order to accommodate the other, to the extent that the comparison winds up saying little about either of them. A case in point would be to consider the reputed concordance of *Estación* and *Ideas* alongside a statement made recently in an insightful article by Stephanie Sieburth: "*La Regenta* is one of the books which comes closer to fulfilling the prescriptions of Ortega y Gasset in *Ideas sobre la novela*."[41] As it happens, this scholar relates the concepts of hermetism and of the provincial novel, concepts that apply least to Chacel's first novel and that conflict with *La deshumanización del arte,* to Alas's masterpiece. Both works do in fact conform to the Orteguian ideal in their distinct, partial ways, yet few modern Spanish novels have as little in common as *Estación* and *La Regenta.*

Further divergence from *Ideas sobre la novela* is found in the break of what little narrative thread existed as the narrator indulges in lengthy digressions of a philosophical and metafictional nature toward the middle and end of the novel. This rupture conforms well to the general avant-garde strategy of defying narrative intelligibility, of breaking with the story line as an aggressive act against convention.[42] Chacel's implementation of this strategy goes against the grain inasmuch as the digression causes a blurring between the narrator-protagonist of the story and the narrator-author, to whom we were introduced in the preliminary autobiography. Here Chacel bursts the bubble of hermetism irreparably: the reader cannot help but associate the musings on writing itself with the novelist herself. This sliding implies a gender-crossing between voices that is more perplexing still; knowingly or not, Chacel plays with the reader's assumptions. Does the sliding back and forth from female author to male protagonist imply that there is no discernible difference between the sexes in their apprehension of themselves and of their circumstances? If this is the case, one still wonders why Chacel chose to "speak as a man." How could this not have been conditioned by the preponderance of male writers and by Ortega's self-proclaimed Age of Masculinity?[43] The very crossing of boundaries calls attention to gender difference. The text supplies a partial answer to these questions:

> Me avergüenza crearle [mi protagonista] muy cerca de mí, prefiero hacerle de mis viceversas. . . . Será de esos hombres que pueden tener una permanente manifestación de "su yo." Fluctuará "mi yo" movedizo alrededor del suyo firme.

[I am ashamed to create him so close to myself, I prefer to make him out of my viceversa. . . . He will be one of those men capable of having a permanent manifestation of "their I's." My swaying "I" will hover about his firm one.][44]

The selection of a male voice is not without a certain irony, intentional or not, since we know that the narrator's consciousness is constantly permeated by those of his *novias* and by the author, resulting in a complex series of Doppelgänger effects.[45] In addition, the fact that a male is represented as writing this in the first place leads to an interesting *mise en abyme* that reinforces the playful gender-crossing subtext: the female author creates a male character with a firm sense of self, who in turn fantasizes about creating a male character with a firm sense of self, who in turn . . . One is reminded of the sisters described elsewhere in the novel as "Chinese boxes," the eldest being distinct only in that all the others are contained inside of her (56). The firm, supposedly masculine "I" is conspicuous in its absence throughout, as if to question the very possibility of its achievement. In this sense the Father's law, in the form of masculine mastery over the narrative, is rejected and denied in favor of permeable character boundaries. This permeability may at first glance echo Freud's finding of permeable ego boundaries in the female psyche, a finding he then uses to claim that female ego development is forever incomplete. In this novel, however, and even more so in *Memorias de Leticia Valle,* the device is employed as a positive technique for illuminating feminine *vivencia,* the view from inside the female body. Stretching of character and ego boundaries has been seen as the literary parallel to the physical extension of self involved in motherhood.[46] This takes place on a textual level in Chacel's writing, even if maternity as a theme remains a lateral issue to the main characters in her novels. Maternity and authorship are compared in *Estación* in that the protagonist-author's digression on the novel he or she is planning to write is simultaneous with the child developing in the lover's body.

The shame involved in writing of a character who is "too close" is also resonant. As Susan Suleiman asserts of the woman avant-garde writer (based on Marguerite Duras's calling her own writing "doubly intolerable"), writing in an antitraditional vein and being female besides makes her position twice as vulnerable.[47] If we venture to presume that Chacel writes through a male mouthpiece in order to alleviate this twentieth-century version of the anxiety of female authorship,[48] then the *glissement* that occurs in the female author persona shows that her search for shelter behind a male protagonist is equivocal; a female voice is in fact struggling to emerge and is playfully mocking the need for an absolute, phallic signifier, a firm "I." The reader then begins to perceive the novel as a search for a voice in a maze of discourses: confessional, avant-garde, cinematic, and philosophical, among others.[49] This meshing contributes to the work's vitality.

Philosophical discourse takes center stage during the first digression (a clumsy label used for lack of a better one, as it is hard to pinpoint where story line ends and digression begins). The narrator rambles on about things, from his lack of a career to thoughts that run parallel to Ortega's well-known tenets that there are no more interesting plots to be invented and that the individual cannot be seen as separate from his circumstances. They contain such echoes, in fact, that they distract from the hermetism of the interior monologue:

> El desenlace, el encasillamiento, la clasificación de mi historia vulgar de mal estudiante que tiene un contratiempo con la vecina y recurre a la burocracia, sin terminar el doctorado. Todos verán con desprecio mi historia vulgar. . . . Maldicen al Destino. Porque no quieren ser cuerpo de su Destino. Quieren que sea algo exterior, los otros, lo que está fuera, las circunstancias. Pero yo no me veo, no puedo verme, más que penetrado de mis circunstancias; me busco entre ellas, y no me encuentro.

> [The unraveling, the pigeonholing, the classification of my ordinary tale of a mediocre student who has a mishap with the girl next door and turns to bureaucracy, without finishing his doctorate. Everyone will look down on my common story. . . . They curse Destiny. Because they do not want to be part of the body of Destiny. They want it to be something external, the rest, what is outside, circumstances. But I do not, I cannot, see myself other than permeated by my circumstances; I seek myself among them, and fail to find myself.] (77–78)

This permeation of Orteguian doctrines, textually interrupting narrative flow, conflicts with the idea of a voice that says, "I have my own personal norm, which I am bent upon imposing. Because that is true satisfaction, that contradiction, that resistance of the current" (80). Yet the regurgitation seems oddly necessary, something that the novelist must get out of her system before finding a voice of her own. Resistance to this foreign matter abounds as well: it may be summarized in the difference between a novel that makes the reader contemplate (Ortega's preference) and one that contemplates aloud. Nor does this novel make the concessions to dramatic interest that Ortega deems necessary "for the human soul."[50] Rather, in a further refusal of mastery over narrative much like the kind that French feminism associates with women writers, it either slows the plot or nearly suppresses it. The fluctuation throughout the work between compliance with and resistance to the Father's law gives new meaning to the final words, "Something has ended, now I can say, 'Beginning!'" (200).

When asked what sort of an impression her *orteguismo* had on the man in question, Chacel is equivocal. The publication history of *Estación* reveals underlying stress in their mentorship. Instead of publishing the entire book as she had hoped, he accepted only the first chapter. The complete manuscript "was mislaid among other papers." She got the distinct impression that he had not read it. When it was finally published, she found that the work "had no resonance whatsoever." When she tried to elicit a substantive comment from the critic Manuel Abril, he would only remark, "You go off to Rome, without saying a word to anyone. You come back with a little book like this and you would have a man read it as if it were Kant." Most surprising is the lack of acrimony on Chacel's part in recounting all this; indeed, she has only positive things to say about these figures who had the potential to extinguish her literary aspirations when they had barely caught fire.[51]

Ortega's *Ideas sobre el cuerpo* are most notably expressed in the essay "Vitalidad, alma, espíritu" (1924).[52] In that essay he seeks to differentiate his thoughts on psychology from those of Freud, which he considers too mechanistic in their separation of the components of the psyche into ego, id, superego, and so on. Ortega does propose his own tripartite division but chooses instead to speak of personality "centers" or "zones," emphasizing their interrelatedness and overlap: the *espíritu,* most closely translatable as the rational mind, which Ortega also calls the "I," the subject of statements of thought, opinion, and will; the *alma*, the site of emotions and vital energy, the "me" as object of external factors that provoke feelings over which one has no control; and the *intracuerpo*. The *intracuerpo* is "the portion of our psyche that lives infused in the body, bound to it and melded with it."⁵³ Herein lie consciousness of physical sensations, the basic instincts of self-preservation, "the attraction of one sex for another," "vitality," and perception of the inner body.⁵⁴

Although Ortega asserts that the body has been much maligned by civilization—more so by Protestantism than by Catholicism—and that both body and intrabody should be studied for their role in determining human nature, by the end of his abruptly curtailed section on the physical he has managed to align neurotics, artists, mystics, philosophers, and women with an unusually acute and therefore unhealthy inner-body consciousness.⁵⁵ The impulse of the healthy organism is to look outward; only civilization has given a positive value—and only in the case of artists, mystics, and philosophers—to something "biologically pathological." Thanks to this phenomenon, woman "enjoys a greater sensitivity to physical pain than other creatures, whether human or animal." On the other hand, woman "is better acquainted than the male with the marvelous respite, which consists of being overwhelmed by another being."⁵⁶ Ortega himself takes credit for doing some of the overwhelming when he proclaims himself a Don Juan who knows how to predict any woman's "quarter of an hour" of vulnerability to seduction.⁵⁷

On a sociohistorical as well as an individual level, Ortega's writing makes abundant use of sexual difference and employs the binary opposition of masculine/feminine, along with youth/age and spirituality/corporality, as key "antagonistic powers" that determine the character of an era. In a manner similar to Jung, he saw the masculine and feminine as traits possible in both males and females. It all depends upon which trait, or "lifestyle," is dominant at a particular time.⁵⁸ For this reason, the Venus de Milo, sculpted during a masculine age par excellence, is a hermaphrodite in his eyes, "a kind of athlete with breasts."⁵⁹ Conversely, from the twelfth century up to and including Ortega's grandparents' generation, the feminine mode has been in power, and "men's suits begin to imitate the lines of feminine dress."⁶⁰ Thus far his views correspond to Nietzsche's on the feminization of culture.⁶¹ Ortega distinguishes his time as one of transition from feminine to masculine values, from mature to youth-

ful ones, from the spiritual to the corporeal, and from an ideal of spir-
itualized love of woman to a "perception of male physical beauty."
For this reason women find themselves being assimilated to the male
point of view in their interest in athletics and automobiles, and
society has become ill-mannered after losing the feminine value
placed on etiquette. Men have become more temperate in their relations with women, ceasing their Dantesque obsessions, but there is
the danger of their resorting to "Doric love," Orteguian code for
homosexuality. Women, in turn, dress and tone their bodies in order
to look boyish and hide their breasts, which were ostentatiously
displayed during the nineteenth century. Ortega does his best not to
gloat over the triumph of masculinity: "As one who has spent his
youth in a feminine epoch, it grieves me to see the humility with
which the woman of today, dethroned, attempts to insinuate herself
and to be tolerated in the society of men."[62]

There is ample cause here for Chacel to have changed genders
textually out of humility and deference to the maestro's way of
thinking, in addition to dread of "forming part of the body of her
Destiny," to rephrase her protagonist's words. What is more, the
attitude displayed in her writing toward the female body is certainly
less liberating than that of Pardo Bazán's *Insolación,* to cite an example from the most recent woman writer assigned major importance in
the canon preceding Chacel. Ortega's attitude may in fact be a reaction to real advances made by women in Spanish society: hence his
criticism pertains to the pedestal effect that resulted from the more
constraining conditions of the nineteenth century. However, to forsake the pedestal and traditional femininity is to become male; for
Ortega there is no definition of femininity other than his grandparents' patriarchal one. Thus, in Ortega's scheme, the female body is
to be subjected still more, though not for the traditional reasons.
Instead, the subjection is required for the emergence of a virile new
society. This brings us to the matter of how the avant-garde, while
ostensibly upholding radical change, brought no respite from pa-
triarchalism. The representation of the female body in the novel is
another case in point.

Victor Fuentes describes the tendency of Spanish avant-garde
writers, and particularly of Benjamín Jarnés, to "break the chain that
unites fathers and sons across generations": this includes a parody of
bourgeois values that turns love into "a matrimonial transaction or

reproductive sexuality."[63] Jarnés, as well as José Díaz Fernández, achieves this parody in part through a mechanization of sex and of the female body.[64] A parallel is found in the Golden Age in Quevedo's satire, which unites the figure of woman with corruption and decay, as it does other objects of men's desire, such as money.[65] Hence, what Fuentes and many other scholars of avant-garde movements have called a breaking of the intergenerational chain might more accurately be viewed as a repetition of an age-old oedipal confrontation between father and son. As Suleiman observes of Georges Bataille and of the avant-garde in general, that confrontation is "staged across and over the body of the mother," who has no active role in the proceedings. Suleiman holds that as long as this state of affairs persists, no true rupture with the past is possible.[66]

In this climate, which appears to have released the old hostilities toward Woman and the body rather than abated them, it is no wonder that what Chacel has to say about the female body in *Estación* is nowhere near as affirming or liberating as the desire-driven narrative by Pardo Bazán. Here there is no sliding into the semiotic mode, or *jouissance*.[67] Instead, true to the sliding of voices and narrative ambiguity, an ambivalence toward the female form is perceived that runs a spectrum from disgust or horror, to fetishization, to a subtle recurrence and pervasiveness. Suppressing it from the narrative, however, is clearly not an option. The avant-garde reaction against tradition means that the conventions of courtly love, carried over into the realist novel, which glorified the idealized and inaccessible female lover and separated her body into praiseworthy parts, must be turned upside down. Consequently, the blazon is parodied in the only poem the narrator feels he can write about his beloved's eyes, a poem that duplicates diagrams found in medical textbooks:

Párpado	....	a	....	Eyelid
Pupila	....	b	....	Pupil
Lagrimal	....	c	....	Tear duct
Pestañas	....	d	....	Eyelashes
				(60)

Scientific discourse here functions to demystify the body, whereas customarily it was the subject of laudatory synecdoche. Likewise, the narrator cannot understand his beloved's chagrin when he compares the tiny veins showing through the skin of her décolletage to a railroad map (105). He meant this as a compliment, to show how observant of her he is. Besides parodying the conventions of courtly love, the narrator tends toward disgust, an attitude that later found much development in the movement *tremendismo:* "The truth is that her mouth is not ugly. But the way her lips turn outward . . . it makes the gums so visible!" (112). There is something about even the best-dressed women that inspires pity in him. He cannot watch his lover move her lips to pronounce *petit* without shuddering (113). When he kisses her goodbye, he feels "more than repugnance . . . fed up, as if I had kissed all the women in the world" (159). After the embrace the narrator leaves France and embarks on ruminations on his future novel, which occupy most of the remaining text, thus turning away from the material world symbolized by the woman's body. Disdain for women in their attempt to conform to the patriarchal feminine ideal is also expressed: a girl wears her sorrow as if showing off a new dress, "like those girls who have been saving up for a whole year to one day show off a dress, stockings, and shoes of the same color; which is for them the height of elegance" (29).

Like male writers of the vanguard, Chacel must take aim at the common enemy: the female body as it is mystified, glorified, and fetishized by patriarchal society.[68] Yet her use of synecdoche and cliché in the parodying of these conventions has the paradoxical effect of creating a space for new significance for the body at the same time. When the narrator speaks, for example, of girls running with their breasts jumping up and down, "like fish freshly caught," there is more at work than in the typical *greguería* (165). These disturbingly active and trapped breasts defy the usual rendering of a passive female body for the male gaze, a convention that male avant-garde writers were not concerned with subverting. They emphasize instead the harnessing of female energy, localized in the body, by power from without. The different focus is plain when we examine a representative *greguería* by her contemporary Pedro Salinas, who compares an unread book to "a rejected virgin lying on a bunch of pillows."[69]

The narrator's adoration of a tango dancer's calf muscle carries the fetishization of women's bodily parts to an extreme that becomes an eloquent critique:

Lo llenó todo aquella pantorrilla. Lo pervirtió todo, nos pervirtió a
todos. Estaba tan bien educada, tan bien informada. Sabía tanto de
tenis como de tango. Con tacón, sin tacón, con media de seda, con
media de lana. Eclipsaba la personalidad de su dueña. Es más: eclipsaba la de su compañera. Era una pantorrilla sola la que estaba en
todo. La que saludaba a la gente, la que ofrecía pastas. Esa
muchacha tiene el pretexto de su pantorrilla. Ella no es gran cosa;
pero su pantorrilla, no cabe duda, está bien.

[That calf muscle filled up everything. It perverted everything, it perverted all of us. It was so polite, so well-informed. It knew as much
about tennis as about tangos. In high heels, without heels, in a silk
stocking, in wool tights. It eclipsed its owner's personality. More
than this: it eclipsed her friend's as well. It was the calf by itself that
was in charge of everything. The one greeting people, the one offering candies. That girl has her calf muscle for an excuse. She's nothing great; but her calf, no doubt about it, is just fine.] (89–90)

Once again, the subversion of cliché introduces an active element
that deforms reality and reinvests the female form with "virile"
power. Besides this tendency in the novel, the female body also ac-
quires new significance in the nearly subtextual recurrence of which it
is the subject. The narrator describes the parts of his house in person-
ifying metaphors for the first several pages, constructing a powerful
image that envelops the main characters. Its patio is "so naked and so
imprisoning," its windows "sleep with their mouths open," its façade
conceals "an extraordinary interiority," and its stairway "does not
welcome the visitor" (15–18). Not surprisingly, it has a seductive
influence on those who inhabit it:

Porque la casa nos ha hecho apasionadamente caseros. Nos tiene se-
ducidos, como esas mujeres que, sin aparentar gran atractivo, al que
se casa con ellas lo encasan llenándole la vida de pequeños encantos
caseros.

[Because the house has made us passionately domestic. It has seduced us, in the way those women who, without appearing very attractive, domesticate the men they marry, filling their lives with
small domestic charms.] (17)

The trope of the house-woman underlies and encompasses the beginning of the love affair between the narrator and his neighbor. It forms a third party to their affair in the form of the personified stairwell, whose sense of foreboding they conquer in time: "Did it [the stairwell] know it would be overcome, we wondered?" (24). It eventually collaborates with them in concealing their romance: "It was caught making a falsely calm gesture as if to say, 'Nothing has happened here'" (26).[70] The reverse trope of the woman-house is represented by the *novia* when he sees in her eyes "the dark hole of open windows." The quality of interiority, ubiquitous in this novel, is further associated with the female body in the aforementioned image of sisters who could fit inside each other "like Chinese boxes" (56).

In sum, and in larger terms, one could also say that the stations and seasons of this novel are precisely those of the female body. Most apparently, the narrator's movements though novelistic space are determined first by the structure of the house-woman and later by developments within the lover's body. The telegram relating her pregnancy brings about his return from France. The narrator's voice is never unflinchingly male in that it is never wholly separated from the female consciousness, whether it be the lover's or the author's. This renders his own consciousness similarly permeable. The gestation of the narrator's aesthetic ideas on the textual surface run parallel to the unstated but implied development of his child in its mother's body. The narrator's presumably male body, in contrast, is scarcely referred to—neglecting Ortega's call for a glorification of the male body. Called "a Gothic boy," he hence leans more toward the spiritual than toward the physical (118).

In addition to the explosion of cliché and the parodying of traditional feminine idealization shared by other Spanish *vanguardistas*, Chacel has incorporated feminine forms that shape the narrative and underlie it. A masculinization of the narrative voice may hold sway on its surface, in accordance with the predominantly male ethic and paradoxical tradition of vanguardism, but this is a cloak that is assumed and discarded. At the same time, the feminization of space is most pervasive. As readings of articles relating to the body written by the main spokesman for this new tradition, Ortega, have demonstrated, suppression of the female body was called for in order to facilitate a new and virile culture. Chacel's first novel pays lip service to this call, but the recurrence of the female body and the investing of feminine bodily parts with uncanny powers prove irrepressible, making *Estación. Ida y vuelta* something more complicated than a novel of apprenticeship for its author; the text preserves a spirit of rebellion that ultimately liberates the work from forgotten shelves of novelistic experiments long past. Chacel's subsequent work would turn in quite a different direction, leaving her first novel as evidence of a short and self-contained career in miniature, and not merely a step on the way to narrative mastery.

Replacement of a Romantic Feminine Subjectivity: *Teresa*

Teresa was written at José Ortega y Gasset's suggestion for a series of "novelized" biographies of famous nineteenth-century Spaniards to be published by Calpe. Its first chapter was published in *Revista de Occidente* in 1930, and the book was completed in 1933. The outbreak of civil war (or possibly another instance of Ortega's ambivalence toward his disciple) meant that it was not published in its entirety until 1941, by Nuevo Romance in Argentina. For Chacel, its only value lies in this *vida errante* it has led, a life similar to that of its subject, Teresa Mancha.[71] Among all of her works it is the one she considers least "her own," partly because of the direct role Ortega played in its genesis.[72] In this sense, the outcome of the battle won by the end of *Estación* seems to have suffered a reversal in the writing of *Teresa,* and in fact the avant-garde tendencies that least conformed to Ortega's novelistic guidelines have disappeared from this second novel. In ways other than its narrative focus, it turns backward, but as no real return to the past is possible, the results are not altogether satisfying. The only one of Chacel's novels written entirely in the third person, its unexpected distancing of author and protagonist makes one question whether the choice of subject imposed upon her was "too close for comfort." Her mission was to rescue the point of view of a well-known tragic female figure. However, Teresa Mancha was not famous in her own right, but because of her role in the life of a famous poet who immortalized her in verse. It also leaves one wondering what had happened to Chacel in the short time intervening to provoke this seeming backlash or what pessimism, perhaps brought on by her return from Italy and a presentiment of the crumbling of the Spanish Second Republic, influenced this morose novel.

As mentioned earlier, Ortega had not been cooperative in publishing Chacel's first effort, even though it conspicuously entered into dialogue with his aesthetics. By accepting an explicit writing assignment from him, she could be more certain of engaging his attention. In 1928 Ortega conceived of the Vidas extraordinarias del siglo XIX series, which would also encompass contributions from Benjamín Jarnés and Antonio Espina. He did so in response to a need he saw in Spain for biographies of national figures, which were popular in other European countries at the time. Furthermore, several of these foreign biographies in translation, such as André Maurois's *Disraeli* (1927, Spanish translation 1928), were widely read in Spain.[73] The collection's goal would be more one of evoking the spirit of the age than one of historical research. Chacel, for her part, confined factual information to what was largely common knowledge through literature, literary history, and press anecdotes. In this last collaboration of sorts with the *maestro*, Ortega's influence became intolerable in that he sent her back to a time that was extremely oppressive to her gender and forced her to view it from the perspective of a vulnerable and ill-fated compatriot.

The formula history-equals-destiny intermingles with anatomy-equals-destiny by way of the novel's foregone conclusion and the representation therein of the heroine's body. Teresa Mancha became the mistress of Romantic poet José de Espronceda. The date of their first acquaintance is uncertain; her flight or abduction from her husband, a wealthy merchant named Gregorio de Bayo, with whom she had a son, took place outside the Hotel Fravart in Paris in 1831. Espronceda then took her to live in an apartment in Madrid, and their daughter was baptized in 1834. They separated three years later, and two years after that Teresa was dead.[74] The subject who may be too close for comfort, equivocally avoided in the creation of Chacel's previous first-person, male narrator, is flatly imposed upon her. Perhaps this formed part of the motivation for her writing in the third person, whereby she could achieve at least the distance this sort of narration afforded her.

In writing the novelized biography of Teresa Mancha, there existed the need to capture the romantic era and translate it into

Chacel's milieu, which she felt required a more ironic stance than romantic prose afforded. This compromise between contemporary and nineteenth-century narrative techniques may be what causes the book to run aground or at least get bogged down in places. Her efforts, while compelling, sometimes result in melodrama and pathos. Chacel is also confined to imagining the life of an individual about whom little is known and who had little importance as an actor in history or even, for that matter, in her own life. Like the life of its subject, the novel at times seems aimless.

The subgenre of fictional or novelized biography was unprecedented for the time; its outright crossing of fact with fiction questions the notion of history itself, in contrast to the traditional historical novel, as Galdós conceived of it, which remained more faithful to the past. Whether the difference is one of degree of subjectivity or of consciousness thereof, fictional biography has only recently come of age, in such titles as Gabriel García Márquez's *El General en su laberinto* (1989). Ortega was endeavoring to renew the Spanish novel while simultaneously answering the demand for biographies, and like many teachers of creative writing, he gave an assignment to his pupils that would both channel their literary energy and give it a definite form. The idea was ahead of its time, while the subject matter forced young writers to look backward at a time when an uncertain present made putting the past in perspective difficult.

Chacel evidently felt the need to explain the idea and her execution of it in an introduction to the 1963 edition. She described the context of uncertainty of 1930s Spain; the exhaustion of the novel as a genre had been announced, and thus before writing a novel, it was necessary to believe that doing so was possible (7). However, in her description of the literary background—the need to fill the space left empty by the realists,[75] the "phantasmal" or "exotic" nature of more immediate precursors, and contemporaneous popular writers who catered to the masses—Chacel does not fully explain why *Teresa* has turned out so differently from *Estación* or why she all but abandoned *vanguardismo*. Other novelized biographies of the same series, such as Benjamín Jarnés's *Sor Patrocinio* (1930), do not turn away so radically from innovation for its own sake.[76] The return to free indirect style in narration, which was ostensibly anachronistic in the avant-garde context, probably has something to do with a concern for evocation of the epoch.[77] But rather than evoking what Chacel calls the "nocturnality" of Teresa Mancha and José de Espronceda's age, the technique recalls the realist writers and, inevitably, Emilia Pardo Bazán's treatment of extramarital sex from a female perspective in *Insolación*. Chacel is unsure of its reception among readers of the 1963 edition of *Teresa*—three decades separate them from the writing of a book that recreates the life of someone living a century before—but she defends the need for an *encarnación* of the figure of Teresa Mancha. As Espronceda's adulterous lover and the subject of his "Canto a Teresa" in *El diablo mundo* (1840–42), Teresa had already, in a sense, been the subject of a biography. However, she remains in the utmost a *persona desnuda,* and the novel works to flesh her out, or in the novelist's word, *encarnar* (9). Rather than fleshing out her story with historical detail, Chacel simply reimagines the poetic text, in prose and from a point of view that would approximate Teresa Mancha's.

As several feminist studies have noted, "Canto a Teresa" is one of the most radically male-centered texts to be found in Spanish poetry. The view of love and disillusionment is one-sided, albeit powerfully so, and utilizes the tradition of woman as temptress to make of Teresa the Eve that causes Espronceda's fall from Paradise. The new liberal-romantic paradigm for subjective experience authorized the individual (in a patriarchal world, inevitably male) to cast his desire as a right. In this paradigm, Woman is on the outside, part of the object world that fails to grant the lyrical self represented in romantic poetry his desires and rights.[78] Much subsequent scholarship has sided with Espronceda the male romantic poet in blaming his lover for his disillusionment, a practice customary in accounts of romantic writers.[79] Little mention is made of how she died in poverty and abandonment after giving up a comfortable life to be Espronceda's lover or of how her happiness in this new relationship was rendered impossible by her having to live as an outlaw in society at large, something that affected Espronceda much less.

Perhaps Ortega chose Chacel to give voice to this maligned figure as a means of delayed poetic justice. He must have perceived that what was lacking in all accounts of this relationship was a feminine subjectivity to complement the masculine one and perhaps reveal its distortions. Chacel, of all the writers to whom he had access, probably seemed the most qualified to reinsert a romantic feminine subjectivity. In this way, Chacel's writing assignment would serve yet another purpose in addition to that of meeting the perceived need for biographies and better novels in Spain, as her male peers were doing. What Ortega might not have realized was the burden he was placing on Chacel the woman author in asking her to singlehandedly redeem Teresa Mancha's life story.

Such an agenda brings feminist revisionism to mind, yet Chacel does not articulate this aim in so many words. Her most immediate concern is of a more personal nature, for "our great grandmothers . . . stupidly given away to any man at all from the beginning of their lives" (21). An anecdote from a Barcelona review supplies the impetus, which is very close to pure feminist rage, for the first chapter: that Espronceda saw Teresa's shoes next to her husband's outside the door of her hotel room in Paris and that their daintiness identified her as a Spanish woman. An aversion to the traditional physical attributes of femininity, which we have seen at work elsewhere in her writing, motivates the beginning of this novel. Consequently, the first chapter recounts instead what was happening inside of Teresa's hotel room, establishing the view from inside the female body, which will follow Teresa through her escape from marriage to a well-to-do merchant into a romance with the poet, followed by concubinage, prostitution, and death. Rather than the deception and betrayal on the part of a woman we see in "Canto a Teresa," *Teresa* traces the deformation of an idol and places the will to evil, or at least perversity, in Espronceda. Here it is Espronceda who disillusions Teresa, for his seeming rejection of social norms is only superficial, and his hypocrisy harms only Teresa, who bears the stigma of being his illicit lover. That Teresa is represented as paying for Espronceda's impulsiveness points out the continuity of patriarchy, even in social orders declared new by a new generation of men. This observation was as relevant for the avant-garde literary politics of Chacel's time as it was for the disapproving society in which Teresa found herself adrift.[80]

The novel presents Teresa as a real woman of her time, insofar as this is possible for the writer. She is not portrayed as remarkable apart from her association with Espronceda; her lack of education makes her too unworldly for scintillating conversation. Although she lives in comfortable circumstances for most of the novel, marginality springs from her aimlessness, confinement, and ennui. The apartment in which Espronceda keeps her in Madrid is both "cocoon" for the lovers and "cage" for Teresa when he is absent (94). For fleeting moments she endeavors to transcend her circumstances, embarking on escapes that in the end leave her worse off than before. A few tinges of romanticism adorn her physical appearance as the poet might have viewed it:

> La cabeza de Teresa, emergiendo de la sombra, recibiendo de lleno la triste luz del farol sobre sus rasgos de una suprema tristeza y, al mismo tiempo, de una fuerza casi sobrenatural, parecía, por el sobresalto y la fascinación que emanaba, la de una hechicera.

> [Teresa's head, emerging from shadows, with the sad light of the street lamp falling full on her features of supreme sadness and, at once, of almost supernatural power, seemed, because of the shock and fascination emanating from it, that of a sorceress.] (79)

At this moment of the text, as often happens in Chacel's writing, a sudden change of light transforms a person or scene. The sadness that immortalizes the romantic poet becomes part of Teresa's persona and combines with her physical beauty to make a witch of her. For most of the text, however, she is depicted as mortal and tragically tied to the flesh. Her body speaks in a language similar to that of *Insolación*, especially in the first chapter, in which she is still united with her husband and shown in an environment constantly oppressive to her body. In the space of these first few pages, her body speaks in a code of burning or fever, sharp headache, nausea, and weightlessness. Like Pardo Bazán half a century previously, in order to represent an ordinary, respectable woman drawn toward illicit love by desire and constrained by social circumstances, the novelist resorts to physical terms that unite the woman author with the female character. Teresa's awakening in this initial episode is particularly reminiscent of Asís's regaining of consciousness with the after-effects of sunstroke: both implore servants to block out the sunlight streaming though their bedroom windows (36). As in *Insolación*, the privileged heroine views the bodies of lower-class women as bestial or monstrous, sensing that social position has been crucial in her freedom from the more complete subjugation and anonymity suffered by women of the masses. When she walks through a lower-class neighborhood and sees poor women, she is frightened of their "spiteful claws" (154). The writing of *Teresa* places Chacel the woman author in a precarious position. Whether he knew it or not, Ortega was sending her back to a time of certain powerlessness and oblivion for women with aspirations like Chacel's. By forcing her to view the world from this woman's eyes, Ortega plunges Chacel into the female anxiety of authorship characteristic of nineteenth-century women writers (or Chacel's great-grandmothers), with its symptoms of physical dis-ease and discomfort and negatively charged bodily discourse.

One of the markers noted in *Insolación* was the representation of everyday life for a woman, which meant care of the body and of dress, instead of a fetishizing view often found in male writers that equates the body and its packaging and focuses on the body and its attributes as finished products for consumption. The process involved in the body's transformation, rather than the result, is in focus. In *Teresa* the toilette takes on excessive proportions, for the heroine has little else with which to fill up her day. In addition, the novelist has little else with which to populate the text. The lack of external happenings to be narrated cannot be wholly remedied by turning to Teresa's thoughts or meditation for substitute novelistic sustenance, since she is to be portrayed as uneducated and unextraordinary in intellectual terms. Interestingly, she is less similar to the author than any of her male protagonists, in that she is a character who feels rather than thinks.[81] This constitutes yet another obstacle to the recreation of an "extraordinary life of the nineteenth century." Teresa routinely spends the entire day preparing for her trysts with Espronceda, and in one instance, she spends three days at her toilette to achieve a special effect. She realizes that she has spoiled the effect, however, when she tells him how long she has worked on it and sees the wonder leave his eyes. The male gaze that dominates her life and dictates her actions is disappointed by her demystification of her own beauty. This grows into one of the many chinks in the love relation between Espronceda and Teresa, culminating in his eventual tiring of her.

Only the woman frozen in a work of art can achieve the perfection Teresa feels is required of her. She admires the candor and richness of nudity in a painting of Eve, with "feet so delicate they seemed never to have tread on anything other than carpets" (76). Her affinity with Eve also addresses the role to be assigned her in Espronceda's fall from earthly paradise. Ekphrasis serves as the only way of making Eve physically present. At a social gathering, Teresa is content with the way her hands fall on her lap, as she had never before attained such an academic pose (108). Chacel's background in the visual arts, and particularly in sculpture, becomes evident in this current of woman as work of art, present to some extent in the tango-dancing lover of *Estación,* passing through the ballerina cousin of Leticia Valle, and reaching its fullest expression in the statuesque dancer Elfriede of *La sinrazón.* In the case of Teresa Mancha, the fact of having no active role in her own life appears to predispose her to envy the perfection of women in static artistic representations.

According to Chacel's recreation of Teresa's adolescence, related in retrospections, she developed a friendship with Mrs. Langridge in England. The description of her house marks the return of the house-woman trope: "When she entered that house, it felt like entering a body" (64). Langridge, with long and bare fingers that bend like legs at the knuckles and a rigid body, herself seems sculpted (65). Her rigidity also imbues her with a masculine quality in Teresa's eyes, and Teresa's attraction to her borders on the homoerotic, a phenomenon we shall see repeated in the adolescent development of Leticia Valle. Teresa tries to imagine her friend undressed: "An irrepressible fantasy settled between her eyebrows: what was there beneath Mrs. Langridge's dress? Was there a body as beautiful as Miss Blake's Eve?" (90).

In the forum of art, shame is suspended so that the female form may be exposed for all to view. Teresa's exposure to the looks of strangers in Madrid is equally beyond her control (as if she were a statue to be looked at) but indicative of her having stepped outside of social norms. Essentially, her body is no longer her own, no longer accorded normal privacy, because of her transgression. After she moves to Madrid with Espronceda, stares follow her everywhere, from the stares of her female neighbors on their balconies to those of men who stick their heads out of passing carriages. From this level of degradation, Chacel makes it clear, it is only a short distance to utter prostitution. Her body gradually becomes totally objectified, a product for consumption, and for the living woman this can mean only prostitution. The theme of prostitution is dealt with circuitously but unmistakably in the latter part of the novel. Textual ambiguity concerning precisely when Teresa becomes a prostitute mirrors the confusion Chacel wishes to recreate in Teresa's own mind, for she was never clearly not a prostitute, from the "transaction" of her marriage (21) to the point where she finds herself on the street. In between there was the loss of self involved in her love for Espronceda, when she perceived that in the act of love her body was truly under another's control (143),[82] and the stealthy overtures of his friends. One of them, Salvador, places his hand on her hip, "heavy like a toad" (112), echoing the toadlike kiss that closes the story of another nineteenth-century fallen woman, Ana Ozores in Alas's *La Regenta*. Her relations with Narciso de la Escosura are especially ambiguous, with traces of initial camaraderie (they are both overshadowed by Espronceda's fame), concubinage, and love affair. Teresa's body emerges as a token in a male-centered exchange economy, but her very immersion in her own physicality (obsession with the toilette and other material components of everyday life) prevents her from seeing herself this way until it is too late.

While much of the imagery associated with the body in *Teresa*—burning, pain, confinement, weakness—is reminiscent of *Insolación*, the pure misery that prevails in *Teresa* concerning all things feminine marks a strong departure. It even stands in contrast to *Estación*, which also showed a release of hostility and a sense of horror directed at the female body. There is comparatively little reinvestment of vitality in the feminine form here, for circumstances militate against it overwhelmingly. Since this time the view is from the inside, there is no escape. The interior, furthermore, has been chosen for Chacel by the *maestro*, and it is one that is hard to redeem. For how is one to reinsert a feminine subjectivity in a personage who has been chosen, not for her own merits, but because of her relationship with an extraordinary man? Chacel was asked to write a biography of an extraordinary life that was so only by male-centered definition. In addition, the very relationship that made Teresa Mancha extraordinary in Ortega's eyes appears to have been what ruined and shortened her life.

Teresa Mancha is notably the only Chacelian character whose death is part of the narrative focus. The third-person free, indirect narration follows her sensations as life escapes from her in the form of rivulets of blood, significantly linking menstruation with the cause of Teresa's demise in a correspondence of femininity and physical vulnerability. The third-person narration that allows the reader to experience Teresa's death also keeps the novelist one step removed from the protagonist, who may be assumed "too close for comfort," in the words of the narrator-author of *Estación*. Chacel states that she had yet to read *Madame Bovary* when she wrote *Teresa*. Both establish the novel of adultery as an additional chapter in the female Bildungsroman, one that follows the supposedly happy ending entailed in marriage. As *Teresa* bridges the preceding century in its treatment of this theme, the results are especially nightmarish, sometimes to excess. It is as if the author herself feared imprisonment in this confining mirror of the feminine form one century ago. The consequences her ordeal had on Chacel's master-disciple relationship with Ortega are revealed clearly in the intellectual battle—fought in physical terms—in her next novel, *Memorias de Leticia Valle*.

The Uses of Seduction: *Memorias de Leticia Valle* and Later Novels

Emilia Pardo Bazán's heroine Asís, married off while quite young to a man many years her senior who soon leaves her a widow, succumbs to a seduction instigated by an Andalusian gentleman with traces of *donjuanismo*. The most salient seduction scene in Chacel's novels occurs in an eleven-year-old girl's confession, in the form of a memoir, to a less believable seduction in which she claims to have been the aggressor. The confessional mode unites *Memorias de Leticia Valle* with Asís's hypothetical confession in *Insolación* and with a feminine tradition that goes back to St. Teresa of Avila and forward through Carmen Laforet's *Nada* (1944), among many others. It is interesting to note that while this confessional mode is not exclusively feminine, it does not become prevalent among male novelists until the 1960s, with Luis Martín-Santos's *Tiempo de silencio* (1962) and Juan Goytisolo's *Señas de identidad* (1966). Chacel the essayist, nonetheless, subscribed to an unusual definition of the confession. She admitted novelists like Cervantes, Galdós, and Unamuno to the confessional canon but omitted St. Teresa (and St. Augustine, for that matter) because of the lack of a genuine feeling of guilt manifested on her part.[83] We can assume that the obstinate Leticia Valle would not qualify in her mind either.

Chacel began writing her third novel in 1937, and she finished the first chapter before leaving France, where she had been living with her son, for self-imposed exile in Argentina. The novel was published eight years later in Buenos Aires. Its first Spanish edition surfaced in 1971, reaching mainly the writers of a younger generation. The readership seems to have increased in the 1980s, to judge by the numerous reeditions, the 1987 Círculo de Lectores standing out among them because of its prologue by Luis Antonio de Villena.

Despite its popularity, this fictional autobiography has received relatively little critical attention. Criticism has tended to focus more upon her first novel, for its relation to Ortega y Gasset's vanguardist activities; on *La sinrazón* as her masterpiece; or on the novels in dialogue, beginning with *Barrio de Maravillas*. Like *Teresa*, with the eruption of war it fell by the wayside and was published outside of Spain, virtually unnoticed. *Teresa*, however, like *Estación*, was supposed to be published by *Revista de Occidente*. Indeed, her second novel had been virtually assigned to her by Ortega. Thus *Memorias* was the first of Chacel's novels that was not written with the explicit aim of pleasing Ortega; it is the first she refers to as entirely her own.[84] The rite of passage takes place textually as well, and the battle is not without casualties. In addition to vanquishing Orteguian influence, Chacel takes on another *maestro*, Sigmund Freud, whose discovery of the unconscious mind she claims to have intuited when she was seven years old.[85] In the process, this novel claims the Bildungsroman as feminine literary terrain and expresses feminine difference vis-à-vis widely read novels of development of the day, such as James Joyce's *Portrait of the Artist as a Young Man* (1915).

Perhaps the complete break with the male mentor accounts for some of the harshness of *Memorias*, and perhaps there is some echo of Civil War strife in its use of seduction for ultimately deadly aims. For whatever reason, there can be no doubt that this memoir has resisted feminist readings. For what could be more unlike feminism than to blame something any outside observer would call child abuse upon the victim herself? Surprisingly, I found that a close study of this invented memoir supports two different readings, at least one of which conflicts with Chacel's stated intention of writing a tale in which the seduction of a grown man can be blamed on a young girl's perversity. The first of these readings casts Leticia as an unreliable narrator who blames herself mistakenly for what has happened to her, internalizing the guilt, as often happens to victims of rape or child abuse. The second reading, closer to what Chacel may have intended, empowers Leticia's body in a turning of the Freudian tables that says more about Chacel as a writing adult woman than it does about adolescent girls. The product of this reading is a fable of subversion through seduction.

Memorias de Leticia Valle combines a principal feature from each of her previous novels in such a way that, despite the youthful narrator, it produces a decided sense of maturity. Here she has found the novelistic voice that will be heard again in the more extensive *La sinrazón*. As in *Estación*, the narration is that of an interior monologue. Here, however, the most avant-garde turns are missing: gone, or nearly so, are the *greguerías*, the linguistic playfulness, the arbitrariness of train of thought, the narrative rupture or refusal to narrate, the "intrusions" of foreign discourses (such as Orteguian philosophy). Like Teresa Mancha, the protagonist is female, and her gender figures prominently in the main conflicts, especially regarding physical representation, in which we see the Chacelian hallmarks of disgust, vulnerability, ambiguity, and finally reinvestment of power.

The confluence of first-person narration and female character make possible in *Memorias de Leticia Valle* a greater approximation to autobiography than in her preceding novels, and the youthfulness of Leticia, who is about to turn twelve when she begins her story, also likens it to Chacel's account of her own first ten years of life, *Desde el amanecer* (published in 1972 but written much earlier). Further exploration of the tie between fiction and autobiography in Chacel would prove interesting (and results indirectly from any study of her work), but here I shall concentrate upon *Memorias de Leticia Valle* as fiction with the body as frame of reference. I shall also discuss how it relates to two works with autobiographical strains that I have privileged as intertexts because of Chacel's well-documented favorable reception of them, in addition to the ample thematic terrain they share: James Joyce's *Portrait of the Artist as a Young Man* and Sigmund Freud's *Dora: An Analysis of a Case of Hysteria*. Joyce and Freud are second only to Ortega and Proust as writers who impressed

Chacel as a young reader. We will probably find how she differs from them as a writer most interesting.[86]

Begun in the midst of the Civil War, when daily reports of the disaster must have been reaching Paris, and published in 1945, *Memorias de Leticia Valle* can be classified as one of the first works of postwar Spanish fiction. As such, it remarkably anticipates the trend toward confessional, thinly veiled autobiography that would become prominent in still more contemporary Spanish narratives. While novels written later often look back on wartime and childhood in an effort to come to an understanding of two key periods, one historical, one personal, *Memorias de Leticia Valle* must naturally hark back to an earlier time if it is to capture the ambience of Chacel's childhood. The novel shows the strains of exile in several ways: Leticia the narrator writes from Switzerland, where she has been taken to separate her from the environment in which she has caused a disgrace her father can only refer to as "unheard-of."[87] and Luis Antonio de Villena has seen a certain nostalgia in her evocation of Valladolid and its daily life.[88] Most powerfully redolent of exile is the alienation felt by Leticia at each moment of her monologue. This is an alienation that is directly stated and not absorbed into the "dehumanized" writing technique of *Estación*.[89] Leticia's mental precocity, reflected in the eloquence of her language, isolates her from her peers, as does her family situation, yet she is still not an adult. She disparages herself frequently as a know-it-all or a bookworm, to cite two of many examples. As a girl she is more prone to cast her zeal for knowledge and literature in a negative light, since this was perceived as an abnormality in the female child's development. In the absence of a feminist cause with which Leticia can identify, in order to be outstanding she must transcend others of her gender in a way that exaggerates even Ortega's elitist position in *La rebelión de las masas*. Once again, Chacel's formation during a largely prefeminist era in Spain shows up in a certain revulsion toward women as a group and the trappings of femininity, even though she empowers the individual female subject.

As is the case in *Insolación* and many other novels by women, the heroine is motherless from an early age. In a novel in which the body seldom comes to the surface of the text, Leticia's sole memory of her mother stands out for its purely physical nature:

La verdad es que nunca pude recordar cómo era mi madre, pero recuerdo que yo estaba con ella en la cama, debía ser en el verano, y
yo me despertaba y sentía que la piel de mi cara estaba enteramente
pegada a su brazo, y la palma de mi mano pegada a su pecho.

[The truth is that I never could remember what my Mother was like,
but I remember that I was in bed with her, it must have been in summer, and I was awakening and felt the skin on my face completely
stuck to her arm, and the palm of my hand stuck to her breast.] (10)

While other memories haunt Leticia, this is one in which she
willingly submerges herself. The dreamlike union with the mother's
body is left unshattered by the term of language and its association
with the Father's law, for Leticia remembers only her mother's smile
and not any words she may have said. She finds that although she has
seen many things since then, she has felt nothing, and she concludes
that this experience alone was love. The counterpoint to this memory
of perfect happiness is one of perfect cruelty: a girl in Simancas
throwing puppies from a bridge to be drowned by the current. Leticia
remarks that she ceased to feel the cold outside because of the intensity of the coldness this produced inside her body. The witnessing of a
pivotal act of cruelty against animals haunts several novels of the
twentieth-century peninsular canon. One is reminded of the pure,
unmotivated cruelty of the drowning of a dog by a group of young
boys described by the narrator Sigüenza in Gabriel Miró's *Libro de
Sigüenza* (1917) and the orgiastic slaughter of the bull during an
encierro in Juan Goytisolo's *Señas de identidad* (1966). The difference here is Leticia's immediate physical response to the incident in
the form of chilling cold within her body. Once more the writing of a
woman author bridges the mind-body gap wherever possible, undoing the notion of mind-body dualism, with its inherent privileging of
the former term over the latter.

Leticia's father is affected differently by the loss of her mother. He
goes to fight in Morocco, "to get himself killed by Moors," but
returns instead with a leg amputated (11). The disastrous Moroccan
campaigns of the early part of the century, which laid some of the
groundwork for the Civil War, thus figure in the text as the father's
attempt at suicide. They also unite the moment being narrated with
the time of writing, when Spaniard was killing Spaniard in a similar

self-destructive war. In a reversal of the maternal figure, his is a physical presence and an emotional absence in Leticia's life. She discovers his alcoholism and concludes that he and her aunt, who lives with them in order to care for the father, have decided to die a slow death. Hence there can be no buffer zone between Leticia and the outside world, and her search for personal autonomy leads to the scandalous result that she confesses in her narrative.

Although the confessional mode of these memoirs links them to Teresian literature and to the first part of *Insolación,* and although Leticia mentions her belief in a God who is the beginning and end of all things, she is at bottom recording her memoirs for no one but herself, in order to hold onto them and to see herself reflected in them. Hence, these confessions lack the immediate *destinatario* of a priest, such as Asís's Father Urdax (although he is but the imagined recipient of her confession) or St. Teresa's confessor(s).[90] They also lack a firm sense of culpability, for Leticia is most unspecific about how guilty she feels. As a confession *Memorias de Leticia Valle* is just as elliptical as *Insolación,* for the central, unheard-of sin is never depicted. Chacel writes around it: a door closes on the girl and her tutor, confirming suggestions planted elsewhere in the text. The reader presumes from Leticia's reticence that "the worst" has happened between herself and her tutor Daniel and either that she is the instigator in the proceedings (her own stated view) or that she simply imagines that she is. She had hoped to convince herself, her father, and others that she was somehow extraordinary, but she looks back on her actions and feels that she has shown herself to be at heart just like other girls. Specifically, it is the physical means she uses to topple her male adversary that unite her with the rest of womankind. She had hoped to transcend her gender and prove herself superior to the feminine masses in a variation on Ortega's paradigm of *mejores* and *masas* in *La rebelión de las masas* (1930).

Villena recounts that Chacel, having read in her youth an account in a local newspaper of a teacher in Valladolid who had seduced a young schoolgirl, decided to write a story in which the reverse happens.[91] Despite this statement, for lack of other evidence, the reader may be inclined to believe from what is known about child abuse that Leticia has merely internalized her blame in the incident. The pairing of this unspeakable act with ellipsis in the narrative leaves an ambiguity at its center in the form of Leticia's barely pubescent body. The ellipsis is necessitated in part by narrative decorum. Villena comments that although Chacel is an "erotic novelist," her love scenes are not "epidermic."[92] I would make an exception for the maternal love scene already noted. As a vestige of her avant-garde phase, the ellipsis may also be motivated in part by the poetic device of suppression of the anecdote (prescribed in the Orteguian ideal of a decelerated novel), as well as by the requirements of Leticia's subjectivity: her unawareness of what is happening as it transpires and her unreliability as a narrator. In her words, Daniel's masculine desire is a certain look that puzzles her, "lo otro . . . lo indefinido" (the other . . . the undefined) (158).

The prelude to Leticia's seduction of him (the provocation of his "quarter of an hour" of vulnerability to seduction, which Ortega claimed he could pinpoint in women) takes place textually in intellectual terms. As the precocious schoolgirl she seeks to impress him at each opportunity with her capacity for learning. This is another feature that makes the book fascinating, for it functions as a fresh commentary on the material the brilliant pupil is learning in literature, history, and philosophy, as well as on Daniel's teaching methods. She calmly notes his progressive restlessness and discomfort in her presence. Leticia's mental maturity leads to a physical seduction, which, though unrepresented, is the central fact of the memoir, bridging the gap between mind and body in a highly disturbing way. For as readers we come to believe in Leticia's power to seduce her teacher mentally, but we are never credulous of, and above all never comfortable with, the idea of an eleven-year-old girl physically seducing the *maestro* as well, especially when her body is portrayed as insignificant. One would assume as well that this seduction could lead only to her loss of honor and consequent ruin, but here the tables are turned in that it is the gentleman who feels compelled to take his life in order to escape dishonor. Leticia, we are led to believe, has the chance to start her life over again in Switzerland.[93]

The memoir has little besides a bare outline in common with Nabokov's *Lolita* (1955), which focuses on a man's desire for a young girl represented as physically desirable. The erasure of Leticia's body from the surface of the text has roots in her own perceived feelings of insignificance, emptiness, and disgust—much the same

elements we see related to the female body in *Estación*. She continually experiences an enormous or insatiable hunger, as if trying to
fill some gap inside. Her confessor blames her craving for physical
comforts on her association with frivolous women, and Leticia cries
as she acknowledges "the disgust with being a woman" that this
evokes in her (49). While contemplating the beauty of her father's
lover, she uncontrollably impales herself in the back on a balcony
door handle. She often describes herself as too smart for her own
good and at the same time physically diminutive or insignificant.
Daniel's condescension exacerbates her and comes to form the motive for revenge. He refers to her as "all head" (hence, no body) and
laughs at her wish to be "a little gentleman" (73, 102). Instances like
these seem overloaded with Chacel's efforts to incorporate a Freudian framework of female psychology no matter how unwieldy the
result, in a way nearly as distracting as the undigested excerpts of
Orteguian philosophy in *Estación*. However, like her first novel,
Memorias concludes by subverting the *maestro*'s influence through
its investment of power in the female body as well as in a female
subjectivity. Leticia's seduction of Daniel in revenge for his belittle-
ment and his consequent downfall have the effect of undoing some of
the injustices of Freudian psychoanalysis toward women.

Just as the facts of the seduction scene are ambiguous, its effects
upon Leticia are not clear-cut. Her memory of it provokes further
physical deprecation: Her language moves rapidly from one metaphor to another to describe this sensation. She alternately feels "split
into pieces," "like a vestige of a plant that has been uprooted," as if
someone could step on her like a mouse, and deserving of being
drowned (alluding to the puppies she saw thrown from the bridge, as
well as to a common punishment for witchcraft). On the other hand,
her desire to set down her story reflects a sense of self that is still vital.
Indeed, the "firm, masculine I" longed for by the narrator of *Estación*
is embodied in Leticia's perseverance and autonomy in the face of
alienation. For better or worse, Leticia has won her battle with the
belittling *maestro* in a way that recalls the narrative stress of *Estación*. The ivy branch outside of Leticia's window in Switzerland
frames the beginning and end of her retrospective narrative. By the
end, she finds that it has grown exactly as much as she had predicted.
The image stretches across from the "little root" the narrator perceives as animating his literary creativity in Chacel's first novel (162).

By creating a seduction tale in the voice of a self-possessed young girl, Chacel empowers a person we would otherwise be inclined to regard as a victim. The question who has seduced whom is raised in the margins of the narrative and is left unresolved. She effects a gyno-centric symbolic inversion of the archetype of rape and seduction inflicted on a younger female in a way that has been linked to women avant-garde writers as a group.[94]

The sexual and political entanglement does not end with Leticia, her father, and Daniel, the two representatives of the Father's law. Other constellations of love, power, desire, and corporeality populate the invented memoir. The memory of maternal love finds some echo in relationships with a few other girls or women, despite the revulsion or disdain she generally displays toward most girls and women and toward the idea of womanhood.[95] Her female tutors, particularly Daniel's wife, and her cousin Adriana, with whose family she eventually leaves the country, are the exceptions. When she is introduced to Luisa, the woman who will give her music lessons and whose domestic life she will shatter, there is an instantaneous identification and mutual attraction. Luisa's maternality is exaggerated: she holds a suckling child, and her thinness and dark-circled eyes give Leticia the impression that she is nursing ten infants (32). Leticia's transference of daughterly affection onto Luisa is made plain when she falls asleep with her cheek resting on Luisa's hand.

However, unlike Daniel, Luisa does not evoke feelings of small-ness or insignificance in Leticia; theirs is a relation of parity and intimacy approaching the permeability of boundaries of the self. When Luisa falls and breaks her leg, Leticia moves into her place: "Who could deny to me that I felt everything that was going on inside of Luisa, as if I myself were inside of her?" (144). Whereas in *Estación* a purportedly masculine narrator is permeated by various, vague others, effecting an ambiguous series of Doppelgängers that cast doubt on the protagonist's autonomy, Leticia's permeability of self is more clearly motivated by the figure of maternal love, leaving her basic sense of autonomy intact.[96] Freud made use of the notion of permeability of boundaries of the self to maintain that the female ego is forever incomplete. Leticia, however, presents a coexistence of permeability of the self and of personal autonomy underlined by the boldness of her actions.

This coexistence causes Chacel's Bildungsroman (or *Künstlerro-*

man, a novel tracing the development of an artist) to stand out in contrast to another that influenced her greatly, *A Portrait of the Artist as a Young Man* (1915), written by James Joyce while he lived in Trieste.[97] In part of the first chapter, Stephen Dedalus is roughly the same age as Leticia. Comparing the first chapters of the two books points to possible gender differences consonant with some that have been noted by psychologists of development such as Erik Erikson and Carol Gilligan.[98] Erikson observed of children at play that girls seem more concerned with games involving interiority, that imagined household scenes in which the sudden interruption of an outsider or the passage through a portentous doorway form girls' basis for fantasy. He invented the concept of the "inner space" as a defining motif in female development; at the time it seemed a more positive view than Freud's reliance on penis envy. On the other hand, boys made more use of vehicles and other action toys; their fantasies involved accidents, crashes, races, and other violent or competitive activities. Gilligan, who also studies gender differences, criticizes Erikson's elaboration on women's development for his interpretation of the "inner space" as a woman's basic lack of identity until others (husband, children) fill the emptiness for her. Gilligan leans instead toward Virginia Woolf's assertions about the caretaking impulse being foremost in women's value system. Gilligan's studies of feminine moral behavior point to the interconnectedness with others that is fostered in women from childhood onward, which finds ultimate manifestation in motherhood and thus gives a more positive value to her assessment of gender difference than does either Freud's view of the incompleteness of female ego boundaries or Erikson's conception of the inner space.

Stephen Dedalus's navigation through his boarding-school environment is rife with competition with his peers. He excels at scholastic competition, but athletic competition makes him painfully aware of the superior strength of other boys. Leticia, on the other hand, barely needs to compete at school because her classmates are not interested in excelling. Something of the critique of Spanish *abulia* (lack of will power), prominent since the Noventayochistas, lies behind her classmates' lethargy, but her disdainful attitude toward her peers is also redolent of disgust with the specifically feminine masses, interested only in domestic skills. Her academic flair makes her an exception; she is immediately recognized as a prodigy and often leads or entertains the class herself. Stephen, like Leticia, perceives his body as small and weak and longs for the creature comforts of home. However, his physical self-perception (or *intracuerpo*, as Ortega would put it) is set in contrast to his perception of his older schoolmates, with whom he actively tries to fit in while maintaining the intense inner life that marks him as an artist from the very first pages. He expresses no shame or disgust toward membership in his own sex. There is, however, a continual sense of defenselessness; Stephen's body is the instrument through which he is punished by peers and superiors and, hence, socialized. In some instances, the ostensible goal of this socialization is productivity, as in the hand-paddling Stephen unjustly receives for not writing exercises when his glasses have been broken. Yet, the pleasure the beating seems to afford the clerical disciplinarian leads one to suspect other motives as well. Stephen's body is hence more exposed to the violent and sadistic-homoerotic impulses of male peers and elders (priests), respectively. By contrast with Leticia's textual body, Dedalus's body suggests the male body's increased vulnerability to forms of physical subjection that occur in social institutions outside the basic unit of the family (which exerts primary control in the lives of contemporaneous women like Chacel), such as organized athletics, military conscription, and penal confinement.

Separation from the mother and from all of womanhood is enforced through physical terms. Stephen's thoughts at school are at first filled with memories of his "nice mother." When a bully ridicules him for saying that he kisses his mother good night, Stephen immediately gives the opposite answer, trying only to give the right response, the one that will satisfy the older, stronger male figure who had previously shoved him into a ditch:

> The cold slime of the ditch covered his whole body; and, when the bell rang for study and the lines filed out of the playrooms, he felt the cold air of the corridor and the staircase inside his clothes. He still tried to think what was the right answer. Was it right to kiss his mother or wrong to kiss his mother? What did that mean, to kiss? You put your face up like that to say good night and then his mother put her face down. That was to kiss. His mother put her lips on his

cheek; her lips were soft and they wetted his cheek; and they made a tiny little noise: kiss. Why did people do that with their two faces?[99]

Stephen's original physical closeness to the maternal thus turns to bewilderment once he is immersed in a peer group of other boys, and because of their forcibly imposed demands he gradually draws away from even the memory of the "nice mother." This female figure is replaced in his mental life of later passages by the figure of the Virgin Mary, also referred to as "Tower of Ivory." An image taken from prayer, it later becomes one of the epithets applied to his eventual flesh-and-blood beloved. The latter half of this progression from intimacy with the mother to sublimation in an abstract religious personage to desire for the lover (with a sporadic but intense rite of passage with prostitutes) lies beyond the scope of the present comparison. However, it is relevant to note that Stephen's complete separation from the flesh-and-blood woman at boarding school is accompanied by his beginning to listen to the voices of (male) poets, who speak to him from across the ages. In this way the artist inside of him is kept alive. Leticia, while precocious in her literary interests, does not express spiritual connection with writers of the past as much as her body becomes their representation. In a climactic passage, she gives a public reading of a Zorrilla poem as part of a tribute to a retired teacher. Her body (both voice and gestures) becomes the instrument through which the romantic poet's verses are heard in the assembly; in effect her body is the text. At the same time, socialization does not force upon her a separation from memories of maternal warmth and comfort, which endure in her consciousness.

The declamation is a pivotal step in her seduction of Daniel. She has memorized every accompanying movement and is told to stand in front, "so that you may be seen well" (127); her performance is also an exhibition meant for her *maestro,* who is in the audience. She feels his heart beating from across the seats and tastes revenge in watching his face turn gloomy, "seeming about to unleash at any moment a terrible event" (130). The reading of the poem forms a space in which Leticia can come to feel the interpenetration of selves that she usually feels elsewhere in the text with Luisa. The intersubjectivity that arises between herself and Daniel is more problematic in that she perceives his masculine desire as an impending danger.

Leticia's identification with Luisa is in the end too complete, for the latter's injury enables the very precocious and somewhat perverse youngster to substitute for her in her marital relations as well. There is little textual evidence of Leticia's physical desire for Daniel.[100] When it comes to Luisa, on the other hand, there exists something of the harmonious physical union described regarding the remembered mother. It is always Luisa who entwines arms with her, upon whose hand she falls asleep, whose tenderness toward her she finds undeserved, and whose sensations she perceives as her own.

In addition, as in other Chacelian novels, the figure of the dancer is prominent, in the form of Leticia's cousin Adriana. The ballerina's body stands not only for perfection of form and discipline; through the dancing woman Chacel finds another way of investing the female form with an almost "virile" power, with no consequent loss of femininity. This replies to and contradicts Ortega's assumption that the female body must take on masculine characteristics in order to synchronize with the Age of Masculinity, which he heralded and applauded. Adriana dances out a love story between a young girl and an old man, making her body the equivalent of a text. When she is asked to give a repeat performance in front of Luisa, however, the spell is broken, implying the ethereal quality and spontaneity necessary for this sort of body-into-text transformation. The treatment of Adriana's dance also serves to focus attention on Leticia's admiration of a female body, one that has been refined through artistic training.

Chacel scholarship has been slow to take note of the current of homoeroticism in her Bildungsroman. As suggested earlier, there are traces of this in her retrospective delineation of Teresa Mancha's adolescence; in all cases (for *La sinrazón* has its representative in the German dancer Elfriede) the artistic body that is admired is foreign (though a relative, Adriana has grown up in Switzerland, and Mrs. Langridge is British). The choice of textual body that is admired and coveted is hence consonant with the ethic of *europeización*, which permeated Chacel's development as a young writer by way of some of the Noventayochistas and the avant-garde under Ortega. In her gravitation toward the foreign physique we might also perceive reflections of Chacel's own liberation via extensive living and traveling abroad from some of the restraints placed on Spanish women. Finally, the increased otherness of the foreign body appears to facilitate the expression of homoerotic desire in Chacel much as it did the expression of heterosexual desire in Pardo Bazán's representation of the refined Andalusian Pacheco.

Through the homoerotic adolescent, *Memorias de Leticia Valle* responds very apparently to Freud's *Fragment of an Analysis of a Case of Hysteria* (1905), otherwise known as *Dora*. Chacel had in all likelihood read this in the 1920s.[101] In this case Freud first posits homoerotism, or what he calls "gynecophilia," as a stage of adolescent development, and as one to which the troubled postadolescent girl (specifically, the hysteric) may return. He recognizes, in his written account, his patient Dora's desire for her father's mistress. In turn, the mistress is married to a man who makes overtures to Dora. She perceptively realizes that her father looks the other way as part of an unspoken agreement. However, Freud suppresses his awareness of Dora's homoerotic inclination from treatment and exhibits a bias toward her feeling attracted to the husband instead, seeming to undergo a countertransference that identifies himself with the would-be seducer. As commentators have suggested, Freud remains unaware that this insistence and blindness probably exasperated his patient so much that she refused to continue treatment.[102]

Both Dora and Leticia are portrayed as troubled and as intelligent beyond their years, uniting female precocity with abnormality, much as Martín Gaite finds these terms associated in the frequency of characters she calls *chicas raras* (strange girls) in Spanish postwar literature by women, such as Laforet's *Nada,* published one year earlier.[103] As much of the feminine body of scholarship that has developed around *Dora* emphasizes, the primacy of her attraction to other women threatens patriarchal norms. This is an aspect of *Dora* that Chacel has incorporated in Leticia's feelings toward Luisa and Adriana. Whether this stage will recede in time for Leticia's entrance into adulthood is left in question. Her major departure from Dora's story lies in her desire for revenge and power, targeting the husband of her love object, and her implementation of bodily means to reverse the existing power relationship. Dora's vengeance, according to Freud, consists in her breaking off treatment "just when my hopes of a successful termination of treatment were at their highest."[104] What Dora has actually deprived him of is her physical presence; in this sense her bodily strategy is one of absence, instead of Leticia's unthinkable seduction. Dora's bodily strategy of absence or deprivation seems appropriate given that Freud has compared himself to a gynecologist, who "does not hesitate to make them [women] submit to uncovering every possible part of their body."[105] Dora thus frustrates the complacent male gaze and shields herself from "the/rapist."

Dora is also notable for its articulation of the relationship between writing and neurosis. Freud equates narrative mastery, or the ability to tell one's life story coherently, with sanity. His own desire for narrative coherence has been indicated as another motivation for his imposition of the happy ending of heterosexual love onto Dora's story; he seeks to avoid the contagion of both neurosis and female homoerotism.[106] The undecidable event at the center of Chacel's memoir, in the form of physical seduction, attests in a sense to a lack of mastery on Leticia's part. Since decorum would in any event prevent Chacel's description of the scene, this taboo crosses over into Leticia's storytelling capacity: patriarchal norms concerning narrative decorum erase the very core of her story, leaving her body in the void. About many other facets of her past Leticia is surprisingly eloquent (there is no recreation of a primitive, juvenile voice as in the first part of Stephen Dedalus's tale), especially in view of the distance that now separates her from the scene of the transgression. Or is it because of this distance? As Freud observed of Dora, when the object of her desire was absent, she became silent: "Speech had lost its value when she could not speak to *him*. On the other hand, writing gained in importance, as being the only means of communication with the absent person."[107] The space between Leticia and Luisa and the temporal space between her mother and herself, more than the impossibility of communication with her ill-fated tutor, form the gaps that Chacel's extensively imagined character writes to fill, in the process presenting her body as a significant part of the plot, but as a compelling absence from the text. The pivotal role of Leticia's body as an indication of who has seduced whom would make its refusal to speak frustrating for anyone like Freud or her tutor Daniel, who would like to view the matter as simple, clear-cut, and lending itself to narrative mastery.

Just as a nostalgia or spirit of place surrounds Castile in Leticia's memoir and reads as a refracted image of Chacel's incipient life in exile, we can also find traces of the Civil War itself in the figure of the missing body, in the conversion of seduction into warfare as the only use of force available to the young Leticia, and in the opposing impulse of a patriarchy that leads to its own destruction. Not surprisingly, the trauma of war often leaves its mark on novels, even novels that do not specifically deal with battles, in the treatment of the body as cadaver or missing body. Natàlia of Mercè Rodoreda's *La Plaça del Diamant* tries to imagine the whereabouts of her missing husband's remains on some wind-swept plain. Pascual Duarte's violent impulses lead him to deprive females, both human and animal, of their lives. The drowned body of Lucía is the one mute and unchangeable fact of *El Jarama* that differentiates the day Sánchez Ferlosio chronicles from countless others. In *Tiempo de silencio* the blundered abortion blamed on the protagonist results not only in a bloody death but, in accordance with the rules of an exchange economy, in his seeing his sweetheart's body rendered lifeless. Much of Juan Goytisolo's *Señas de identidad* is concerned with a search for the father's murdered body and the events surrounding it.

In addition to confronting Freud, *Memorias de Leticia Valle* puts to rest once and for all the Father's law as represented by Ortega. Leticia triumphs via seduction over her belittling tutor in Chacel's first book that was not written with Ortega's wishes in mind. Both a feminine subjectivity and a female body are categorically empowered, and this time there is no turning back. In *Teresa* it was evidently difficult for Chacel to have to narrate the viewpoint of a woman who is not extraordinary in mind, but rather in her relations with an extraordinary man. With *Memorias de Leticia Valle* Chacel gets a second chance to write a novelized (auto)biography. This time she freely chooses her subject: a girl with no name for herself in society at large who reinvents herself in mind and body and brings about the destruction of her male mentor in the process.

Chacel returns to a masculine narrator-protagonist in *La sinrazón*, written from 1950 to 1958 and published in Argentina in 1960. It continues the first-person, diary format of *Memorias de Leticia Valle*. The possibility of a firm, masculine voice is not at issue here as it was in *Estación:* Leticia has paradoxically settled that question by accepting "the body of her Destiny" and relying upon its permeability and interiority as strengths. Much happens in this sprawling work, but single events seem of little consequence, at least in the eyes of the morally indifferent and remarkably self-centered narrator-protagonist Santiago Hernández. Like Leticia Valle, he is trying to understand himself by setting down the story of his life. He is also haunted by guilt, though it appears that moments of "unreason," rather than evil, are the causes inherent within himself. The "unreason" referred to in the title also emanates from an Unamunan definition for faith (in turn borrowed from a chivalric romance that left a bewildering impression on Don Quijote). Perhaps the idea behind this is that Santiago is in need of faith to resolve his conflicts, yet as happens with Unamuno's writing, one is left with the impression that resorting to conventional religion would not be the ultimate answer for such a restless soul. The reader learns at the end that this is a dead man's tale, for Santiago is found mysteriously dead (an implied suicide), a device that emphasizes the power of writing in giving permanence to a life that has already vanished from the scene.

The matter-over-mind reversal of Freudian dogma entailed in Leticia's vengeful seduction of her teacher reaches hubristic extremes in the representation of Santiago's *intracuerpo*. He becomes convinced, after several astonishing coincidences, that he is possessed of a telekinetic power, or the ability to move objects by willpower alone. He imagines himself bridging the gap between mind and matter in this way, and the interrelation of these two elements is accordingly reinforced. In *La sinrazón* bodily discourse approaches the fantastic in a narrative that breaks no natural laws of any other kind. In fact, most of *La sinrazón* is devoted to pure contemplation, further evidence of Chacel's effortlessly turning toward Unamuno after ceasing to follow Ortega.[108] Nonetheless the tie between matter and mind in the context of a masculine character who is inclined to view himself as a god ends with his frustration at the loss of this fantastic power, which apparently leads to his suicide. It is irresistible to find in the treatment of masculine telekinesis a reference to male impotence: guilt after an extramarital affair appears to be responsible for the suspension of Santiago's power to move things mentally.

Santiago's transgressions, overwhelming feelings of guilt, and resulting death have much to do with female characters, and with his estrangement from and attraction to them. Two feminine poles inhabit his life: his wife Quitina, with whom he has several children, and a ballerina, Elfriede, with whom he has a youthful affair and, later, an adulterous liaison that eventually ruins the lives of all concerned. Far from losing his head in passion, Santiago proceeds logically in doing the illogical and creates chaos, leading him to reverse Pascal's maxim: "La raison a ses passions, que le coeur ne connaît point."[109]

While corporeality may be but a secondary concern in this contemplative novel, the representations of Quitina and Elfriede illustrate the triumph of an almost classicist form in Chacel's later writing: the female body is subsumed under the figures of mother and dancer. In each of these functions it is shown to have powers that fascinate the male narrator, whose own body is barely alluded to. What emerges as well, then, from the bipolarity of feminine bodily discourse is the lack of a discourse for representation of the male body. Santiago finds in his perhaps only imaginary telekinesis his only possible concrete relation to the physical. When this vanishes, he has no other source of power upon which to rely, and his character caves in. Like Daniel, he is emasculated by guilt.

The young ballerina Elfriede's body is disciplined and finished, like a work of art. In fact, Santiago begins to flirt with her by comparing her features to those of various sculptures in a museum where they meet. This fascination with the body of the dancer and the use of ekphrasis to represent a perfected, classicist vision of the female form perpetuate a motif found in Chacel's earlier novels. The expressiveness of a dancer's body in motion is carried over into Elfriede and Santiago's relations, in the significance he accords each part of her body. He describes his feeling for her as fleshly, but not sexual, transforming contact into contemplation. The contact of their bodies is also related as dialogue or communication. Elfriede's transformations from day to night, wakefulness to sleep, and from one emotion to another continue the importance of body as process (rather than product) previously noted and add further meaning to her body for the narrator:

> Yo pensaba en su llanto como flujo, como emisión de humores femeninos que habían manado de sus hontanares; lágrimas, sangre, dispendios de vida. . . . Mirando el cuerpo de Elfriede, extendido en la cama, dilatado por su abandono al sueño, me gustaba imaginar su pelvis ancha, en la que reposaba su vientre inmóvil como un lago,

donde ocurrían fenómenos de sedimentación, de erosión, de germinación, y saber que si tocaba la planta de su pie con la punta del dedo explotaría en gritos y carcajadas, cosa que no puede pasar con un nenúfar.

[I thought about her weeping as a flow, as the emission of feminine humors that had sprung from her sources; tears, blood, excesses of life. . . . Looking at Elfriede's body, stretched across the bed, expanded by its abandonment to sleep, I liked to imagine her wide pelvis, in which her still belly rested, like a lake, where phenomena of sedimentation, erosion, germination were occurring, and to know that if I touched the sole of her feet with my fingertip she would explode in shouts and laughter, something that cannot happen with a water lily.] (377–78)

The dancer's body casts a spell over the narrator because of the combination of static perfection of form it has achieved and the dynamic, distinctly feminine flux or flow that is more than skin-deep and cannot be captured in a static image. The complement to this pole of feminine physical attraction is Santiago's wife. Their relationship is a paragon of the Unamunan heterosexual bond, in which the maternality of female toward male outweighs all else. Their first meeting, when he bends over to tie her shoelaces after a tennis match, establishes that in his mind she was always obviously destined to bear children with him:

Tardé unos segundos en llevar a cabo esta faena, concienzudamente, y durante ellos Quitina se borró un poco ante mí, la emoción que me producía su proximidad se convirtió por un instante en una perfecta paz, como si estuviese atando cuidadosamente, con habitual meticulosidad, la zapatilla de nuestro hijo.

[I took a few seconds to fulfill this task, conscientiously, and meanwhile Quitina was erased a bit from in front of me, the emotion produced by her closeness turned for an instant into a perfect peace, as if I were tying carefully, with a customary meticulousness, our son's sneaker.] (65)

Quitina is also described as physically beautiful, but her instant and eternal spiritual union with the narrator gives her body little chance to take shape in the text. In accordance with the Unamunan vision of the only true love between man and woman being one that casts the latter in a maternal role, Quitina's body is referred to almost exclusively as the vessel and nurturance of one child after another. When pregnant, she is in a "vegetative state . . . a pure fleshly being, of pink silk" (146–48). Once the cycle is completed, Quitina is at the mercy of the baby, a small but voracious little beast (123).

Santiago's inability to reconcile body and soul, either in himself or in his partners Elfriede and Quitina, is another factor that leads to his ultimate destruction. The compartmentalization in his mind of Elfriede as communicating body and Quitina as productive body isolates and makes abstract these possible facets of the female body. The lack of reconciliation and of integration causes his interpersonal relations to disintegrate. He feels compelled to resume his affair with Elfriede after he has been married to Quitina for several years and eventually wrecks the trust existing among all three, shattering his marriage. Afterwards, when he finds that his mental telekinetic power, which had perhaps compensated for the absence of his textual body, has deserted him, he self-destructs.

There is much that is worthy of study in Chacel's masterpiece, her favorite work, although she laments its lack of popularity in her homeland.[110] Since my primary concern here is an elaboration of the physical, particularly its figuration in the conflict between Chacel and her early mentors, I will move ahead briefly to make a few comments on the first of her novels that are written completely in dialogue. The trilogy that begins with *Barrio de Maravillas* (1976) lies mainly outside of the scope of this study, for it collects the voices of a series of characters who are developed from one book to the next without a descriptive narrative overvoice. The seemingly disembodied voices, however, do have something to say about the female body, above all the adolescents in *Barrio de Maravillas*, to which the present remarks will be limited.

Barrio de Maravillas, published in Spain in 1976, after Chacel's repatriation, returns to the early years of childhood. The female body enters the text most prominently in the form of ekphrasis, in characters' descriptions of sculptures in the Prado and the National Archeological Museum, and more cryptically in the onset of puberty ("crossing the Rubicon"). Isabel is interested, above all, in sculptural renderings of the human form and speaks of the softness of the marble that composes a sleeping Ariadne.[111] Most of the works mentioned are mythological and allegorical figures that make use of the figure of Woman. As the girls whose speech constitutes the novel come to terms with their own bodies—always associated with adolescence in Chacel's work is the original disgust with finding out that one's body unites one with the masses constituted by other women—they search the artists' portrayals available to them for a solution to their uncertainties. These academic bodies thus take on vital meaning for them, but their mythological or allegorical connotations keep them a step removed from real women and hence unable to fulfill the girls' quest for identity. Will not the breasts of the statue of Tragedy fall from her chest like tears, since she seems to be crying with her entire body, one character wonders (281).

The female characters are also made conscious of their developing bodies by the comments of male companions, who jokingly call them *estetas, tetas, esteticas* (aesthetes, breasts, aesthetics—little breasts). When Montero recites a poem by Morenas de Tejada that ends with "y yo, sobre tus sienes, escribiré el poema / de una blanca corona de blancos crisantemos" (and I, on your temples, will write the poem / of a white crown of white chrysanthemums) (241), the point is taken about how much of literature has already been written on the female body, leaving the women in question to decipher and reclaim this territory for themselves.

Barrio de Maravillas in this way follows the novelist returning in her imagination to a time when she had yet to begin her reclaiming of the female body in her writing as *vivencia*. Elena and Isabel, inseparable friends who come from very different social classes, are surrounded by male-created representations of the female form. At the same time that they search these works for reflections of themselves, they seek to channel their own creativity and find a space for themselves among the artists. Silence and ellipsis shroud actual events; like the girls, the reader feels sidelined by lack of access to the story that occurs outside of their dialogue. The novel ends suggestively with their increased confusion regarding what their roles should be—as women, as artists, and even as political activists. At the conclusion of

Barrio de Maravillas, the young women are left looking at the half-clothed statue of the allegory Tragedy and wondering not only "what do they think of us?" but also "what do we think of us?" (282). Many of Chacel's novelistic practices have sought to answer this question through a constant interplay of female mind and body confronting cultural paradigms.

3.

Mercè Rodoreda

Mercè Rodoreda (1909–83) leads us into the distinct terrain of Catalan literature, encompassed within Spanish national though not linguistic boundaries. Her difference in the context of Spanish literature emanates from three sources, for she wrote as a woman, as a Catalonian, and for the greater part of her career as an exile. Regionally esteemed for her articulation of Catalonian heritage, she has been rediscovered outside of the Catalan canon because of a freshness intensified by her threefold decentered perspective.[1] She has been widely read in Castilian as well as in the original versions and has been translated into at least nine other languages; in English she has enjoyed particular popularity.

Rodoreda's resurgence has much to do with her thorough integration of feminine physical experience into social settings where men hold sway. Her balancing of the vulnerability of female characters against their considerable inner strength creates a tension that makes her fiction both politically engaged and engaging to read. Her heroines, no matter how closely aligned they may be to traditional feminine roles and symbolism, are never passive victims. Rodoreda constructs their bodies inextricably alongside their voices, deepening and problematizing the processes of motherhood (and daughterhood), sexuality, and aging from a perspective inside of the female body. Besides its active participation in the shaping of story lines, the female body in Rodoreda's novels assumes many disguises and forms of codification. Spread over the surface of the entire text, it is found encoded in the rich variety of flowers and vegetation that wend their way into every novel. The jewelry and clothing that decorate and cover it tell their stories of the text-body connection, as do the statues, ornaments, and household interiors that become associated with the feminine. The significance of the female body in male-dominated exchange economies of money and power recurs constantly through the institutions of marriage and prostitution. While the model of maternal love seems an apt parallel to Rodoreda's narrative nurturance of her characters, the bond of motherhood as it occurs in her plots is often blighted or riven. The recovery of lost maternal love often appears to underlie or motivate heterosexual relations (especially in the case of the young, troubled woman who meets a benevolent, older man). The erotism appropriate to mature lovers finds its way into her novels relatively late in her career, and when it does, energetic landscapes and seascapes often parallel its representation. The body as a truthful text and consequent unweaver of social deception is salient in all of her female characters, and toward the end of her career it to some extent characterizes the male body as well. What the Father's law has separated or alienated, the body serves to connect once more.

I will begin here by discussing the primacy of maternality in relationships many critics have interpreted as paternal, mainly in the context of Rodoreda's first post–Civil War novel and greatest popular success, *La Plaça del Diamant* (1962). The fact that a reliance upon superficial Freudian frameworks has misled some critics has been deftly noted by Jaume Martí-Olivella. He establishes instead a double articulation based on the simultaneous presence and absence of mother figures. The protagonist is involved in two types of pursuit, one symbolic, with the father as goal, and one semiotic, seeking the mother.[2] The latter quest forms a chain across the narrative as daughter first expresses nostalgia for the lost mother and then confronts the experience of motherhood herself. I will elaborate upon this quest, as well as on the conflict between authorship and motherhood as evidenced by sundered maternal bonds. I will argue that this conflict emanates from the patriarchal privileging of mind over body.

Physical description in Rodoreda often includes birthmarks, scars, and other markings connected to the past that bring the body into focus as the slate for these signifiers. Furthermore, the epidermic or morphological traits and habitual gestures often proliferate in hereditary fashion; as they pass from one generation to the next, they fill in gaps in chains of ancestry, untangle webs of deceit (the body does not lie, and it keeps fewer things silent than do characters in dialogue), and bring about an interplay of biological versus social or environmental influences in development. For a heroine uprooted from her original family, the body holds out hope as a puzzle whose solution may restore her lost social identity. In the second section below, I will deal with the workings of physical markers in Rodoreda's second acclaimed *novela de protagonista, El carrer de les Camèlies* (1966).

A floral obsession shows up increasingly in Rodoredan fiction, with apparent connections to classical femininity and to nostalgia for her Catalan homeland (it begins while she is in exile). I examine some of the ways flowers and vegetation subsume the female body and encode it, along with other codes of physical inscription, in the third section. Beginning with *Jardí vora el mar* (1967), the sea becomes more than a backdrop; the erotic and the maternal are united in this image that parallels textual bodies and sometimes engulfs them. Through Rodoreda's most complex work, and the last of her more successful novels, *Mirall trencat* (1974), I will examine the confluence of accumulating codes for the body, with special attention to clothing, jewelry, ornaments, and, most important, the dollhouse, in conjunction with bodily discourse and a new, personal (and for this reason gynocentric) remythification of the feminine.[3]

Writing in Catalan, Rodoreda has somewhat less historical motivation for seeing women as divorced from literary tradition than do writers in Spanish; the Catalan canon included many recent precursors who often wrote about themes considered taboo for women, though they often did so under cover of male pseudonyms.[4] Still, not one of the Rodoredan novels with which I deal here depicts a woman in the act of writing.[5] For protagonists she deliberately chooses women low on the socioeconomic scale whose lives are not concerned with the written word (their real-life counterparts often could not read or write). Her writing consequently effects an almost maternal rescue of her novelistic creations. José Ortega has included the choice of such characters as one aspect of a technique of hers that he calls *ingenuísmo* (literary primitivism).[6] Her choice of protagonists also relates to the author's social status as the daughter of a petit-bourgeois family who could not afford to continue sending her to school while she was still young.[7] She began to make her way in the literary world by dint of her journalistic work.

Compared with the other novelists studied here and with women authors of her generation in general, Rodoreda is less elite, and it is tempting to see this as a factor in her convincing ventriloquy, which seems to bring to life marginalized (but ultimately victorious) women of the masses. The displacement of narrative voice across class divisions takes the place of the confessional mode—associated with a first-person narrator closely related to the novelist—which has been noted in the works of Pardo Bazán and Chacel. The distinction is a subtle one, for as Rodoreda asserts, all of her characters are ultimately herself. Nonetheless, her practices conform more to the testimonial mode than to the confessional. Her testimony brings to life a subject in vital dialogue with her physical self as well as with a particular community, reuniting a body and mind despite their social estrangement. This testimonial aspect is in turn broadened by a tendency toward the uncanny and the fantastic, which are also interwoven into the narration of daily life, so that the circularity of fable gives an added dimension to her heroines' testimonies.

Joan Ramon Resina has observed that the intellectual function is suppressed in the narration of Rodoredan heroines and that this makes everyday life and objects, and ultimately historical events and a sense of a specifically Catalan community, more immediate and more real.[8] His linking of these texts with the concept of a minor literature that evokes a certain oppressed sociohistorical community through the very use of its language (Catalan) in recreating colloquial speech and in naming places and things underlines the testimonial quality. However, Resina is disquieted by what he deems a "deterritorialization" of the author—a minimization of the importance of her attachment to the Catalan community—inadvertently enacted by American feminist critics practicing hermeneutic readings. Resina does make some concessions to the importance of gender in Rodoredan writings, but he places the body in the same category as "things" that are named and used to indicate the passage of time.[9] An either/or fallacy plagues his dismissal of feminist scholarship on Rodoreda, for the resulting exclusion, while perhaps effecting a "reterritorialization," would impoverish any reading: the spirit of place that is evoked is often directly related not only to a geographic location but to the protagonist's inhabiting of a female body. Cultural specificity alone fails to explain the dynamic double-voicing of Rodoredan imagery where all things physical are concerned and hence misses part of what makes her novels vital for all potential readers. The territory Rodoreda reclaims in her novels is also that of a female body inextricably linked to a particular woman's consciousness, universalizing her work. Fortunately, Resina's reading does not wind up being an equally hermeneutic one, at the service of regionalism, for he does allow for the importance of class conflict and for some possible implications of Natàlia/Colometa's gender, including her lack of education and her experience of the self as somehow continuous with the external world.

Carme Arnau has analyzed the central role of childhood in the entire corpus of Rodoreda's fiction.[10] Although I agree with the emphasis she places on idyllic childhood and nostalgia for the lost paradise (particularly in the spatial representations of *Mirall trencat*) juxtaposed against adult hypocrisy and corruption, I will argue that there is more at work than a repetition of the Edenic myth. The representations of objects within the paradisiacal garden are polysemic and primarily aligned with the semiotic quest and hence with maternity and the female body. I will also show how the accumulation of tropes and codes for the female form display a clear striving toward transcendence, surpassing the limits of realist and even avant-garde fiction. Existing mystification of Woman has understandably come under fire for helping to keep women in a subordinate state. Rosario Castellanos has elaborated on how this relates to the Hispanic tradition: "Throughout history . . . woman has been, more than a phenomenon of nature, more than a component of society, more than a human creature, a myth."[11] Rodoreda finds an alternative to the psychological-realist perspective with a perceptible political agenda in her subversion of the traditional "feminine mystique" of Woman viewed from without by the male writer. Through the repetition and opposition of motherhood, markings, plants, accoutrements, and ornate interiors, as well as the techniques of marvelous realism (from the late 1960s onward), Rodoreda arrives at a new gynocentric mystique, reaching from realism to the fantastic in her literary evolution.[12] It stands to reason that the raw materials of this remythification, as well as Rodoreda's careful naming of them, stem from the Catalan soil that nurtured her in youth and remained in her memory as she lived and wrote in exile in Switzerland until her return to Spain in 1974.

Sundered Maternal Bonds in *La Plaça del Diamant*

In his discussion of the epistolary works of Madame de Sévigné (Marie de Rabutin Chantal, 1626–96), Pedro Salinas sets up two coexisting though seemingly contradictory links between the maternal and the literary. His main thesis is that the mother-daughter dyad was the relationship that enabled the marquise to write her masterpiece, a collection of letters of advice and news to her absent, married daughter Madame de Grignan. In addition to feeling motherly affection, Sévigné must have harbored a desire for literary fame and the ability to achieve it, or her missives would not have endured as texts but rather would have remained in the category Salinas considers plain letters, lacking or falling short of literary aspirations. Without the underlying, prior condition of a maternal bond, however, Sévigné would never have initiated her creation. But Salinas suggests that the "literariness" of the resulting work undermines the relationship between mother and daughter. Literary fame is posited as more enduring than the merely mortal fame that comes from physically giving birth. Thus, in the larger, enduring picture of literary history, Sévigné's daughter becomes an addressee or character in her mother's discourse instead of "a woman of flesh and blood." Salinas holds that maternal love motivates a literary creation that, "though addressed to the daughter, makes of the mother the outstanding one."[13] Why does Salinas see this as going against nature? His thinking hinges not only on the placement of the mental or spiritual over the physical or maternal on the patriarchal hierarchy that we have seen at work elsewhere but also on the commonplace of maternal abnegation: it is somehow unnatural for a mother to steal the limelight from her full-grown daughter, when the youthful charms of the latter are assumed to be more appealing and maternal love itself is supposed to be of the most altruistic and self-sacrificing order. Salinas's critical paradox is a cultural blueprint swallowed whole, but he is correct in sensing that it will be accessible enough to the reader to form a building block for his argument, since it draws upon deeply ingrained attitudes.

The view of motherhood and writing as incompatible is another obstacle to the writing woman in Spanish tradition. For Julia Kristeva, maternity is a process or filter that places a woman on the threshold of nature, corporeality, animality, and culture.[14] She builds on Simone de Beauvoir's view of the female self as a divided one: the reproductive task imposed on her by both biology and culture fragments her into the conscious individual, on the one hand, and the perpetuator of the species, on the other. The two sides often find themselves at odds.[15] I suggest that the process of maternity as it is culturally constructed is a vestige of the "female anxiety of authorship" that has persisted more tenaciously than other obstacles that confronted the writing woman of previous centuries.[16] While it is common enough to find complaints launched against male novelists for using their personal relationships—with wives, lovers, friends, children, colleagues, and others—as raw material for plots, when it comes to women writers, who are potential if not actual mothers, the stigma against violating the most sacred of human relationships, against an egocentric employment of the experience of mothering, can be viewed as a veiled monstrosity. Just as the mind and body, or text and body, rarely coincide in male-centered tradition, becoming the physical creator of another human being must be incompatible with authoring a text. If it is the text that grants the writer immortality, then the offspring are somehow slighted, and vice versa. In broader and more ridiculous terms, art has been seen as what man creates instead of bearing children. Its symbolic or token importance places it on a higher level than the bodily act of giving birth. While in these pages I will concentrate on the problematizing of motherhood as an enhancement of the representation of feminine experience, we should not lose sight of the positive purposes served by the maternal mode into which Rodoreda often steps in the nurturing of her characters.

The ingrained idea of the incompatibility of authorship and motherhood seems to influence some of the mother-progeny configurations that occur in Rodoreda's fiction. The double bind of a maternal figure that constitutes both a presence and an absence in narratorial consciousness, noted by Martí-Olivella,[17] appears in two moments: a particular heroine's longing for lost union with the mother and her relations with her own offspring. In *La Plaça del Diamant* (1962) the first moment initiates the continuous structure of "two lovers" inherent in the name of the eponymous public square, *di-amant*. There is always a prior love to whom the heroine feels she owes allegiance but who has deserted her in the present. The resulting schema of the heroine's psyche proves similar to Nancy Chodorow's observation that even after a heterosexual resolution of the Oedipus complex in adolescence the primary attachment remains the mother, rather than the father, who is added onto the dyad. Thus, for women the oedipal struggle is ongoing, and the internal (bisexual) triangle is retained.[18]

In Rodoredan fiction there is seldom a bond between parents and offspring that is both satisfactory and lasting. The effect on one level is to present very early childhood as a time (associated with a particular place) of happiness and perfect love to which return in later life is impossible. It is also evident that the author has sometimes deliberately incorporated the Freudian family romance in the form of an Oedipus complex, most apparently in Cecília's conscious quest for a father in *El carrer de les Camèlies* and in the mother-daughter rivalry of *Mirall trencat*. Her heroines tend to wind up rescued by older men of a higher social status for whom the label "paternal" is appealing. However, I find that the representations globally of a sundered and sought-after perfect union in childhood make the semiotic state of maternal love, a state shattered by the Father's law, primary. It is the Father's law that functions in Rodoreda's writing to destroy maternal relations.

The presence of motherless heroines, who are copious in the tradition of precontemporary women writers and appear frequently enough in works by male Spanish realists, typifies Rodoreda's work as well. Natàlia of *La Plaça del Diamant* was orphaned of her mother while very young. She begins her monologue as a teenage girl at a dance meeting the young man (Quimet) who will become her husband. Her thoughts stray from the here and now, rendered with meticulous details of dress, music, and scents, to her absent mother no less than four times, in a singsong repetition that mimics a lullaby.[19] All these allusions incorporate a comparison of Natàlia, the speaking subject at the present moment, and her mother, elsewhere in time or space: "My mother dead years ago and unable to give me advice and my father married to someone else."[20] The plaza where this opening scene transpires also stands for 'Natàlia alive' as opposed to 'deceased mother': "My mother in Sant Gervasi cemetery and me in Diamond Square" (10).

Each reference to painful separation from the mother is closely accompanied by a reminder of the sharp physical pain being inflicted on the heroine by the elastic waistband of an ill-fitting petticoat: "And my mother dead and me standing like a fool and the elastic band squeezing my waist, squeezing as if I were bound up by a wire like a bunch of asparagus" (11). Here as in *Insolación* and *Teresa* an article of feminine clothing restricts the body in the same way that the social guidelines prescribing its use restrict the wearer. The petticoat finally falls to the ground, and the maternal memory recedes into the background, when Natàlia runs away from Quimet. She has entered into her first significant relationship since the loss of her mother (her indifferent father echoes Leticia Valle's emotionally absent surviving parent), putting an end to the daughter's mourning for her mother, which had also been a mourning for her own loneliness. When Quimet meets his end years later in the narrative, Natàlia undergoes a similarly long-lasting and debilitating mourning period. This establishes her character as one in whom the early loss of the mother has left an indelible impression that forms the paradigm for each successive relationship; the resulting mourning is primal in her emotional history, just as Leticia Valle felt that her emotions began and ended with her mother's memory. Natàlia's subsequent attachments to the men in her life—first Quimet, then Antoni—bear the stamp of the sundered mother-daughter bond, in the first case because of this prolonged mourning period, in the second because Antoni also "lived only to take care of" Natàlia. Here as elsewhere the surprising discovery of an older man who proceeds to take care of the heroine, solving all her troubles in an uncanny way, has more in common textually with the maternal memory than with the encountering of a father figure, as an interpretation based on an overly religious adherence to psychoanalysis might conclude.

Kathleen McNerny has commented upon the contrast between the heroine's seeming passivity and her inner resources, which buoy her along despite great adversity.[21] The episodic structure of this and other Rodoredan novels and their following of an outwardly passive heroine as she ascends the social scale by associations with more powerful men likens them to the popular genre of the feminine romance, or *novela rosa,* not wholly accidentally. In a far-reaching investigation of the American version of this fictional commodity, Janice Radway has detected a repetition of the triangular feminine sexuality described by Chodorow. The heroes who fulfill all the heroines' desires usually display a nurturing attitude of unconditional love. In addition, "the desire to recover the life-giving care of the primary caretaker" is what motivates the reading of these romances by women, who are usually homemakers or women involved in care-giving occupations themselves. From a combination of close readings and interviews with consumers and writers, Radway concludes that the goal of all romances, "despite their apparent preoccupation with heterosexual love and marriage," is the "reestablishment of that original, blissful symbiotic union between mother and child."[22]

Of course, it is not difficult to perceive fundamental differences in the handling of this double articulation in Rodoredan fiction and its handling in the *novela rosa.* Radway affirms that the reading of feminine romances fulfills needs that are both "combative and com-pensatory." In the first place, the reader must turn away from the chores constantly requiring her attention just to consume romances, and in the second, she must emerge from the interlude feeling re-plenished.[23] To this effect, the romance must follow a formula, and there can be no surprises. (Tzvetan Todorov distinguishes the popu-lar from the literary genres in that any example of the latter consti-tutes an innovation, an evolutionary step forward.)[24] Carmen Martín Gaite, while maintaining a similar definition of the Spanish *novela rosa,* reminds us of the particularly misogynist nature such texts assumed because of the broad social influence of Francoism and par-ticularly of the Sección Femenina (Women's Section) of the Falange. For this reason, she views the eruption on the scene of a novel like *Nada* as diametrically opposed to the popularity of the *novela rosa.*[25] In the realm of ideology, the Rodoreda novels examined here also stand in contrast to the conventional and orthodox popular literature as it was fostered by the Franco regime. Furthermore, they have proven enjoyable to a wide variety of men and women who would never dream of reading romances. That does not, however, prevent Rodoreda from utilizing some of the material afforded by this fic-tional commodity to suit her own aims.

The maternal quest is complicated when Natàlia herself begins to bear children, uniting her with her own lost mother in a way that defies verbalization. From the start, she relates feeling an inexplicable shame when she feels herself prodded by her mother-in-law to determine whether she is pregnant and when she hears her husband boast, "I've got her nice and full" (61). There is something here of Kristeva's "impossible syllogism of motherhood"—"it's happening, but I'm not there"—to be enveloping an Other at the same time that one is invaded by it.[26] Mother-becoming, in contrast to narrative mastery, lies almost entirely outside the realm of the will. The discomfort or impossibility of putting this into words bursts forth in the delivery scene:

> Y el primer grito me ensordeció. Nunca hubiera creído que mi voz pudiera ser tan alta y durar tanto. Y que todo aquel sufrir se me saliese en gritos por la boca y en criatura por abajo.

> [And the first scream deafened me. I never would have thought that my voice could be so loud and go on for so long. And that all of that suffering would come out of me in screams through my mouth and in a baby from below.] (65)

What is unusual in Natàlia's remembrance is not only the explicit attention paid to painful childbirth, a process glossed over as natural and/or mysterious in most male-authored texts. Inarticulate utterance and giving birth are united in this paroxysmal scene, which pushes Natàlia from the role of (orphaned) daughter to that of mother in her own right. She truly crosses the threshold between the symbolic and the semiotic. In her memory she appears to watch herself do these things, as if she were someone else (as in Kristeva's "it's happening, but I'm not there"). The conflict between authorship and motherhood carries over into the problem of Natàlia's remaining the speaking subject during her subjection to the involuntary spasms of her body. In this way, Rodoreda's double-voiced text illuminates a specific aspect of feminine *vivencia* for both the writing woman and the rescued feminine subjectivity Natàlia, a Catalan Everywoman. The inarticulate cry that pushes her over the threshold of motherhood is echoed much later in the cathartic scream with which she bids farewell to her youth (actually, the reproductive phase of her body) when she returns after menopause and after the cataclysm of war to the home she had inhabited as a young mother. In each of these instances, bodily events beyond her control prompt a response that cannot be captured in language.

Surprised at her own strength during childbirth, she is made to feel that she has endangered her son's life in the very act of pushing him into the world: "And when everything was about to end, one of the bedposts broke and I heard a voice saying, and as beside myself as I was I couldn't tell whose voice it was, 'You were about to smother him'" (65). Guilt worsens as the child turns out to be unhealthy and the mother's body malfunctions. She has trouble ejecting the afterbirth ("the child's house"), and only one breast lactates. Soon, the infant seems to be melting away like a cube of sugar for lack of appetite. Once again, blame rebounds on the narrator: "The people downstairs must have heard him crying, and it started to get around that we were bad parents" (66).

The gradual accumulation of doves on their rooftop, instigated by Quimet in order to collect their eggs, works as another vehicle for maternal discourse. The first dove is trapped and coerced into staying when it is wounded; when its death years later coincides with the confirmation of Quimet's death on the Aragonese front, it signifies the end of Natàlia's childbearing period more so than the expiration of Quimet himself, about whom there was nothing dovelike. Some doves are described as "pious women going into church" (81). They become an integral part of the household, related in a bodily metaphor with the apartment as body, the coop as heart, and the doves as circulating blood. In the meantime, her children are neglected flowers (120). When the doves seem to have taken over the household and Natàlia's very existence, she does battle with them by subverting their maternal instincts, picking up the eggs so that the mothers will abandon them on the roof: "They rotted with the chicks inside, still half-made, all blood and yolk and the heart first of all" (133).

Natàlia's own attachment to her children is affected similarly by the onset of war, the absence of her husband, and the lack of sustenance. All these conditions convey intrusions of the Father's law into her private world; she obliquely relates awareness of the actions of men in the world outside of the home. During the war she sends her eldest off to a camp for refugee children to lessen some of her financial burdens, although she knows that the brutal and negligent atmosphere there will change him entirely. When she returns to reclaim him, he is no longer a flower: "He was another child. He had changed on me" (172). She repeats the ruptured mother-child dyad that darkened her own childhood. Finally, when she is most destitute, the emaciated appearance of her children makes her decide to kill them and herself. A male enterprise, the Civil War, almost turns her into the murderer of her son and daughter out of helplessness. The frustration incited by this lack of power is presented as more powerful than Natàlia's maternal feelings. If the horror of this situation was foreshadowed by her sabotaging of the birds' nests, it is reflected afterward in an even grislier form in the image of the pregnant rat she catches in a trap, its dead young emerging from the burst body.

The horror involved in blighted motherhood, whether caused by natural or man-made occurrences, forms a chain from beginning to end in *La Plaça del Diamant*. First there is the premature separation from a loving mother, leaving Natàlia at the mercy of her father, her stepmother, and her employers. Once she marries, her husband and the mother-in-law who spoiled him set out to make her body productive. Until the conclusion and "senyora Natàlia" 's resignation, a prior, more compelling love always draws her away from the present. That expressions of love in the novel are maternally encoded is clear from the insistence on the image of the navel: the midwife instructs her that it is the center of the person and that "before birth we are like pears; we have all been hanging from this cord" (67). This alternative feminine knowledge is repeated throughout. Natàlia dreams of being dragged around by her umbilical cord as punishment for subverting the maternal instincts of her doves, showing her subconscious agreement with the midwife. The final resignation to her life as "senyora Natàlia" comes at the conclusion, after she lets go of pent-up frustration in the form of a scream and carves the name Colometa, almost as an epitaph, into the door of her previous home. She expresses her love for Antoni by stopping up his belly button with her finger "so that all of him wouldn't pour out of there" (254). Rodoreda's centering of the person around a maternally marked example of synecdoche (the umbilical cord) stands in contrast to the insistence on phallic power and domination over passive bodies one finds in male novelists who seek to recreate the harshness of postwar Spain. Juan Marsé in *Si te dicen que caí* (1973) is a prominent example; his text effects a hyperbolic inscription of the body, but what results from the abundance of marked, violated, and tortured bodies is alienation and loss.[27] Rodoreda's female protagonist perceives war's rupturing of the chain of being in a way that vitalizes the female body.

The series of riven maternal bonds also implies a questioning of the notion of a maternal instinct. Maternal nurture is presented as something that may be learned or unlearned and that may in fact show up in the guise of heterosexual relations. It is important to note that the older men who redeem Rodoredan heroines are described as incapable of intercourse (except for Esteve in *El carrer de les Camèlies,* a novel in which the symbolic quest for the father predominates) because of either age or injury. If we avoid the interference of Freudian configurations, we can unite the prevalence of the maternal motif in Rodoreda with a maternal motivation underlying these redeeming relationships. The strangeness and alienation involved in being a mother, however, is as difficult to reconcile in the context of Natàlia/Colometa's life as it is with the act of authorship for women writers. Motherhood is presumed more natural and hence deserving of more attention than the writing of books in the life of any woman. Yet Rodoreda represents motherhood as strange even for a woman unlike herself, a woman who is not possessed of an almost biological drive to write. For Natàlia/Colometa, motherhood is an activity foisted upon her by her occupying a woman's body. Quimet, in contrast, has an ironic pregnancy of little consequence: in his gut he harbors a worm, which he proudly displays in a jar after it comes out. Like Chodorow, the author of *La Plaça del Diamant* leaves one with the impression that the role of mothering is bestowed on women as "a product of a social and cultural translation of their childbearing and lactation capacities. It is not guaranteed by these capacities alone" (30). The insights of *La Plaça del Diamant* effectively blur the categories of physical and intellectual creation, of bodily and verbal discourse, and of semiotic and symbolic realms. This blurring dissolves the paradigm of motherhood as either miraculous or natural and instinctive in dominant discourses and creates a feminine subjectivity engaged in a continuing dialogue with the body.

Writing-on-the-Body in *El carrer de les Camèlies*

Colometa/Natàlia's maternal body uttered sounds and brought forth another body as expressions of suffering, problematizing motherhood in a way that continues throughout the work. Hers is a communicating body, while the bodies of the men who concern her (her son, her two husbands) do not disclose their secrets and thus become sources of worry for her. The next novel Rodoreda published also relies on a female narrator who recounts her own story with a high degree of subjectivity. But *El carrer de les Camèlies* differs from *La Plaça del Diamant* in many respects. The narrator is a foundling who runs away from her adoptive home with a boy who takes her to Barcelona's shantytown. After his imprisonment she becomes a mistress or prostitute for a string of other men, until one buys her a house as a parting gift and she is able to practice her profession with some degree of stability. For the greater part of the text she is more subject to social marginalization than Natàlia/Colometa. The major historical event, once again the Civil War, is less perceptible because the heroine is so far removed from society at large. Her circumstances and psyche are portrayed as more troubled, although it is the reader and not the narrator who realizes that something is wrong. The theme of motherhood hardly has a chance to take root, for Cecília was just an infant when she was separated from her own mother, and she remembers nothing of her origins. Her own desire to be a mother, which becomes an obsession for part of the novel in the form of a recurring dream, is never realized, as she has an abortion or miscarries each time she is pregnant. Motherhood turns out to be incompatible with the heroine's way of life, for in the end the physical abuse she has sustained from men renders her body incapable of bearing healthy children. Her final pregnancy ends in the still birth of a baby described as having a malformed heart.[28]

José Ortega accurately brings out the importance of solitude as a constitutive element in the two monologued, Civil War novels. His analysis follows the muted effects of the war as they are stated in Natàlia and Cecília's monologues, and he details the representation of the two narrators' fundamental powerlessness as women in the broader social arena of Barcelona. However, instead of implementing literary psychoanalysis, he succumbs to a psychologistic tendency, making these two women seem like patients in a case study. Similarly, his treatment suffers from a depth fallacy by speaking of Natàlia and Cecília as if they were consciousnesses to be probed rather than textual representations of the same. Joaquim Poch, a professor of psychiatry in Barcelona, has gone into much greater detail to develop extensive case studies of Rodoredan heroines.[29] While these works by Ortega and Poch testify to the resonance of Rodoreda's characters for psychoanalytic discourse, the resultant schematic symptomatologies ignore the double-voiced inflection of her writing, situated at the crossroads of female subject, body, and culture. This life-affirming quality of Rodoreda's writing and the very elusiveness of the characters she invents refuse reduction to a particular neurosis or psychosis.

As the more obviously troubled of the two heroines, Cecília does seem a likely candidate for the diagnosis of narcissism. She gazes into a mirror to see "what has fallen in love, and outside of the mirror that which enamors" (54). In contrast, she finds that the bodies of other women, particularly their elbows and knees, often disgust her. Like Leticia Valle, another heroine whose quest involves a connection to the symbolic realm, Cecília feels a basic discomfort when she sees herself physically connected to others of her gender. Her attention to the surface of her body is presented as part of a larger quest that entails divining her family origins and determining whether anyone, specifically a father, has ever loved her or will ever do so. Thus, her body provides an array of physical clues, like a map that has been nearly but not quite erased. This draws her body into focus as the slate for signifiers that might connect her, in her eyes and the eyes of those around her, to a niche in the social hierarchy. The body as a conveyor of symbolic significance rather than as a means of experiencing fragmentation marks a departure from the previous novel and signals the symbolic quest for the father as being in the foreground of what is still a double articulation of the heroine's desire. Cecília's brushes with romantic love are still characterized by the maternal care customary in both the *novela rosa* and Rodoredan fiction in general.

In several respects, *El carrer de les Camèlies* develops along more fantastic lines, without, however, completely forsaking the practices of psychological realism. Cecília is a foundling whose origins are unfathomable, surrounding her with mystery and linking the story to a tradition more ancient than that of realism, ranging from fairy tales to the biblical story of Moses among the bulrushes. The circularity of the narrative structure, which ends with her confronting the watchman who first spotted her in a basket on the eponymous street, calls attention to the final impossibility of determining her origins. In addition, her actions are less accountable for the reader, even according to what is known about her motivations. Why, for example, when her life on the street becomes unbearably rough, does she never return to the comfortable and safe household where she was raised? Another force, a fate to which she freely submits, appears to be at work determining what direction her life will take and manipulating her like a doll through the Barcelonan underworld. Because of the many travails and coincidences, she comes to resemble a fairy-tale heroine, but thanks to the conviction and intensity of her language, she never loses credibility.

The pull of an unstoppable fate draws Cecília along through a string of disappointing or abusive relationships and upward in economic terms. At last this invisible fate guides her back to the watchman who originally found her, and she hears him reiterate the story of her discovery. The only new information the tale reveals is how she got her name. The haphazardness of her story, combined with its predestined circularity, makes this work more obviously a flight of the imagination. When she is in trouble, Cecília is always rescued in the nick of time by someone who steps in out of the blue. At the same time, the lower social status of this heroine, particularly in the depiction of daily life in Barcelona's shantytown and her working the Ramblas as a prostitute, root the work more firmly in a real urban landscape and introduce the sordid details of marginalized life that readers sooner associate with naturalism-realism or their exaggeration, *tremendismo*.[30] All this makes it a hybrid fantastic-realist work. On the one hand, readers may be tempted to "diagnose" Cecília (as Ortega does) as though she were a troubled young woman; on the other hand, this circular picaresque, with its quest for lost ancestry, obeys none of the rules of character development of its genre. Cecília does not change mentally over time, for example, since she is portrayed as quite dissociated from the events and people in her life. It is her body that shows the passage of time; when she looks in the mirror, for instance, she finds her breasts "not so fresh as before" (using a word that would be appropriate for wilting flowers as well).

Arnau uses the term *mythic* to describe the gradual transformation in Rodoredan fiction that begins to take root here and becomes more noticeable in later novels. This word may be misleading, however, because of its lack of specificity and because it alludes, deliberately or not, to Northrop Frye's literary categories.[31] What increases over time is more appropriately termed the *fantastic content,* which Todorov has defined as a quality occupying the duration of a reader's hesitation between deeming the events being related as uncanny (unusual but still explainable by natural causes such as dream, madness, or intoxication on the part of the narrator) and deeming them as miraculous (only a supernatural explanation remaining).[32] For Todorov, the fantastic is a genre in and of itself and is partially defined by its manipulation of the reader; the reading time itself is accentuated, as numerous clues guide the reader through disquieting terrain and indicate the role he or she is to play.[33] In the latter respect, the fantastic content of this text does not gain it entry to the subgenre of the fantastic; its destination is closer to the realm of what Irlemar Chiampi has called "marvelous-realist," in which elements of the fantastic are incorporated into narrative reality and presented as of a piece with it, passing up the shuddery effects of wonders presented as belonging to another world.[34]

Chiampi's model of marvelous realism is an even more adequate description of the workings of *Mirall trencat,* in which ghosts gradually take over the house that has become equated with familial structure in an almost natural way. Rodoreda's marvelist-realist leanings thus show affinity with the Latin American "Boom" novel, which often utilizes cultural substrata to create a reality permeated with the fantastic. With this in mind, we might look to the stratified nature of Spanish-Catalan culture, in which a nationality is superimposed upon a clearly defined regional culture, as drawing Catalan literature closer to the sort of sociohistorical context that gave birth to the term *marvelous realism* in Latin America.[35]

It is as difficult for Cecília to decide whether she has risen on the social scale as it was for Lazarillo de Tormes at the end of his tale. She has a house and has become a professional, although not of a respectable sort. When asked to sum up her life, she places the accent on romantic quest and vagaries: " 'What did you do with your life?' I was about to tell him that I had spent it looking for lost things and burying love affairs, but I didn't answer, as if I had not heard him" (268).

As the novel approaches the marvelous in style and substance, we see the body taking on deeper symbolic values as well.[36] Although Cecília refers to her physical appearance much more often than Natàlia does, the description does not enable the reader to visualize her. Instead, it serves to "mark" her body and that of other characters, establishing connections to broader meanings. She mentions the dimples in her cheeks several times, when her lovers place their fingers in them and laugh. When she wishes to make an old man who knew her when she was growing up recognize her, she places his fingers there as well. The repeated gesture is the probing of a mystery; some reference to sexual penetration is present in it, but given the overall importance Rodoreda assigns to the navel as "center of the person," the dimples recall the heroine's umbilical gap and her miraculous appearance from out of nowhere.

During a time when she is being kept by a married man in a small apartment, Cecília finds herself spied upon from all directions—by her next-door neighbor; by the doorman, who stares at her legs; by a man across the way, who takes pictures of her; and by an anonymous phone caller, who seems to keep track of her comings and goings. The effect is one of growing entrapment; she feels that both her body and her living quarters are on display and hence not really her own. Later, in contrast, when she has acquired a place of her own and some economic security, she returns to the scene of her entrapment, this time exhibiting herself boldly to the neighbor and the doorman who had intimidated her when she lived there.

As a foundling infant Cecília was first identified by the local watchman, who spotted her as female because her ears were pierced. Unknown to anyone else until the end of the novel, he writes the name Cecília Ce on a piece of paper before handing her over to the adoptive parents he chooses for her, who christen her with this name, thinking it was put there by her mother. When Cecília finds the now aged watchman at the end of the novel, she learns that he had been interrupted in trying to write "Cecília, Cecília," echoing the weeping of his childhood sweetheart's mother when her daughter had died. This writing on the body remains the only source of information, misleading or otherwise, regarding Cecília's identity. It is a misplaced signifier taken from a dead girl and uttered by this girl's mother as a pure expression of sorrow.

In the absence of people to speak for her, Cecília's body is asked to do so. On the day of her discovery she is shown to neighbors and undressed so they can look for markings on her skin that might provide some information. Throughout her childhood, Cecília's bodily parts supply her adoptive parents and their acquaintances with the basis for ample speculation about her parentage. The fact that her earlobe is attached to her cheek is cited as evidence that she must be descended from thieves (15). Cecília overhears this as well as other pieces of gossip that cast her as the illegitimate daughter of a noblewoman or a singer. A woman identified only as wearing a violet dress affirms that her father must have been unusually handsome, because Cecília has "the face of a nymph and of a saint" (16).

Cecília is represented as dissociated from these developments, which should have some emotional impact on her, until the end of the passage in question. When the shape of her hands leads someone to exclaim that her father must have been a pianist, she bursts into tears. Instead of reacting verbally to emotional pain and stating her feelings, Cecília's usual response is a spontaneous and physical one, either voluntary or involuntary: she tries to burn her ears to erase this oft-mentioned bodily clue (39); when she sees the only man with whom she really falls in love, Esteve, with his wife, the realization of the inevitable end of their affair presents itself as an illness: "Because it was as though I were dying, burned by love and vomiting" (226). Kristeva has written of oral disgust as the most archaic form, associated with denying the boundaries of the self and rejecting the separateness of the mother.[37] Often the connection between physical reactions and Cecília's affective life is left unarticulated, another aspect that lends the work its fantastic overtones. Her body is the substitute for gaps in her subjectivity. Instead of mind over matter, we have matter over mind, for Cecília's body is seen, in the instances of miscarriage, for instance, as reacting in a way that determines the story line, while her conscious mind has little impact on events other than to recount them. If, in fact, she has spent her life, as she tells the watchman, looking for lost things and burying love affairs, neither her body nor the text that develops around it will allow her to do the latter entirely.

One of the lost things Cecília seeks is a father. This makes her a rival of other women, ever on the outside. She grasps the hand of another little girl's father and follows them down the street until the girl pushes her away; she attempts to take over her cousin's boy-friend. It is clear that her social powerlessness is what leads her to desire a strong father for protection and comfort and as the source of a definite social signifier in the form of a name and a family. When love comes along in the narrative, however, it is portrayed in such a way that the primariness of a maternal or paternal figure is ambiguous. How does she fall in love with Esteve? The scene is unquestionably one of motherly care, for after seeing that she has been attended to in a clinic after her miscarriage, he sets her up in a house and proceeds to bathe her:

> Me lavó poco a poco, sin decir palabra. Parecía que el tiempo se hubiese detenido. Luego me llevó en brazos hacia la cama, envuelta en una toalla, y me sentó en su regazo. Toda yo olía a jabón y agua, y tenía frío, y el pelo mojado me hacía cosquillas en la espalda.

> [He washed me little by little, without saying a word. It seemed that time stood still. Then he carried me in his arms over to the bed, wrapped in a towel, and sat me in his lap. All of me smelled like soap and water, and I was cold, and wet hair tickled my back.] (219)

Upon awakening the next morning after this idyllic love scene (the only such purely pleasurable one related by Cecília), she plays at giving new names to each part of Esteve's body. She places her hand over his breast, calling it "the sun of a man." When she reaches the sex she hesitates, however, and is interrupted by his calling her a thief. The bodily part that would irreparably separate the lover from the maternal figure remains nameless, keeping alive the double articulation of Cecília's quest on the semiotic and symbolic levels (220). The unnameable part of the kind and nurturing lover has its counterpart in the purposefully hidden part of her cruel lover. The latter wears an eyepatch for some reason she never learns, covering the instrument of male gaze that invades her private life. Duplicity is evident in the physical representations of the men who deny the protagonist her desires. The controlling lover with the eyepatch is on the other hand the one who demands that Cecília reveal herself the most; he drugs her so that she will be unaware of his physical possession of her, has her followed, photographed, and monitored, and finally hands her over to a friend for his amusement.

Although the families who search the baby Cecília's skin with curiosity do not find any scars or birthmarks, these kinds of markings show up in other characters here and in other Rodoredan works, always in a significant manner.[38] Male cruelty often underlies the scars described on women's bodies. Cecília recalls an older woman, beautiful in her youth, who bore a scar on her neck where a jealous lover had stabbed her, leaving her for dead. The pattern of feminine resilience in the midst of adversity, prominent in Cecília's own vital trajectory, is apparent in the way this woman survives, by dragging herself to the balcony to call for help, leaving a trail of blood behind her (16). When Cecília catches a glimpse of her lover Esteve's wife, a shock that will bring about their breakup, she notices above all the scar extending from her temple to her neck (226).

In tandem with the blurred map formed by Cecília's body, uniting her with a father or mother she can never know but only daydream about, the scarring process establishes a link between the physical markings of women and the pain inflicted by the abuse or absence of certain men in their lives. Furthermore, given Cecília's inarticulation of her underlying problems (something the reader, particularly one familiar with psychoanalysis, infers), her body serves as an indicator that communicates directly, spontaneously, and without the capacity for lying. The male body, however, as evidenced by its hidden and unnameable component and the wearer of the eyepatch, does not carry out a similar function. This casting of the female body as a communicative organ that does not lie, in contrast to words and other socially mediated forms of communication governed by the Father's law, is a staple of Rodoredan fiction. As her work progresses toward the purely fantastic, we see it come into play still more in *Mirall trencat*.

I hope to have shown that in place of the usual character development of psychological realism, Cecília bears traits that give her the fantastical quality of an orphaned fairy-tale heroine. What charges her story with meaning applicable to the adult world is its metaphorical relation to the otherness of one's own body. As Cecília and the reader search her body for clues to her origins, the encounter with the body as a strange vessel becomes clear, much as Natàlia/Colometa dramatized the strangeness of the maternal body. Cecília is prodded by the speculation of those around her to move from wondering about the maternal link (Who am I like?) to seek her symbolic link to the world (What is my name?) and seeks herself fruitlessly in successive erotic bonds with strange men. Just as her maternal quest is aborted by this uncertainty, Cecília never manages to become a mother herself, except in dreams. The mystery of her origin remains intact at the conclusion. Her name was given her by a stranger. Her name for this stranger means sadness, mourning, loss. Cecília's body is still a vessel cut loose from its moorings, and she drifts on.

The Matriarchal, Marvelous Dollhouse: *Mirall trencat*

As Emilia Pardo Bazán and Rosa Chacel have done in their different ways, Mercè Rodoreda makes of the female body a signifying text in its own right, and not just the projection of male desire. The questions of maternal linkage and of bodily writing contribute to this project in the two *novelas de protagonista*. In her two subsequent novels these issues persist, along with a new development. The proliferation of codes for physical inscription distinguish *Jardí vora el mar* (published in 1967 but written from 1959 to 1966) and *Mirall trencat* (1974). The form of codification that stretches from the beginning to the end of her literary career is the floral: Natàlia's name recalls the plant species *nadala*, or rose of Jericho, used to predict the opening of her body in labor and the outcome of delivery as part of feminine folklore; Cecília's vital trajectory is associated with the garden where she grew up, particularly the cactus blossom that blooms the night of her appearance and the vine she follows up the garden wall in order to make her escape. The narrator of *Jardí vora el mar* is male and hence distanced from the female form. However, since he is a gardener, his musings are obsessed with the flowers and plants he tends, and these in turn become aligned with the female characters, such as Rosamaria. The floral motif serves to extend bodily significance to surrounding objects and landscapes, permeating the surface of the text. In addition, Rodoreda's use of this traditional trope for the female body has a twist: rather than the passive and fragile beauty of the flower, she highlights its vitality and hardiness as part of a gynocentric remythification of Woman.[39]

The unbridled sea, closely associated with the Catalonian Costa Brava, gains prominence in *Jardí vora el mar* as another vehicle for the representation of the body and of desire. In this move from the urban locations of the first two novels to the almost pastoral country house where the narrator works, the streets of Barcelona give way to landscape and seascape. As she does with flowers and other plants, Rodoreda employs the sea as more than a backdrop: its watery environment unites the erotic and the maternal as the medium for pure semiotic drives. The sea has a speaking part in this novel, seemingly usurping narration from the mild-mannered gardener:

> Las olas iban y venían . . . ¡paf! espuma y retrocedamos, y otra vez hacia adelante, y . . . ¡paf! espuma y retrocedamos . . . ahora nos vamos, ahora venimos, lamida a la arena y otra vez con nuestra agua, siempre con nuestra agua, siempre las olas con su agua, que las deja y no las da, siempre simulando que venimos, en verano y en invierno, y ahí tenéis dos conchas, y a ver si nos alcanzáis.
>
> Venga, venga, venga . . . ahora venimos, ahora volvemos.
>
> [Waves came and went . . . splash! foam and we go back, and again forward, and . . . splash! foam and we go back . . . now we go, now we come, licking the sand and again with our water, always the waves with their water, which leaves them and doesn't give them, always pretending we are coming, in summer and in winter, and there you see two shells, and let's see if you can catch us.
>
> Come, come, come . . . now we come, now we go back.][40]

The gardener, a bit of a voyeur as well as an eavesdropper, catches glimpses of women disrobing and diving into the waves at night; one of these is the serpentine, sirenlike Miranda, a Brazilian servant who tempts the head of the household. A heartbroken lover drowns himself as if to regain the lost happiness of childhood. Here as elsewhere in Rodoreda, the drowning character seeks to initiate a return to the womb because adult life, separated from the object of love (for which the primary model is always maternal), has become intolerable. The sea thus forms the reservoir for pure energy and an entire spectrum of drives: it holds eros and thanatos combined. As mentioned, it also anchors the narrative in Catalonia with its Costa Brava (Rough Coast). For this reason, Arnau sees *Jardí vora el mar* as a turning point after which the dominant image of Rodoreda's novels will be the sea.[41] The sea is given prominence in the work of several contemporary Catalan women authors, such as Carme Riera ("Te dejo, amor, el mar como recuerdo"), Nuria Amat, and Esther Tusquets.[42]

In *Mirall trencat* there is a convergence of the tendencies exhibited in earlier works: blighted motherhood in tandem with maternal motivation of romantic quest; bodily writing as a map relating to an obliterated past and to a larger network of meanings; the profusion of flowers and other plants, which come to be associated with Woman, just as the garden is the place associated with feminine childhood and adolescence; the sea as a medium for the free flow of semiotic energy as well as a womblike environment that can only be regained by drowning. In addition, *Mirall trencat* focuses on the jewelry and clothing that adorn the female body and develops a parallelism between the human body and dolls. Its centering on a family home establishes the interior as an extension of Woman's inner space, and this interior is in turn ornamented with objects whose description imbues them with larger than usual significance. When the children begin to play with a dollhouse within the house to reveal secrets about their elders, the dollhouse becomes fully established as a metaphor for the author's novelistic creation.

Written between 1968 and 1974 and first published in 1974, *Mirall trencat* (Shattered mirror) departs from Rodoreda's previous, monologue novels in that a third-person focalizer, uninvolved in the proceedings and impersonalized, narrates the majority of the text. Her longest novel as well, it is divided into three parts, each comprising thirteen to twenty-one short and therefore episodic chapters. Each chapter focuses on a particular character or pair of characters (in a few instances, a plant or animal) and follows the consciousness of the person(s) closely, relating both "inner" thought processes and "outer" happenings. Spanning three generations of a family, the narration resembles overlapping panels as each successive group gradually takes over from the preceding one.[43] The story also inevitably hovers about the family home and its fortunes, making of the interior of the Goday-Valldaura-Farriols mansion a stable and uniting space, one that contains the eponymous mirror. Like the remaining people and plants, the existence of the mansion is transformed by the onslaught of Civil War troops, leaving the structure that had housed the matriarchal family in a dormant state, its stately mirror shattered.

Metamorphosis, often a characteristic of fantastic literature, enhances the marvelous-realist technique; physical changes caused by aging are related as naturally as a dead woman's reappearance as a spider. Supernatural beings, such as angels and skeletons, are glimpsed in visions that could be explained as intoxication or dreaming, but the question is left unanswered by the otherwise omniscient narrator. While many male authors have written in a marvelous-realist vein, it does seem that here the technique is at the service of Rodoreda's gynocentric renovation of the feminine mystique: it reinvests traditional tropes for femininity with an active, often magical, power. Further implications of the fantastic in Rodoreda have been observed in women's writing as a whole: C:iplijauskaité posits the tendency of "feminine novels" toward magic and mysticism and their return to the prerational as an antidote to phallo-logocentrism (214). One can go still further to find a search for a goddess lost in patriarchal religions: when self-definition for women takes a turn for the marvelous the goal may be recreation of a female deity.[44] All of these are definite interpretive possibilities in Rodoreda's late, pronounced trend toward marvelous realism. The trend toward redefinition of divinity, accompanied by the fantastic mode of writing, is reflected in other maturing women writers, such as Pardo Bazán and Chacel. But one must also take into account the influence of Latin American new narrative, particularly the mutual admiration of the author and Gabriel García Márquez.[45]

War itself appears as an almost supernatural phenomenon. It begins with hushed rumors that a few generals in Africa are staging a rebellion, continues with the occupation of Republican troops (captained by the illegitimate son of the matriarch) in the house, and ends abruptly with the phrase "and once the war had ended."[46] It is followed by the last owner's decision to demolish the house and build a modern apartment building. In contrast to the prolonged descriptions of everyday life and thoughts, and especially the erotic memory, the accelerated narration of war turns it into a fantastic erasure of the slate. The focus on female characters that inhabit the house necessitates the representation of war as inexplicable, alien, and uncontrollable. This male enterprise results in the evacuation and subsequent demolition of the house, superseding both the matriarchal structure and a symbol of Catalonian prosperity.

Curiously, the focus broadened from a single character to the fortunes of a family and their home is accompanied by a heightened sense of closure. The conclusions of previous works do not give the impression that the last possible detail has been recounted, since the protagonists remain alive. Arnau finds that in *Mirall trencat* the author, "like a demiurge, creates at the start of the text a universe of great opulence that she will completely annihilate at the end of the novel."[47] Her exercising of the power to evaporate characters is reminiscent of what has been viewed as a depopulation (a killing off of characters) at the end of romantic works, a device that eradicates the body and concludes with a movement toward spirituality.[48]

The pull of the voice of a female character who rises from lowly origins to a better life, partly through her own designs and partly through physical charms—the sort of character to which Rodoreda gravitates in her monologue novels—exerts an influence even on this novel, deliberately planned as one centered on a family. For this reason, Teresa Goday emerges as the matriarch and most salient figure of the Valldaura family, even though in other respects the familial structure preserves the rules of patriarchy, such as those against acknowledgment of children born out of wedlock. This tension often uses the body as a slate or site of conflict. In the prologue the novelist reveals the primacy of Teresa as character long before the plot was conceived; her general outline had taken shape before *La Plaça del Diamant* was written. That Teresa, when introduced, has a mother, whom she helps to sell fish at market, distinguishes her from Natàlia and Cecília, but the similarity goes deep as well: "a beautiful woman . . . internally prepared to ascend the social scale with that ease that a person, especially a woman, often has after being uprooted from her surroundings by a particular destiny" (11). Once more the intersections of the *novela rosa,* with the picaresque and with elements of *tremendismo* and the *novela social* produce a variegated work that takes a turn for the strange or revolting just when the exquisite has been on display. Surprise inversions at the end of chapters, ubiquitous in Rodoreda's novels, facilitate the sliding between subgeneric discourses. The narrative's continuation even after Teresa is no longer physically present allows more space for the physical codifiers that take her place. And in effect another upwardly mobile, independent woman, Amanda, formerly Teresa's servant, occupies much of the ensuing narrative.

At the story's outset Teresa is as "agile as a deer" and has to help her elderly husband descend from a carriage. Her body parallels in vitality the rising and then waning fortune of her family as a whole. It is decorated with minutely described jewels and delicate articles of clothing and mirrored in a proliferation of dolls, statues, ornaments, and plants on the ample grounds of the estate. Her declining health, physically inscribed by her swollen and useless legs, signals the end of plenitude for her family and the property they inhabit. It is then that another group of bodies, the servants, who shower outdoors and cavort with their "thighs of stone," become the focus of bodily discourse and the obsession of the decadent *senyoret* Eladi, who spies on them from a hole in the shed. Like prostitutes in literature, female servants constitute another "set of potentially dangerous resigned female bodies at the disposal of the bourgeoisie."[49] In this narrative they reinforce bodily vitality in its purest form, devoid of the accessories that gradually become the main event in the world of the *senyorets*.

In addition to featuring the multiplicity of consciousnesses, generations, and social classes and the more concentrated focus on the building they inhabit, *Mirall trencat* travels farther back in time than any of Rodoreda's previous novels. As in *La Plaça del Diamant,* the sense of history is communicated indirectly through everyday events (*intrahistoria*) and only resoundingly and disastrously in the case of the onset of war, which breaks the mirror. The time span gives the novelist a chance to recreate the nineteenth century, which she imagines must have been feuilletonesque, rife with the intrigues of illicit affairs occurring of necessity in an age in which love and marriage were rarely concomitant, the resulting illegitimate children being raised secretly. It is interesting that the interpretation of the past relies on a popular genre—the newspaper serial or the penny dreadful—which is known to have influenced the realist novelists of that same period. Hence, *Mirall trencat* will be at least two paces removed from *las cosas tales como son* (things such as they are). The very literaturization that kept the realists from carrying out this project to the letter enters into Rodoreda's imaginings quite consciously. Another important aspect in *Mirall trencat*'s grand design is the dollhouse, which the novelist refers to as one of the keys to understanding the work (21).

There is perhaps no paradigm for feminine creativity more archetypal than the dollhouse, which Erikson unites with the imagination of girls at play in his pioneering gender-based study.[50] By introducing a dollhouse as a plaything for the children of the Valldaura household, Rodoreda playfully alludes to her manipulation of characters in the house she has created and their double role as mere toys and as beings invested with life by the imagination. Much has been made of the author's statement in the prologue of the 1982 edition to the effect that *La Plaça del Diamant* contains not only things but, above all, a character, Colometa (8). She is aware of her own belief in the independent existence of her characters, and thus there is nothing ingenuous about her conviction that "an author is not a god. He cannot know what is going on inside of his creations" (13). She takes this into account in their representation, taking care not to overstep the boundary between her consciousness and theirs. In the last analysis, it is the reader who benefits from the author's claimed nonintervention in the inner workings of her characters, for it leaves behind the sort of gaps in the text that are held to be what motivates the reader moving through a text. In the end, this conception of characters as autonomous beings in tandem with the author's moving them through plots of her own design (as children invest dolls with an inner life) repeats the pattern of maternal nurturance. Since in literary creation it necessarily takes place in a ludic fashion, the model of the dollhouse is especially appropriate.

When Teresa's favorite grandchild, Jaume, disturbs the inside of the dollhouse "in order to see the faces of the mamas and papas," his search refers on another level to the illegitimate children who grow up together with legitimate ones in the house or in the story not knowing they are siblings (Sofia Valldaura and Jesús Masdéu, Ramon and Maria Farriols). Their biological ties keep them together, enclosed in the larger structure of the house, while their unsanctioned social lineage necessitates deception. Nature and culture thus occupy the house in their struggle. The house itself, like the sea, becomes aligned with the maternal body in this way, much as in Colometa/Natàlia's retention of the "child's house," the placenta. Ramon's disturbance of the doll figures also foreshadows the violent death that awaits him because of his upsetting the status quo. Social order dictates the need for secrecy regarding true biological links, and it proves an implacable force until the larger structure and the house are both destroyed.

There is a doll-like quality to many characters populating the Rodoredan microcosm; this quality is explicitly stated regarding some female characters. Colometa/Natàlia's friend Griselda's mint-colored eyes, freckles, and silken hair lead to her being referred to as a doll (84). Natàlia's young daughter resembles a doll when she is dressed up, as does Quimet's mother when she lies in state. When Marcos, one of Cecília's more abusive lovers, decides to take control of her life, he speaks of her in doll-like terms: "We shall change Cecília, we shall dress her and undress her, make her laugh and make her cry" (135). The vulnerability of women in a weaker social position vis-à-vis more powerful males or circumstances is expressed through the simile. It also reworks an archetypal paradigm for the feminine imagination at play. Thus it is heroines, more so than male characters, who are dressed and adorned and manipulated through stories. There is nothing childish about the author's resorting to the things of childhood; on the contrary, it shows that she recognizes what is childlike or ludic in the nature of literary creation and translates the process into the realm of female experience. Like Cervantes with Maese Pedro, García Lorca in his puppet plays, and Unamuno in *Niebla,* Rodoreda plays with the reality/unreality of her creation, and like Cervantes and García Lorca, she resorts to an artificiality and plasticity of the body to achieve this aim in the figure of the doll. What is unusual in her work is the way these two textual bodies, the flesh and blood and the doll, seem to coexist (although this might be said of García Lorca's play *Don Perlimplín*).

An interplay is established between women who are doll-like on the one hand and lifelike dolls on the other. The dress and features of the latter are described with the same meticulousness as the heroines themselves.[51] The two approximate each other in the social symbolism of Jaume and the dollhouse and in the feminine figurines that often decorate Rodoredan interiors and gardens, such as the statue of the patroness of sailors "with a girl's face" that stands in the Valldaura garden (219). While the doll code is an obvious reference to women's lack of freedom, it also leads to a situation similar to one perceived in García Lorca's theatrical use of puppets: a plasticity that makes the body a primary referent and results in a corporeal obsession and the dissolution of conventional oppositions of good and evil or life and death, which cease to have meaning in the puppet or doll world.[52] And in effect the doll-like bodies of *Mirall trencat* remain signifying texts even beyond death: an entire chapter narrates the gradual postmortem changes in Eladi's body as a further reflection upon his life, and Jaume's corpse continues to emit signs that incriminate his murderer.

We first meet Teresa married to the generous and elderly Nicolau Rovira, and he is immediately beset with the question what to give her for their first anniversary. A black lacquered Japanese wardrobe with gold and mother-of-pearl inlay failed to hit the mark; she prefers a diamond brooch in the shape of a bouquet of flowers. As Arnau remarks, this novel is "incrusted" with jewels, giving "shine to the fictional world."[53] Besides a weakness for flowers, the choice of the brooch also indicates a desire for power: Teresa knows that she will get a high return for such a gem should she sell it surreptitiously. This she does, but with the intention of paying child support for her son, the offspring of a premarital affair with a married and penniless lamplighter. And so the entangled undergrowth of *Mirall trencat* begins. The child, Jesús Masdéu, grows up as her godson in the home of the lamplighter and his wife and becomes a painter of religious scenes and a few profane subjects, like "The Mermaids' Rock" and "The Adulterous Woman."

Embedded in the third part of the book, just before Teresa's death, is her recollection of her first lover, Miquel, calling her "a doll in the shop-window of the world" (283). She decorates her bedroom with a white porcelain statue of a nymph of just about her own height. When a suitor bends over Teresa, he notices her long eyelashes and her thick hair like a silken helmet. The third-person narration permits the reader more of an outside viewpoint on the doll-like Teresa, with her innocent eyes and luminous beauty, than a first-person narration would, but physical description of the sort that generates a mental image remains at a minimum. Instead, at every turn there is reference to the brooch shining from her chest, her love of touching her possessions, the ruby necklace given her by her second husband, Salvador Valldaura, on the birth of their daughter Sofia, the grey pearl she presents him with on their moving back to Barcelona, the earrings her lover renders as homage, her hat with peacock feathers, and her dresses of moire, satin, and silk. Clothing and jewelry as extensions of the female body become primary elements in the representation of bourgeois womanhood of a bygone age, making the wearer doll-like. Transformation from the doll-like state to the flesh-and-blood takes place mainly on the level of memory, when protagonists remember erotic attachments and desire animates their bodies. In the doll state the pearls, rubies, and other gems that adorn the body suggest that most uniformly suppressed organ of feminine pleasure, the clitoris. Wealth is concentrated in the gem just as sensitivity is concentrated in the clitoris; thus, different desires or "appetites," both of which Teresa possesses, are conflated in the prevalence of jewel imagery.

The most intense love of Salvador Valldaura, Teresa's second husband, was a violinist he spotted in an orchestra. Bàrbara's pallor, serenity, and delicate lines reflect a cool Austrian beauty Rodoreda counterposes to Teresa's brilliance. His gift to her is a bunch of light-colored violets with no fragrance. Bàrbara appears all in black on a night when the memory of her mother, who abandoned her as a child, seems to have overcome her. She recalls a nightmare she had at the time, of being trapped inside a mirror, and insists that Salvador cover a mirror on the wall with his cloak, whereupon they make love. Salvador learns several days later that she has drowned herself. In this extremely accelerated episode the author introduces a character unusual in her work (a non-Spanish woman) and brings together the memory of a beautiful but negligent mother, reawakened in turn by the physical tenderness of a man, and the flowers, dress, and furniture appropriate to impending self-destruction. Any character that wishes to cover up the mirror (of fiction) displays an intention to exit the text. Submersion in water as a means of escape functions as a return to the womb and a chance to mend a broken maternal relationship. As far as Salvador is concerned, the episode provides another set of repressed erotic memories (the first being Teresa's falling in love with the impoverished and already married Miquel, the father of her firstborn) that will return to haunt the character's consciousness in later years. Repressed memories of a failed first love are presented as the cause of death of Salvador and two other characters. As Bàrbara demonstrates, the always present failed previous love has an inevitable maternal origin. Death, related to a return to the womb, is also apparent in Ramon's reflections on having drowned his brother, when he remembers Jaume "like a giant fetus in water with no belly . . . dying in the water a death with no corpse to bother anyone, inward, inward, where the water is colorless salt in his lungs" (221).

The episodic or feuilletonesque structure becomes evident in the chapter immediately following Bàrbara's suicide, when Salvador meets Teresa for the first time and becomes involved with her. His melancholia, inattentiveness to Teresa and later to their daughter Sofia, and eventual premature death from apoplexy (the sign of a repressed emotion that explodes) indicate that he never really forgets Bàrbara, however. And herein lies the particular relationship of this book with the popular serial: Episodes and adventures succeed each other seemingly without rhyme or reason, but their traces are never wiped away altogether. They form part of a rich undergrowth, the "involuntary memory" Rodoreda, like Proust before her, names as the source of novelistic writing (9). "Secret memories" accumulate gradually and in nonchronological order throughout the text.[54] Furthermore, ties of the flesh (erotic links, kinship) preserve the underlying involuntary memories in the face of the denial and repression dictated by the social milieu. The translucence of water, gemstones, and mirrors proves attractive but unattainable for people as they accumulate experiences that leave ineradicable traces, impeding their return to childhood, of which these crystalline elements form reminders.

The streak of *donjuanismo* borne by Eladi Farriols, who marries Teresa and Salvador's daughter Sofia, targets women's accoutrements and selected bodily parts: "In addition, his weakness was not the ladies: it was the performers. Ladies intimidated him; on the other hand, for a girl in a sequined dress, or disrobed beneath feather boas and gauze, he would have sold his soul to the devil" (100). This fetishization chains Eladi to the female form—an older servant says he has "skirt sickness" (138)—but only in its most exquisite manifestations, for real physicality makes him queasy:

> Y recordaba una noche de un verano violento en la que Armanda había ido a verle con un dedo vendado, la venda ligeramente manchada de sangre. . . . Le dieron ganas de echarla a empujones. Des-

pués, cuando estaba a su lado, veía siempre aquella venda manchada de sangre. Quizá por eso acabó con Armanda.

[And he remembered a tumultuous summer night when Armanda had come to see him with a bandaged finger, the bandage lightly stained with blood. . . . It made him want to push her out of the room. Afterwards, when he was by her side, he always saw that bandage stained with blood. Maybe that was why he was finished with Armanda.] (215)

Just as sexual and economic power are often linked in Rodoreda's novels, she also makes Eladi economically dependent on his wife. His wedding night resembles a ritual of enslavement, the bride demanding that he kiss her foot before embracing her. As time progresses, Eladi becomes a skirt-chasing but basically impotent romancer whose fetish is kissing the underside of women's toes. His dandified demeanor is also adorned with care by the author, but his body is more of a conspicuous absence until his death, when an entire chapter relates his lying in state. A playful irony surrounds the representation of the lifeless male body, which suddenly becomes an object of attention: his delicate nostrils and handsome features are upset by a belly that is already starting to swell (a monstrous male pregnancy similar to Quimet's intestinal worm) and an eye that refuses to stay closed.

The next lateral offshoot of the matriarchal family after Teresa's son Jesús Masdéu results from Eladi's dalliance with a performer named Pilar Segura. As her stage persona Lady Godiva, she sits naked, but for her hair, atop a man disguised as a horse and sings ballads. Her body is described more explicitly than that of any other of Rodoreda's characters: "Her face was barely visible, half-hidden by the hair that reached the small of her back, but her legs and thighs, her belly, that freckle on her breast and her mother-of-pearl skin . . ." (113). As *artista,* akin to Chacel's dancers, hers is a body that belongs to the public, just as it belongs temporarily to Eladi, whose mistress she becomes during his long engagement to Sofia. Afterwards she is seen mainly in photographs, and in the physique of her daughter Maria, who goes to live with the Valldaura-Farriols family. The mother's abandonment of Maria, like Bàrbara's abandonment by her mother, culminates years later in the daughter's suicide, when memories of lost affection are reawakened by an affair with a man. The maternal voice seems to speak to Maria from the sky, telling her that she is not alone; hers is the first of the spectral voices that speak toward the end of the novel. Out-of-the-body experience is part of the movement toward spirituality in *Mirall trencat:* Maria narrates an entire chapter from beyond the grave. She beseeches workmen not to remove her possessions, which keep her floating about the premises, unlike "the truly dead," who move on to another world. The attachment to objects of daily life, which Resina saw as one of the important links between the individual and the sociohistorical community in *La Plaça del Diamant,*[55] thus takes on fantastic overtones in *Mirall trencat,* defying death. Arnau also remarks on the free flow of the imagination that takes hold in this novel.[56] The themes are similar to those of earlier novels, but they are embellished with a higher degree of marvelous realism as well as eroticism, the ultimate aim of which is bodily transcendence.

It is Sofia who plans the care of her stepdaughter, her husband's illegitimate daughter. On her wedding night she looks up from the garden at the bedroom window "in which she would have the girl live." It was Sofia's mother, in turn, who had made the newlywed couple spend their tumultuous first night in the mansion, "so that its memory would be kept within these walls." One generation of women after another thus helps to enclose and manipulate those to follow in the inner space of the (doll)house, keeping the narrative centered on it. Sofia's physical strength, in contrast to Teresa's agility and magnetism, is more brutal in her treatment of her husband, whom she bites and kicks. She also sets traps in the house for her husband by hiring the most attractive servants she can find, for the amusement afforded by his attempts at seduction in various rooms of the house. The house itself is more than the passive spectator reflected in the title; its furnishings are richly described and form objects of enchantment or hiding places for the inhabitants. The lion's mouth whose tongue must be pulled to ring the doorbell never fails to make an impression on visitors. Just before dying Teresa clutches a rubber pear attached to a cord for ringing, echoing the image of the umbilical cord as a stem from which everyone has at one time hung like a pear iterated by the midwife of *La Plaça del Diamant.*

The servant girls of the mansion, unlike the ladies, are devoid of opulent ornaments. Instead, Rodoreda describes their daily public showers, during which they comment openly on each others' bodies: "Your breasts are made of lemons, Olívia, two small lemons, yellow from the sun" (257). The maids thus enjoy a certain freedom, even if they are used as pawns in the dynamics of the Farriols' marriage. They gradually take over the scene as the physical vitality of Teresa wanes. One of them, Armanda, through her own resourcefulness discovers the game of Eladi's flirtation and plans for her future by saving her salary; at the novel's end she is the only "survivor" from the old days untouched by personal catastrophe.

In addition to physical appearances, gestures constitute another sort of "body language" represented as hereditary in *Mirall trencat*. They form a second set of links between the socially sundered but biologically tied sets of parents or grandparents and offspring. Teresa sees nothing in Jesús Masdéu that is hers until he shows an inclination to touch things. Maria, like Eladi, has a habit of placing her finger under her nose in thought. It is in this way that Armanda perceives that Eladi is Maria's father. Ramon's gestures hark back to those of his fishmonger grandmother. The separation between these pairs, brought about by social structure, and the deceit that suppresses knowledge of their connections, is undone by the ultimate truth of the physical, since learning these mannerisms would have been impossible. Hence the body functions, both in form and in gesture, to legitimize relationships declared illegitimate by the predominant rules of patriarchal society.

The physically warped son of Sofia and Eladi, Jaume, was born prematurely. His spindly legs and enlarged head give him the appearance of a fetus, and, in fact, when he plays at Teresa's feet he would like to "go into grandmother, become fat grandmother" (152). When he is murdered by his jealous brother Ramon, a purple ring appears around his neck well after he is fished from the water, telling the tale of his violent death. As usual, it is Armanda, unfettered by the need to maintain appearances, who is able to "read" the bodily writing:

Deslizó hacia abajo el pañuelo blanco de seda que cubría el cuello de Jaume y Teresa pudo ver una señal oscura que le surcaba la piel; una gargantilla morada como la gargantilla negra de la tórtola. "Cuando

el médico le ha mirado aún no le había salido la señal." Armanda
corrió con un dedo la raya oscura: "Esto no es cosa del agua, señora
Teresa."

[She slipped off the white silk handkerchief that covered Jaume's
neck, and Teresa could see the dark mark that furrowed his skin, a
purple neck ring like the black neck ring of a turtledove. "When the
doctor looked at him the mark had not yet shown up." Armanda ran
her finger along the dark stripe: "This did not come from the water,
Miss Teresa."] (168)

As might happen in a detective novel, the body reveals clues that
turn a supposed accident into a murder. Similarly, after her husband's
death Sofia finds a discoloration on her foot where she forced him to
kiss her on their wedding night. In a novel much concerned with
secrecy, the body works as a text that deals in truths more often than
does the characters' dialogue. Not only does bodily discourse refuse
to lie; it refuses to keep the secrets required for the smooth function-
ing of a bourgeois pre–Civil War family.

The erotic body occupies a similar position in *Mirall trencat*,
where it is more intense and explicit than in Rodoreda's other novels.
The narrators of the monologue novels either display a naiveté regarding the sexual (Natàlia's fear of "dying split in half" is not
replaced by mature desire), or translate love into the longing for
motherly care (the love Esteve affords Cecília) or a willingness to be
abused in return for sustenance (when Cecília states, "He did as he
wished with me," there is no doubt about her meaning), or sublimate
it more thoroughly into their surroundings (the gardener of *Jardí
vora el mar*).[57] As the sea speaks momentarily for the semiotic drive
in *Jardí vora el mar,* taking words out of the gardener's mouth, we
find a similar dialogue that confounds the boundaries between characters in the incestuous love of Maria and Ramon, which comes to
the surface as they bathe in the sea. There is also the unlimited sexual
desire of Teresa, equated with her appetite for life, which leads her
body to undergo a complete metamorphosis when she is in the throes
of passion:

Las uñas de Teresa, rosadas y tiernas, en los momentos de pasión
parecían hechas de furia. . . . Los labios de Teresa a la hora del beso

de amor, abiertos y entregados, y los labios a la hora del beso amistoso, ligeramente irónicos, ligeramente maternales.

[Teresa's fingernails, pink and delicate, in moments of passion seem made of fury. . . . Teresa's lips when she kisses amorously, open and proffered, and her lips when she kisses amicably, slightly ironical, slightly maternal.] (179–80)

It is only during such metamorphoses, wrought by desire, that Teresa the magnificent doll completely recedes from view and becomes carnal. Like the passage above, the most powerful love scenes in *Mirall trencat* are contained in retrospections relating memories of repressed love. We see the same pattern in Salvador Valldaura, Eladi Farriols, and Teresa Goday: a first, true love that is thwarted by death or poverty becomes an obsession that leads to melancholia and finally "explodes" (apoplexy, fever), causing death. The story of Teresa's most intense love, her love of Miquel Masdéu, is not recounted in detail until just before her death, accentuating its permanence. Bodily discourse thus helps to "fix" the importance of these erotic memories in the text. It controls narrative flow, causing retrospections and leaps into the future that defy the order of chronological time. Although the Father's law prescribes their total repression, the body brings the reality of past loves to the surface. Even the least romantic of characters is hard put to dismiss past amorous intrigue:

El había hecho el amor durante años con Teresa: una repetición infinita del mismo gesto y de las mismas palabras. Como el carbonero, como el estanquero, como el presidente del consejo de ministros. El mismo gesto, pero cada cual con un acento distinto del de los demás. ¿Teresa había sido su fuente de vida?

[For years he had made love with Teresa: an infinite repetition of the same gesture and the same words. Like the coal man, like the pond keeper, like the president of the ministerial council. The same gesture, but each with an accent different from the rest. Had Teresa been their source of life?] (175)

Despite the staid notary's thoughts to the contrary, the narrator asserts that even years after the conclusion of their affair Teresa's house (no longer her body, which has been ravaged by time) is still his center of gravity. That he should still feel propelled by this old desire seems unbelievable to him, yet Teresa's form via its extensions—the mansion, the cherry tree ("The cherry tree still blossoms, Teresa Goday de Valldaura" [180]), and countless other signifiers—defies the passage of time by continuing to exert an influence. Her body, as much as her house, is also seen as a leveler of social classes among men. Her lovers come from up and down the social scale, and in wartime the house becomes a temporary refuge for Republican soldiers led by her son born out of wedlock. Her body is the terrain on which social classes are forced to confront each other.

The free flow of semiotic drive, or desire, is unleashed here more than ever by immersion in water. The stronger role played by water as imagery is mirrored on the level of the writing itself in the pronounced fluidity of the *style indirect libre* of many passages that seem to forsake punctuation as feelings run strong. In such a passage, water works as a medium for the communication between Ramon and Maria, whose biological kinship was kept a secret from them until they fell in love. Ramon's inner voice usurps the narration, as the sea does in *Jardí vora el mar,* as he swims alongside his sister:

> Maria en un lecho azul del agua y a lo lejos una barca en torno a las burbujas de espuma de la ola sólo tú y yo hasta el fin del mundo solo con la lluvia, solos con las tormentas, cada rayo para honrar tu nombre Maria hermana mía.

> [Maria in a blue bed of water and in the distance a boat around the foamy bubbles of the surf you and I until the end of the world alone in the rain, alone in storms, every lightening bolt honoring your name Maria my sister.] (220)

Taken alongside the fire imagery accompanying desire in *Insolación,* aquatic codification of eros may seem a radical change, but as one of Freud's insights discloses, the substitution of fire or burning for the natural liquid by-products of sexual activity ("love makes things wet") involves a mere flip of the subconscious coin. Freud finds the antithetical relation of fire and water at the bottom of a dream, with the latter being closer in a physical sense to the dreamer's subconscious fear of sexuality.[58] More primal is the relation of water to the womb, and this type of placental imagery has in fact come into play in other novels by Rodoreda as part of the maternal quest. Immersion in water signifies the original pleasurable state of union with the mother. A burning sensation is associated with the repressed erotic memory repeatedly in Rodoreda; desire that is acted upon is encoded as water. The woman-child Maria sees herself as a composite of these elements when she realizes that she is in love: "Her face in the water was the face of a creature with eyes of water, with saliva of water: a creature made of water and fire. A flame leapt up inside her soul: high. A flame of love without knowing what love was" (238).

The element of fire enters the picture, and takes over from water as medium of desire, when love turns from pleasure to pain, in this case the pain of having fallen in love with someone to whom she is too closely related, someone of her own flesh and blood. The double articulation of Maria's desire is evident in the fact that her longing for the lost mother appears as inseparable from her longing for the male lover.

The interplay of doll bodies and flesh that is somehow "too real," hence incapable of maintaining lies for the preservation of the status quo, adds significance to the many and varied bodies of *Mirall trencat*. Acting on erotic desire is what differentiates the vital body from the doll, and a character may pass freely from one state to the other. The repression of the erotic impulse, as well as the riven maternal bond, propels characters toward death by interfering with a generalized appetite for life. Teresa is the major representative of this appetite for life; there is playful irony in her calling out for the workmen she mistakenly believes are visiting the house even after she is half-deaf. The cross-generational sweep and marvelous realism of such Latin American novels as *Cien años de soledad* show a clear kinship with *Mirall trencat*. The difference in the latter lies in the matriarchal structure of the household, the use of the body as text in unraveling social deceit, and the paradigm of the dollhouse, toying with the barriers of reality and fiction and acknowledging the maternality and hence nondivinity of the flesh-and-blood author. The sum of the various codes that have traditionally been applied to Woman from without call attention to themselves here by their very excess and by the active roles they inevitably assume in producing meaning and shattering the topos, the mirror that has reflected Woman from predominantly male perspectives. Rodoreda reclaims these codes at the same time that she reclaims the female body as the dwelling place of feminine subjectivities, indispensable in achieving the spirit of place and time for which she is justly acclaimed.

4.

Body Politics in Novels of
Franco's Spain

From the uniqueness of Mercè Rodoreda's decentered viewpoint I now turn to a group of novelists who stayed in Spain and whose work overlaps her postwar novels chronologically. As the fiction under analysis drew closer to the present, I began to find the common threads in physical inscriptions between female and male authors to be more salient than before. I do not mean this as an apology for broadening the focus to include male authors in the foreground. In writers who grew up and began to publish in the more recent past, one finds fewer reasons to oppose male and female physical inscription diametrically, as was warranted by the gender politics of Emilia Pardo Bazán and Rosa Chacel. Protagonization of the text by a speaking body, the extreme of the body-as-text, begins to manifest itself increasingly in novels written by men. Part of what brings them together in terms of bodily discourse, at least those writers who stayed on in Spain and wrote under the dictatorship (1939–75) of Francisco Franco, is the overwhelming presence of forces of social subjection acting upon all bodies, male and female. There are still differences that remind the reader of the gender of the person writing, but they exist within the confines of a novel that exhibits the scars of a lacerated body public and the fetters of an authoritarian state. At the same time, Spain cannot remain absolutely isolated from the far-reaching revolutions in thought and behavior taking place in the rest of Western culture during these decades: some of these changes, such as the rapid evolution of gender roles, filter into Spain despite policies of isolationism and Spanish moral superiority.

As samples of what the body undergoes in the novel of dictatorship I have decided to focus upon three novels that stand at important crossroads in the trajectory of contemporary fiction: Camilo José Cela's *La familia de Pascual Duarte* (1942), Carmen Martín Gaite's *Entre visillos* (1958), and Luis Martín-Santos's *Tiempo de silencio* (1962). Each one contains a markedly physical focus that I have not seen addressed very specifically in criticism. In these three novels, spanning twenty years, sociopolitical protest must take a subterranean route if the text is to survive censorship. This intensifies what Peter Brooks has called the mutual "somatization of the text" and "semioticization of the body";[1] repressed or surpressed material is bound to show up in the body, which cannot lie or hide as easily as words alone. I believe that the subterranean channeling of protest into textual bodies is also the key reason why male- and female-authored narratives of this epoch share more common ground in their representations of the body as *vivencia*. The subterranean challenge to authority noted by Spacks as necessary to women writers from the very beginning is now de rigueur for men as well.[2] Upon closer scrutiny, however, the effects of gender on perspectives vis-à-vis the body, and particularly the female body, are still apparent.

Whatever judgments and opinions circulate regarding Nobel prize winner Camilo José Cela, his short masterpiece *La familia de Pascual Duarte* has enjoyed a resonance unequaled in post–Civil War Spanish narrative. Although it was rejected by the first publisher to consider it, the novel was soon heralded as the resumption of literary activity after the paralyzing martial hiatus. Critics have published commentaries dealing with its original use of narrative voices, its oblique commentary on the Civil War and life under the Francoist regime, its psychoanalytical, existentialist, and anthropological content, its lexicon, its style of so-called *tremendismo,* and its images of women. One facet that has been central from the start, and which I will examine from the corporeal viewpoint, is the protagonist's continually threatened sense of masculinity. For Paul Ilie, this is the key for understanding the antihero Pascual's behavior, which oscillates between passivity and outbursts of escalating violence that seem to be "detonations of a latent explosive charge."[3] Besides noting the role played by frustrated masculinity, Ilie aims true in localizing these violent responses in Pascual's textual body. Writing of one of the first in a series of sadistic acts, Pascual's killing of his hunting dog Chispa, Ilie affirms that "all we know is that [Pascual] is literally possessed by turbulent organic changes and driven to kill. The situation is nearly identical to that of a stimulus followed by a reflex; in other words, it is the body that provides a response."[4] It is interesting to note that the root of the term *tremendismo,* often used in a derogatory way to characterize this and other Spanish novels of the 1940s, is also physical: it comes from the Latin *tremendus,* "capable of producing tremor."[5]

The rest of the text elucidates the ties between physical and social determinants that provoke the reflexlike response of violence in certain passages. For the most part, Pascual recounts his own story eloquently; the reader infers that he is not a beast but a man caught in the hold of an untenable situation. The burden of acting as a fully masculine person according to social definition falls upon Pascual thanks to his possession of a supposedly male body. The burden exerts itself on Pascual in the form of a bodily subjugation that he finds intolerable. His rebellion against the pressures of masculinity in his particular milieu sounds out all the more stridently for the recent turmoil of the Civil War and the harshness of its aftermath, when executions of "enemies of the state" were a daily occurrence. While Don Juan refuses the channeling of his body into a subjected and productive state through the pursuit of pure pleasure, Pascual Duarte strikes out at those around him as a shrill proclamation of "masculine difference" issued in a culture of violence. Woman has represented the Other, difference in the face of the masculine norm, in many discourses. Pascual's explosive complaint runs a parallel for those of his gender: he feels different from the established norm of masculine conduct, and he expresses his difference in the face of a Law of the Father incarnated in "the distinguished patrician" Don Jesús. At the same time, he projects blame onto the maternal body that engendered him and frustration onto seductive female bodies that incite him to act the male sexual role. Pascual's body emerges at odds with all other textual bodies—male, female, and animal.

The reading of any literary text other than a recitation by the author presupposes the absence of the physical person producing the text. The reader encounters this disembodied voice in a more or less private setting, and in the case of a novel, for a prolonged period of time. In *La familia de Pascual Duarte* this fundamental absence supplies the seed of the conflict. The text positions itself in the gap between the voice or consciousness of the protagonist and the reflection of him as a physical reality cast back by those around him. We have access to Pascual's *intracuerpo;* we perceive his physical comfort around inanimate and familiar objects that pose no threat to him.[6] Many of these objects have a metaphorical or metonymical relation to male sexual organs, such as the rock upon which he sits after hunting, the pair of trousers he likes to use as a pillow, the chair and the bed he remembers from his honeymoon, and the shotgun he cradles between his legs. But the body itself, with its absolute signifier, is the only clue that could resolve the problem of his *hombría* (manliness), and of necessity it remains outside of the margins of discourse. The words substituted for it can never suffice to silence the constant doubts and threats to which other characters subject him, and an unending cycle of violence results.

As Carlos Jerez-Farrán affirms, the protagonist appears to feel the need to assert his manliness, which has been placed in doubt, going to the extreme of "hypermasculinity," the tendency toward a projection of exaggerated masculinity.[7] Anthropologists have used *hypermasculinity* to describe some of the behavior of men in rural Andalusia, where a rigid hierarchy keeps some peasants in a state of economic impotence. Pascual's overcompensation in equally oppressive Extremadura seems similar, but added to this is the complexity of the literary text. Its signs can slide from one meaning to the next and give way to a constant deferment of meaning. For this reason *La familia de Pascual Duarte* yields physical inscriptions that go beyond the landless southern workers whose masculinity turns into a vulnerability to be constantly defended. Because of the displacements and deferments of meaning to which I now turn, the narrative produces just as many reflections of an urban and "modern" subjectivity arising from a capitalist system as it does of the nearly feudal country caste system, to which it bears similarities that are plainer but more superficial.

As in countless female-authored texts, the strategy employed to narrate from the corporeal vacuum is the confession; this time the man-to-man rapport of the confession has special consequences. This strategy throws into relief the power relations between a subjected body and the channeling force of society, incarnated in the confessor. Michel Foucault proposes that the confession replaces the *ars erotica* in Western civilization from the Middle Ages onward and that it is one of the principal rites used in the enterprise of producing truth.[8] As in *Insolación*, the confession implies a discourse between an individual and a configuration of power and knowledge that requires the former to account for transgressions. The idea of threatened punishment and the reward of forgiveness accompany the confession, whether explicitly or implicitly.

According to Pascual's explanations, the necessity of confession has two causes: the persistence of memory, which will not allow him to forget the crimes he has committed, and the desire to unburden his conscience publicly. Elsewhere he observes that confessing has always afforded him a sense of physical well-being, like a bath in warm water. Hence, Pascual's confession emanates from an internal imperative implanted in his very thought processes. Nobody asks for or requires of him his autobiography, but the need to confess has taken root and provides him the opportunity for self-justification in writing. As Foucault notes, the confessional rite is so deeply ingrained in Western culture that it even seems to spring spontaneously from the subject, although this does not mean that it ceases to be part of subjection to an outside authority. As previously noted in women writers like Teresa of Avila and Emilia Pardo Bazán, the confessing woman necessarily confronts a patriarchal power structure and opens a space for feminine difference and for the expression of female desire. Through Pascual, Cela has chosen a marginalized male voice who writes from a jail cell and who knows that his body will soon be obliterated by the state.

As usually happens in the dynamic of the confession, Pascual addresses an entity from a higher moral or social level, vaguely identifiable as a paternal figure. The addressee, Don Joaquín Barrera López, was a friend of the cacique Don Jesús, the count of Torremejía, who was Pascual's final victim. The story is filled with absent fathers, and the very inaccessibility of the paternalistic count comes to justify his murder in Pascual's mind. Similarly, Pascual's own father, absent because of his withdrawal into alcoholism and subsequent death during a rabid fit, abandons him in a predominantly feminine world populated by his mother, his sister, and later his wife, "the three malignant crows." Jerez-Farrán observes that this lack of a paternal model with whom to identify intensifies the protagonist's insecurity regarding his manliness. The count takes the place of Pascual's father in a symbolic way; he toasts Pascual condescendingly on his wedding day. But he lives in a different, more comfortable world and abandons Pascual in the socioeconomic margins of a backwater town. This second father is doubly intolerable because of his oblique but inescapable influence over the protagonist, who in turn desires his acceptance and approval. The frustrated male-to-male bond provokes the homosocial wrath of Pascual, many of whose physical encounters with men are colored with homoeroticism, leaving his masculinity on still shakier ground.

As witnessed by his motive for killing his hunting dog, who displayed "the gaze of confessors, scrutinizing and cold," Pascual's apparent docility hides a strong resentment against those who yield the power of a confessor over him.[9] It is no surprise that his confession is addressed to a stranger who was the count's friend, a paternal figure several steps removed from the protagonist's daily life. This man does not ask for his tale or even know him; it is as if the truth itself desired to come to light. The letters from the count's friend and other voices of authority that frame Pascual's story testify to the presence of an audience attentive to his confession for the purposes of hearing and judging it. As Germán Gullón states, the men who make up the jury that condemns Pascual ahead of time are not his equals "but rather pillars of the community, those *tertulia*-goers, priests, doctors, and Civil Guards who presided over postwar Spanish social life."[10] The frame positions Pascual as ever on the defensive, and this position leaves his masculinity in constant doubt. The more he desires their approval, the more he approaches the danger of homoerotic desire, as in the ambiguous scene where a heart-to-heart talk with a priest almost turns into a romantic interlude.

In this way Pascual's subjection to outside authority extends to his discursive mode and to the frame that encompasses his story. His lack of power has its correlate in the focus of his semioticized body. The final image of Pascual's body is that of an ambiguous text that sparks antithetical interpretations: one of the witnesses to his execu-

tion finds that he accepted his fate like a man, while another claims
that he wailed and dragged his feet like a coward. Only his future
wife, Lola, can assure him beyond the shadow of a doubt, after she
provokes him to take her by force, that "you really are a man" (56).
Aggression momentarily persuades Pascual that his body grants him
the status he desires; the rest of the time weakness, impotence, and
ambiguity characterize his mind-body nexus, or *intracuerpo*. According to Ortega y Gasset, a heightened bodily sense can be a positive
attribute only in the case of artists and mystics. For women and
others who exhibit it (as Pascual does), it is a source of misery. By
listening to his body and using it to inscribe meaning in the text,
Pascual makes himself vulnerable in a way that "real men" should
not. They should only act, as Lola tries to teach him.

The boldness of one of Pascual's first enunciations in reported
dialogue contrasts with the confessional mode of his narration, a
dichotomy repeated throughout the text: "Look Estirao, I'm a man
and I don't mess around with words! Don't tempt me!" His rival's
retort takes aim at the corporeal absence: "But how is that, since you
haven't got anything for me to tempt you with?" (42). El Estirao
demonstrates the hollowness of the threat (Pascual is indeed a paper
tiger), and Pascual describes his anger as a thorn stuck in his side, a
thorn that digs in deeper with each new provocation. From the
beginning the imagery that conveys Pascual's interactions with other
men has a sexual and therefore homoerotic element: Pascual likens
himself, as the loser in the exchange, to the female penetrated by male
aggression. On this occasion Pascual does not react, but his hypermasculinity explodes later when he stabs Zacarías in a barroom
brawl and when he pounces on his mare and stabs her, hearing her
breathe deeply with each thrust.

The paradigm of male aggressor and female passive recipient of
aggression invades Pascual's relations with all textual bodies. From
the first paragraph, the guiding principles of masculinity and femininity appear as the crucial sources of physical inscription, even though
Pascual speaks of males as the only possible subjects:

> Los mismos cueros tenemos todos los mortales al nacer y sin em-
> bargo, cuando vamos creciendo, el destino se complace en variarnos
> como si fuésemos de cera y destinarnos por sendas diferentes al

mismo fin: la muerte. Hay hombres a quienes se les ordena marchar
por el camino de las flores, y hombres a quienes se les manda tirar
por el camino de los cardos y de las chumberas. . . . Hay mucha diferencia entre adornarse las carnes con arrebol y colonia, y hacerlo
con tatuajes que después nadie ha de borrar ya.

[We mortals all have the same skin when we're born, and yet, as we
grow up destiny delights in changing us as if we were made of wax
and in sending us along different paths to the same end: death.
There are men ordered to walk among flowers and men sent down
the path of thistle and prickly pear. . . . There's a big difference between adorning one's flesh with rouge and cologne and doing it with
tattoos, which afterwards nobody can erase.] (21)

There is little doubt that Pascual groups himself with those who
are indelibly marked by their experiences. The luxuries of the fortu-
nate in life bear unmistakably feminine associations: flowers, an
innocent smile, rouge, cologne. If this is the life that Pascual envies, he
expresses a desire to be free of the burden of acting the male role and
leading a harsh life. In the paradigm he sets up, the only alternative is
traditional femininity. Throughout the text, however, Pascual finds
unbearable any hint of his being effeminate, such as his acting the
passive role with El Estirao and hearing the priest call him "a rose on
a manure heap" (47). He suppresses an urge to run and embrace
some companions he overhears defending his actions; something
always interferes with any display of affection for those of his gender.
His protest of the social subjugation that marks his body brings
about an intolerable confusion with a devalued opposite sex. Pascual's response, as always, is rage. His son's early death seems to him
further evidence of his lack of manliness, and his wife does not
hesitate to hit him in his weak spot: "I'm sick to death of your body!
Of your male flesh that can withstand nothing!" (98). The engender-
ing power of the female body oppresses him as much as does pressure
from other males; only after he has destroyed the womb in the person
of his mother does Pascual find that he can breathe easier.

The envy of feminine attributes, isolation from other males, and
pressure to play the male role make life in society worse than a prison
for Pascual. He writes that he would have preferred to have stayed in
prison after his first crime: his other crimes would never have oc-

curred, and he would not be facing execution. The irony of his situation is that "freedom" leaves him naked and exposed to all evil. The more direct and visible physical confinement of incarceration is comforting compared with the subtle and pervasive subjection his body undergoes in society at large. Here is where the central conflict leads to arenas other than the rural backwater in which Cela sets the story, for this subtle form of subjection that comes from various and shifting directions is the hallmark of modern, urban life under capitalism. While the protagonist complains of the docile productivity required of the modern male, the setting expresses nostalgia for a more "primitive" social order in which sex roles were more clearly defined and such confusion would have been far less likely. This double-voiced quality finds its echo in the writing itself, which strikes the reader as much more polished than an uneducated peasant could have produced (even with the help of his "transcriber"). As Leon Livingstone has suggested, all possible solutions to the discrepancy between Pascual's background and his eloquent use of the written word leave one dissatisfied: the author's ironic presence is felt, calling attention to the artifice of the text and to its deception.[11]

The writing, just as much as the type of social subjection described, pertains more to the educated city-dweller than to the marginalized peasant. In this sense, we find an almost romantic quest for a simpler and more authentic way of life. In Pascual's problematic gender identification there is nostalgia for undisputable models of femininity and masculinity in the face of sex roles that are in a constant evolutionary process. In his reaction against the oblique control of absent authority from shifting and distant sources there is nostalgia for a "primitive" society in which contact with others was more direct and more physical. In his choice of violence to bridge the mind-body gap, there is nostalgia for an imagined past when alienation from one's own body was not so extreme.

Cela dramatizes the dilemma of a contemporary man who listens to his *intracuerpo* and finds the alienation from his body intolerable. A lost world of absolutes seems the only solution, but since this is not available, the subject would rather remain locked up. The cross-fertilization of popular and high culture that enlivens much Spanish literature through the ages takes place in *La familia de Pascual Duarte* as well. We have already witnessed Rodoreda's recycling of a popular feminine form, the *novela rosa*. Here Cela uses the *literatura de cordel*, pulp novels exhibiting a fascination with outlaws and violent transgression, as a vehicle for the expression of frustrated male desire. This genre provides the paradigm of a violent man turned against the world in which Cela can situate the cry of masculine difference in a culture of violence. Pascual's reclaiming of his own body entails a radical separation from the female form; during his act of matricide, his mother gouges out one of his nipples with her teeth. Still, without the confirmation Lola's body provides, Pascual has no concrete proof of his manhood: in most other situations his body functions as an ambiguous text with sliding signifiers. We will see this attraction alternating with repulsion toward the female body again, with more complexity and less mourning for a lost utopia of absolutes, in *Tiempo de silencio*. For now let us turn to a novel that takes a more feminist perspective on the issue of physical subjection: Carmen Martín Gaite's *Entre visillos*.

Between the publication of Cela's first novel and this, Martín Gaite's second work of fiction, the Spanish novel undergoes a major shift in focus. From the "egographic" novels of the forties, centered around a single protagonist and often written in the first person, novelists begin to favor the distance of a third-person narration that encompasses a wide cross section of society. The trend toward the "social novel" (or *neorealist,* named for its affinity with Italian directors like Vittorio De Sica) appears as early as Cela's *La colmena* (1951) and takes hold with classics such as Jesús Fernández Santos's *Los bravos* (1954) and Rafael Sánchez Ferlosio's *El Jarama* (1956). Along with the change in narrative mode comes a change in ideological orientation, from the individual anguish of existentialism to a greater sociopolitical commitment (also associated with Sartre) within the limits of a regime hostile to criticism. Still, there is no way to classify the movement monolithically, as a group of writers with common goals or even a common aesthetic.[12] Martín Gaite's depiction of a number of young girls coming of age in a provincial capital is a case in point: she privileges encountering a male-dominated society as a crucial element in her Bildungsroman. Cela and Martín Santos treat specifically female aspects of coming to terms with social norms in passing if at all, in keeping with their focus on male protagonists.

The city where these women go about behind curtains and blinds is recognizable as Salamanca, especially since the author grew up there. However, she conspicuously omits a feature that comes to mind for all those familiar with Salamanca, its magnificent university. The omission reflects the suppression of the intellectual function in the lives of these women, whose families do not encourage them to pursue their studies. It also serves to throw into relief two other landmarks that do make appearances, the casino and the cathedral. Social life, which for these girls means finding a suitor, revolves around the former. And the cathedral tower hovers in the background of communal life; its clock keeps watch at all times like a gigantic eye.[13] In speaking of this novel and the "social novel" in general, it is tempting to see the perspective as one of "camera-eye objectivity."[14] Nonetheless, I find that the author has chosen details in a highly selective way that produces a poetic rather than an objective view of reality, as well as a strong political message. In nearly all instances the spatial constructions of *Entre visillos* exhibit a sense of confinement and the impression that characters are being watched or overheard.

Much of *Entre visillos* concerns itself with the arrangement of interior spaces and the movement of textual bodies through those spaces. We first encounter Tali, one of the more central characters (the one we identify with the author as an adolescent), discussing with her friend Gertru the latter's impending coming-out party. Gertru draws up a floor plan of the place where it will be held so that Tali, who declines to attend, can visualize the event. This drawing up of a floor plan encapsulates the project of *Entre visillos*. While Rodoreda employed a dollhouse motif to strengthen the narrative nurture of her characters, Martín Gaite constructs a series of oppressive dollhouses ruled by the Father's law that enclose the characters and restrict movement. Furthermore, Tali is being made to view something disagreeable from her perspective; the reason she has declined to attend the party is that she cannot stand to see her best friend taking a different path in life from her own. Gertru's entry into society will coincide with her leaving school and preparing herself exclusively for marriage to her fiancé. Like the floor plan Gertru produces, *Entre visillos* will introduce readers to a place where the lines are always already drawn according to status quo, not according to one's own specifications.

Despite the preponderance of dialogue, which occupies more than half of the text, the spatial constructions of *Entre visillos* stand out for their concentrated form and for the way they shape the dialogue and the movements of characters. Each short description of a setting is overdetermined by enclosure and crowding; there can be no privacy for Julia, who sleeps in the same room as her sister Mercedes, who in turn is ready to divulge her sister's secrets to attract the attention of a man. Meanwhile, the youngest sister, Tali, can hear their conversations through the room partition. When the outsider Pablo Klein shows up to teach at the girls' high school, his arrival takes him from a crowded train compartment to a station wagon filled with other passengers.

The women of *Entre visillos* continually navigate close quarters cluttered with other bodies.[15] At the casino two girls must "fight the current" of bodies traveling in the opposite direction to get to the dance floor (67). In a hotel-room party the landscape is littered with couples; in order to escape, a woman goes out on the balcony but finds herself locked out with a strange man. Characters are repeatedly depicted looking through doorways or out of windows at goings-on outside. Many of the encounters between characters begin with one running into the other in a doorway; Tali utilizes this device when she pretends to "bump into" her teacher Pablo. The crossing of a threshold into a dwelling place is a significant moment often included in the narration; what is important is not only that characters are entering through a doorway but the way they enter. Pablo steps aside to let his Tali pass; Elvira goes from one room to the next gracefully and in control of her home domain.

A confession more explicit than any discussed thus far—an actual sacramental confession—transpires between a priest and Julia, whose gravest sin is having entertained erotic thoughts about her boyfriend. True to the architectural overdetermination of *Entre visillos*, it takes place in the appropriately cramped place, a confession booth. As anyone who has grown up Catholic can attest, nothing makes one feel more stifled than pushing aside the heavy purple drapes, kneeling in the darkened, phone-booth-sized confessional, and waiting for the priest to slide open the soundproof panel.

City streets and squares afford no freedom; they are extensions of the confinement of interior spaces. Thanks to the cathedral's gigantic eye, nobody's actions go unnoticed. When some of the girls play jokes and laugh before going home, a friend admonishes them, "Don't make fools of yourselves. People are watching" (15). The provincial capital is like a house turned inside out; one of its streets is "ugly and long like a hallway" (14). The young women always go about in groups, or *bandadas,* or else on a man's arm, as if for protection. When Tali walks alone, she is surrounded by teasing soldiers. From a perspective on the outside, both physically and figuratively, Pablo is aware of the effect of social structure on his pupils and expresses it in concrete terms: "I walked at a leisurely pace towards the pension along empty streets, and looking at the windows of the buildings, I imagined the stagnant and heated life that boiled in their interiors" (219).

The language of *Entre visillos* repeats the patterns of confinement and suffocation present in its interior and exterior spaces. In dialogue characters often use the verb *ahogarse* (to drown or suffocate) to describe their condition. Elvira claims to be suffocating from the compassion heaped upon her after her father's death (it reminds her of the lengthy mourning period that awaits). Tali runs inside to escape after her first heart-to-heart talk with Pablo and finds that the stairway of her home asphyxiates her (188). Finally, Pablo decides to leave the city and its problems and head for Madrid because he feels smothered (253). Similarly, the verb *desahogarse* (to vent, unbosom oneself, get a load off one's chest, etc.) encodes the reverse motion, like Tali unburdening herself and revealing how the conformity of other women annoys her (222) and Elvira writing a love letter to Pablo that she regrets later (94).

The repetition of *ahogarse* and *desahogarse* combines a physical and an emotional response that reinforces the parallel between architecture and social stricture, which in turn gives shape to the novel. Apart from communicating their constant suffocation, the bodies of these women speak little, mainly with sighs and tears. Tears flow freely, especially when a character mentions a particular man who interests her. Crying is the only discourse other than confession for the expression of (frustrated) desire. These women may not bear the ingrained tattoos of Pascual's body or otherwise exhibit the more violent subjection to masculine norms, but the "rouge and cologne" they wear are nonetheless reminders that their bodies are not wholly their own. The accoutrements of femininity serve to limit physical freedom: in several instances women refrain from running or sitting down because of their high heels, stockings, or delicate dresses. When Pablo kisses the casino hostess, the first thing he notices is the bitter taste of her lipstick. Unlike the perspective of Leticia Valle, the selective focus behind the novel seems to view conformist women with compassion rather than disgust. Gertru, for example, has no idea of her fiancé's deception, to which the reader is made privy.

The late nineteenth and the early twentieth century saw the machine and mechanization become prominent metaphors for the body and bodily processes. In the mid-twentieth century the rise of synthetic materials supplied another source of imagery. Martín Gaite fits this in nicely with the motif of artifice in female glamour when some wisecracking young men call a group of girls who look too perfect "cellophane girls" (100). In contrast, Tali refuses to beautify herself and consequently looks younger than her peers. She props up books on her knees and reads in bed, while Gertru stores her books away in the back room (a place for half-forgotten things that occupies a more central position in Martín Gaite's 1978 novel, *El cuarto de atrás*).

Men are represented as having greater physical freedom; they make the passes the women must dodge and are less confined to their homes. Also, men and the one female outcast, the casino hostess, gain some sort of escape from their surroundings through intoxication. We have already seen the use of alcohol to help loosen moral constraints in *Insolación;* in *Entre visillos* and subsequent novels to be examined, alcohol or other drugs are increasingly utilized as an escape from immediate reality and sometimes as an entry into an alternative one. There is no denying that mood- and mind-altering drugs and their relation to the body are a growth area for physical inscription in the latter half of the twentieth century, partly as a reflection of actual society and also as a way of carrying the body one step further as meaning-producing text. At any rate, the hostess's indulgence in alcohol marks her as a fallen woman, while Pablo finds her to be the most sincere and authentic of the grown women he meets in the city. Pablo's eccentric viewpoint encased in a foreign male character breaks up the otherwise strictly binary gender relations in this cross section of a provincial upper middle class. His presence reflects the subtle attitude changes, specifically regarding sex roles, that were inevitably filtering into Spain during the fifties.[16]

Much as the sea represents unbridled drives and provides a medium for desire among lovers in Rodoreda's works, in Martín Gaite's the riverbank just outside the town walls constitutes an oasis of temporary freedom. Julia's boyfriend takes her there on his brief visits. Pablo leads his students by the banks as part of his perambulatory method of opening their minds, but the headmaster cautions him against such heterodoxy. Elvira opens her heart to Pablo there and allows him to kiss her. While there, she recited part of a poem by Juan Ramón Jiménez that speaks of roots stretching downward and wings stretching heavenward. Elvira interprets this as the duality of body and soul. Because her body weighs her down in public, she wishes she could be all ethereal soul. Still, her longing for Pablo is quite carnal, and he becomes fed up at last with her hypocrisy. He resorts to coaching Emilio, who desperately wants her hand in marriage, on how to propose to her successfully. Emilio wins her over simply by not crowding her as he had been doing until that point and by offering her a quiet country retreat where she will have a room of her own.

In the osmosislike diffusion at the end of *Entre visillos* several characters set out for their own space outside of the suffocating atmosphere of the provincial capital: Emilio and Elvira to the country, Pablo and Julia to Madrid. Tali is running alongside the train that carries her teacher and her sister; although she is still too young to escape, she seems determined not to slide definitively into the stagnation that surrounds her. The avoidance of closure at the end of the novel has the effect of loosening the restraints the rest of the work has constructed for the characters: we can hardly guess whether they are headed for "happy endings," but we know that their current stagnation and confinement cannot continue in defiance of bodies with a desire to break free.

A male-dominated power structure determines parameters, limits, and movement. Given the dearth of imagery and scene settings, the few objects caught by the selective focus stand out. The "eye" of the cathedral clock, a portrait of General Franco on the wall at Elvira's house, and a tile depicting the Cristo del Gran Poder (Christ of the Great Power, a famous Sevillian icon) are all aligned as male-oriented symbols that keep vigil subtly but powerfully in the background. Tali must beg her father to allow Julia to go to Madrid and be with her boyfriend. No corresponding female authority figures can be found: the mother of Tali, Julia, and Mercedes died in giving birth to Tali. Since Tali does not remember her mother, she has created an internal image of what her mother was like. It is nothing like the oval portrait she sees at the cemetery, hence, unlike her sisters, she does not cry when she visits the grave. The absence of Tali's mother—caused by Tali's advent—and the daughter's subsequent re-creation of the maternal figure leads us back to the issue of the abundance of motherless heroines in fiction authored by women.

The difficulty of finding a model in the women of previous generations for the increasingly independent women of each new generation seems to underlie this conspicuous textual absence. Janet Benjamin has examined how the mother in psychoanalytic discourse is viewed as something from which the child must separate in order to be whole; the father, on the other hand, is the model of enterprise and dynamism in the world. This leaves independent-minded girls without a same-sex model with which to identify; in addition, there is a great temptation, not to truly separate, but to remain bound, out of fear, to the mother's will.[17] While Freud finds this to be a consequence of the "nature" of gender differences, for Benjamin it is the consequence of a pervasive social bias to which Freudian discourse contributes. Benjamin's critique of the Freudian developmental schema also extends to attitudes toward the maternal body that we see represented in these three texts.

For both male authors discussed here, the maternal body, and to some extent the seductive body, is threatening and engulfing and must be separated from at all costs, even through violence. For the female novelist, the maternal body represents a bewildering and frustrating sense of loss that leaves one alone in the world, while the real menace is the power granted absolutely to men. As in the case of Leticia Valle, a male teacher intervenes to open to the heroine the doors onto the realm of masculine knowledge. For Leticia Valle, the effort ends in a disastrous seduction provoked by male condescension. Tali finds herself deserted by her tutor, who nonetheless has given her back something of herself. In short, no covert hostility ignites against the male purveyor of knowledge, but he is delineated against a background of more articulated and more systematic dominance of men over women.

In the last of the novels written under Francoist dictatorship to be studied here we reach a crossroads between the "social novel" and the "new novel" of the 1960s and 1970s, which placed emphasis on experimental modes of narration, demystification of dominant discourses, and the individual rather than the collective protagonist. Luis Martín-Santos's *Tiempo de silencio* (1962) may truly be considered the culmination of the former trend and a bridge into the latter that would never be surpassed. Bodily imagery is central to the plot and discourses of this novel, the first effort of a young psychiatrist and political activist who died in a car crash before completing his second. This especially compelling chapter of political anatomy in the Spanish novel has motifs of castration, confinement, and subjection to socially defined requirements of masculinity pertaining to the male body and notes of entrapment and mermaidlike enticement associated with the female body. Heat symbolizes the medium of friendship, attraction, and nurturing among textual bodies, for male-female relations as much as for relations between men. True to its rootedness in the *novela social,* the collective protagonist has an active role; hence Madrid and, by extension, Spanish society as a whole are also endowed with the physical features of a distinct body. Another body, the construct Iberian Man and its subcategories Plains Man of Castile and Mountain Man of Asturias, emerges from the narrator's mock anthropological discourse. The inscribed bodies of *Tiempo de silencio* combine in the multiple discourses of its *polifonía* and in its kaleidoscopic panoramas of the social reality of Madrid in 1949 to form a multifaceted representation that poses both formal and ideological challenges to the prevailing novelistic tradition.[18]

Much of the criticism that has concerned itself with physical representation in *Tiempo de silencio* does not go beyond the commonplaces of mind-body dualism, for example, the protagonist's physical limitations and their effects on his free will. The political aspect of mind-body interplay is equally important. As I hope to prove, what turns the body into a limiting factor is the subjection imposed on it from without by particular power structures. At any rate, in his discussion of the relation between "external" determinants and free will in the actions of the protagonist Pedro, Alfonso

Rey enumerates three *facticidades* that infringe upon the characters' capacity to act freely and pursue their Sartrean vital projects: the limitations of the body, the need to coexist alongside one's fellow man, and having to live in a society divided into antagonistic classes (200). By grouping the body with these external determinants, Rey overlooks political implications and maintains the duality of mind and body in a more absolute way than does Martín-Santos, pitting the striving of inner self against a physical shell that blocks not only transcendence but even personal fulfillment. I find, however, that the writing of *Tiempo de silencio* keeps alive a more dynamic give-and-take between thought processes and physical reality, of which the body is a key element. Not only does the author's background as surgeon, physician, and psychiatrist sharpen his awareness of the inseparable nature of the mental and the physical but his writing inscribes the body more thoroughly than has the writing of any of his male predecessors in Spain, making this yet another sense in which *Tiempo de silencio* breaks with the past and introduces the "new novel" in Spanish fiction in 1962.

A good deal of Martín-Santos's creative use of the Spanish social body appears to be motivated by his half-veiled subversion of the writings of Ortega y Gasset and essayists of the Generation of 1898.[19] They liberally used bodily metaphors for Spanish society, such as those found in Ortega's *España invertebrada,* in order to ignite a flagging national will, bemoan the lack of an elite, and instill the value of social cohesion. In Martín-Santos's hands, bodily codification becomes an instrument in the decentering of this discourse and the twisting of the Spanish social body into an anthropophagic figure like Goya's Saturn devouring the smaller, individual bodies of its children. The cancer Pedro studies in lab rats is mirrored and magnified on the collective scale of society, but no "iron surgeon" (Joaquín Costa's phrase) could possibly treat it, and in fact no such person appears on the scene. Pedro is more concerned with furthering his research career against all odds, and in the end he only manages to get himself sent back to the provinces to look after the individual bodies of his countrymen as a physician.

Unlike the Saturn myth vividly depicted by Goya, in Martín-Santos's work the female body is cast in the role of the anthropophagic collective protagonist. As Jo Labanyi has noted, Martín-

Santos's writing is unmistakably informed by a reading of Erich Fromm's *Escape from Freedom*, which equates the willingness to submit to an authoritarian state with a desire to return to the protection of the womb, even if it means that a symbolic castration must result.[20] Accordingly, in the pension where he lives, Pedro finds himself surrounded by the presence of "three generations" of the female form, not unlike the three Fates or malignant crows who come to dominate the scene of Pascual Duarte's home. In any case, Pedro is lulled into contentment in the presence of the "three goddesses," each one perched upon her pedestal, and enjoys the titillation of the youngest, who is simultaneously offered to his gaze but withheld from his possession as she sways back and forth on a rocking chair. The reader is privy to unappetizing facts about this all-female family unit, while Pedro would just as soon remain ignorant so that he may continue to bask in their splendor. But the image that emerges from the grandmother's soliloquy is patently monstrous: her daughter, the mother of Dorita, appears more masculine than her lover, Dora's effeminate father. The grandmother, in turn, laments the "final sinking of [her] life as a woman" and waxes poetic about the sweetmeat of her granddaughter with authentic lust. The three generations are just different faces of the same amorphous female monster, hideously complete in itself and capable of spawning future generations with only a little help. And it looks as though Pedro will soon be netted and employed for this purpose.

While Pedro is held in place by the warmth of this feminine hearth, his laboratory rats also respond favorably to the "female heat" given off by Muecas's daughters in the shantytown. These girls are from poor but hearty stock, conceived in a "Toledan belly," once again bringing into focus the cataloguing of human genetic types common among nineteenth-century anthropologists (and practiced by Marcelino Menéndez Pelayo in his *Historia de los heterodoxos españoles*, 1880–82), which had persisted as a justification for authoritarianism in the prevailing discourse of Francoist Spain. Codifying the poor (such as these provincial Spaniards, recent immigrants to Madrid) as a separate race in biological terms makes their economic condition seem innate and deserved. Martín-Santos ironically echoes this condescending discourse while making clear that social upheaval lies at the root of their low standard of life: in these makeshift accommodations for the masses who have moved to Madrid to better their lot, the most elementary of social laws have dissolved. Muecas and his daughter-concubines are the most blatant example. In a passage that skillfully employs free indirect style of quotation, we follow Muecas on his imaginary ramblings through his estate and find him master of all he surveys. In reality, exerting sexual dominance over his daughters is the only way he can cast himself as a "patriarch," and Martín-Santos alludes to the biblical comparison of elderly King David sleeping between two young girls for warmth to ironically sanction Muecas's incestuous ménage. As an astute self-made man, Muecas has displayed know-how in utilizing his only natural resource, "female heat," for pleasure and profit, until he unwittingly engenders a next generation in this way. Here the incest taboo, which the narrator had claimed did not exist in this barely civilized environment, does cause Muecas to make a biblical sacrifice (under the abortionist's knitting needle) of his daughter Florita so that she will not carry the child to term.

When Pedro is asked to participate in this illegal abortion, he is ensnared by the female body in another sense. His fruitless entry into Florita's womb (she is already dead) with medical equipment is a prelude to his being swallowed up by the underground caverns of a prison, where he and the narrator will describe in minute detail how each feature of the bare surroundings contributes to the sense of confinement, tedium, and powerlessness.[21] There is a constant interaction between his physical subjection to imprisonment and his thoughts as he vainly tries not to think and to exonerate himself for his blunders. It is evident that Pedro does not seem to exist in a body of his own, since it is rarely referred to, and then always in relation to other bodies and to engulfing or imprisoning structures, up to and including the train cabin in which he leaves Madrid at the end. The erasure of his body—for he does not even have a physiognomy—throws into relief the other bodies that act upon him, such as Dorita lying in bed, a body he cannot distinguish from the heat that surrounds it. In this tensely written passage, a "third eye" guides Pedro across the room toward intercourse with the desired object, but what is evidently the male sexual organ is encoded as the instrument of objectification, the pure male gaze. Hence, what little corporeality he might have been accorded in this passage is suppressed, and Pedro remains a nonentity in terms of his relations with other textual bodies, whose pull he is powerless to resist.

Even Pedro's friendly wanderings with Matías are determined by the heat his friend exudes, which will keep Pedro at his side until the wee hours of the morning: "They remained submerged in another, lower form of existence . . . where friendship did not make itself known as spiritual comprehension but rather as animal heat on the shoulder."[22] Their masculine ritual of Saturday night amusement includes the poisoning of their bodies with alcohol, in the narrator's ironic clinical language, and a visit to a brothel that has drawn dozens of anxious men to its door, to expel all but the select team of Pedro and Matías. Once inside, the besotted Matías is more interested in dramatizing his oedipal conflict than in actual physical contact. The prostitutes are characterized as worn-out and unappetizing but lustful, an instance in which Martín-Santos employs physical representation in a nineteenth-century way, to morally brand and censure socially stigmatized behavior by making the body fit the "soul."

As in *La colmena,* the ubiquitousness of prostitution and the conniving to trade valuable virgin flesh for economic stability in marriage serve as reminders of the desperation of *los años del hambre* (the hungry years). Both works emphasize that the harder times are, the more conspicuously does the female body take on the value of a currency in a male-oriented economy. As a representative of the most elemental female figure, Muecas's wife Encarna/Ricarda is so purely physical that she thinks in images, which must be related to us by the narrator; she is the only foregrounded character who never speaks for herself. What Encarna, the incarnation of downtrodden peasantry and motherhood, remembers most vividly are dancing at a festival in her town, glorying briefly in her youthful body, and having transmitted life, "as her only possession," to her daughters. Her connection to the physical is so immediate that knowing that her daughter's body is undergoing an autopsy makes her weep aloud and feel the pain as if she and Florita were still one and the same body. Her sorrow goes beyond mere ignorance of the lifeless body's incapacity to feel further pain: her vital connection to the daughter is such that she actually experiences the postmortem surgery as an invasion of her own body. Encarna's alignment with the flesh, with motherhood, with the peasantry and immigrants to Madrid, and with the earth itself is so complete that she exists almost entirely outside of the symbolic realm of language. But when she does speak, as she does in order to clear Pedro of guilt in Florita's demise, she is incapable of the deception made possible by language.

Against the carnality of women like Encarna, who stand for the Spanish motherland; the prostitutes, who sell or lease their bodies; and the fallen bourgeoisie like Dorita, who must use her charms to reascend the social ladder, there exists the counterpoint of icy, upper-class women like Matías's mother, well-preserved and narcissistic. First we are introduced to the *damas mideluésticas*—a neologism for women of the American Midwest. These frigid but robust females never married and now channel all their energies into causes like the American Society for the Prevention of Cruelty to Animals. Because their kind does not exist in Spain—the fake anthropologist whom Pedro has internalized suggests that the *macho ibérico* renders all such women reproductively active and fettered to domesticity—scientists there need not worry about excessive cruelty to animals in their experiments. Unhindered by the watchful eyes of these midwestern superwomen, the scientists in Pedro's lab have perpetrated an array of experiments whose only purpose seems to be the sadistic torture of laboratory animals. The theme of the sadistic impulse is taken up later in the famous bullfighting passage, which expresses wonderment at the glee with which Spaniards view their compatriots' being skewered on taurine horns and unites the narrator with the collective protagonist in asking, "What bull do we carry inside of us?" Although throughout the novel much of social behavior is explained in genetic terms, it is always in a context that belies its sarcastic meaning. It is evident that the real explanations are more complicated and have to do with the antagonism between social classes, a history of social upheaval, and an unyielding hierarchy of authority—all larger causes relating to a Spanish "complex" that the novel as a whole seeks to elucidate.

While the female form at its most oppressive is numbing, deadening, and smothering, the infliction of pain comes at the hands of male figures. These range from the scientists in Pedro's lab, to the *mago* (shaman) who performs the crude abortion, to the murderous Cartucho, who believes he is taking a life for a life, one token for another, when he stabs Pedro's fiancée. The example of the prison is emblematic: while Pedro's descent into the underworld repeats the pattern of womblike entrapment in the rest of the novel, the figure whose authority keeps him there is symbolic of male patriarchal power raised to an absolute level in the absence of human rights. In the conversation, or semblance of one, that takes place between Pedro and his jailor the latter's accusation and threats are rendered in a shorthand of generic phrases in parentheses that take the place of actual communication, revealing the one-sidedness of the exchange. Hence, Pedro's forced submission to an authoritarian state takes the physical form of a return to the womb, while in words his sentence is dictated by a spokesman for the Father's Law with whom it would be useless to argue.

The protagonists as a group are connected by their inhabiting Madrid, a city with a body of its own and a will, or at least a force that it exerts over immigrants from the provinces. As Pedro's assistant Amador explains the advent of Muecas's family, "Madrid has a strong pull" (38). What is different about the urban body is that it wears its organs on the outside: "In this way we can finally understand that a man is the image of a city and that a city is the internal organs of a man placed on the outside" (18). Thus the city is an inside-out body, exposing what most bodies keep hidden. By the same token, one can never step outside of this body as long as one is within the limits of the urban space. The power of envelopment of this body also functions in an inside-out fashion, so that in this man-made space one can die or be killed but never get lost, "because that's why the city exists (so that man may never get lost)" (19). In some sense the city can be said to think the thoughts of its thousands of inhabitants: "We can also understand that the city thinks with its brain of a thousand heads distributed among a thousand bodies, though all are united by a single will to power" (18). The chaotic enumeration of citizens that follows ridicules the Falangist ideal of an esprit de corps uniting all to rebuild society: Madrid the all-engulfing and all-knowing, inside-out body is an anarchic assembly of human atoms on a collision course, and the authoritarian ideology that seeks to glue it together and regulate it is revealed as a sham.

By extension, public gathering places in *Tiempo de silencio* are represented as maternal spaces of containment imbued with a certain consciousness. Pedro becomes aware of this as he enters the café, with its bohemian literary-artistic circles: "Already he has been incorporated into a community of which, despite it all, he forms a part and from which he could not disentangle himself without difficulty. Upon entering the place, the city—with one of its sharpest consciousnesses—has taken note of him: he exists" (78).

In the arena of foreign affairs, Spain the collective protagonist is best represented by Dorita's grandfather, the *glorioso militar* who regaled his wife with beatings and infidelities and whose military career, from the disaster of 1898 to the catastrophe of Anual in 1921, mirrors the history of Spanish colonialist domination, or attempted domination, during the period preceding the Second Republic. Tellingly, his body bore the scars of his parallel campaign of male dominance over conquered foreign females: one of the local *tagalas* he pursued in the Philippines left him with a venereal disease that blocked his tubes and rendered him sterile. The fact that he is long dead serves to close the chapter definitively on the possibility of Spanish colonialism. Past glory remains, along with the man who symbolizes it, a memory over which the doting widow (symbolizing part of the Spanish body politic) will brood endlessly.

Pedro concludes, too late, that all this time the city has served as his incubator, coaxing him into heat so that he would make the mistakes that now seal his fate. Just as he was continually swallowed up by Madrid and other more specific spatial constructions in the novel, in the conclusion he is expelled or perhaps even excreted from the monstrous maternal body. The near erasure of the male body in the text leaves Pedro with little ground on which to stand: his body is overshadowed by the richness of other signifying bodies in the text, leaving him to face the ultimate obliteration of his masculinity, castration. If Pedro bends this way and that and strays from his vital project, it is because his own body is not represented as a strong base from which to resist the influences of other bodies—both literal and figurative, individual and social—in the text. In the end he finds himself, as Rey aptly states, "summed up with the other silences" of his time and place. Also, he is subsumed into the fake anthropological category of Iberian Man, subcategory Castilian Plains Man. The physical anthropologist of the past has reached forward and trapped Pedro within a preconceived mold; his anatomy plus his milieu is his destiny.

Pedro at last begins to listen to his own body, but in a negative sense, as one of the castrated and voiceless, as one whose organs have been washed out of the inside of his body. The failure of his vital project entailed in the loss of his research scholarship is a punishment for his having violated, not a law (for he was not convicted), but a social sanction against abortion, an operation that takes place within the body of a woman but whose legality and morality are often decided in social forums, making an individual decision the subject of public moral scrutiny and legislation. In this way *Tiempo de silencio* illustrates how complete the control over the individual as a physical entity was in Spain under Franco. The novelist uses a stratified and multifaceted set of discourses to convey the multiple restrictions placed on the individual body by the collective body in Madrid of 1949. Submission to a fascist ideology appears as the cause of extreme examples of physical subjection. The protagonist struggles against the forces of subjection more visibly than against his perceived physical limitations.

In the works of Cela and Martín-Santos the male body speaks and becomes a text, but what is notable about that text is its ambiguity or lack of substance. The pure male gaze serves men as the instrument of objectification, and in the past male characters were privileged as all "subjectivity" (gaze plus consciousness) and no body. What Pedro seems to prove, however, is that no onlooker can remain uninvolved in what he witnesses, even through the microscope. Once he becomes involved (as in Florita's and Dorita's situations), the corporeal void of the male character turns into a strategic weakness, leaving him at the mercy of other bodies. Hence, Cela and Martín-Santos both enunciate cries of difference against supposed advantages of the male subject in patriarchal society; in these mid-century decades it is easy to overlook the fact that gender shifting is not the exclusive product of feminism: men also question the role imposed upon them by their possession of a male body.[23] The hallmark of male perspective is still the territorializing of the female form as source of engulfment or entrapment, harnessing the male body and putting it to work for the perpetuation of the species and of existing social institutions. Martín Gaite portrays women who carry out this task in a different way. For her, "cellophane girls" are made, not born, and they owe their existence to a complex of pressures exerted upon them in a male-dominated world. The girl who chooses to disobey conventional wisdom and invest in herself has a place in Martín Gaite's novelistic world, but her motherlessness suggests her lack of female models and precursors. She has broken the inter-generational chain of amorphous female creatures rendered in the monstrous all-female families of Cela and Martín-Santos.

5.

Nomads and Schizos: Postmodern Trends in Body Writing

THE CONCLUSION OF *Tiempo de silencio* has Pedro in a train headed for the provinces after losing his research grant, musing with sarcasm on the way his ambitions have backfired. Despite the obvious failure of his plans, a certain lack of closure leaves the reader in doubt about whether this may in fact be a not so unhappy ending after all. Joseph Schraibman, for example, interprets the downscaling of Pedro's career aspirations as a paradoxical "cure" for the quixotic impulse that had driven him to seek a cure for cancer in a country that could not and would not support his expensive research (Pedro's hero, Ramón y Cajal, had to accomplish much of his work abroad or with foreign funding). In the process he had turned into a mad scientist with no regard for humanity, as evidenced by his willingness to use Muecas's daughters as experimental specimens to determine whether the particular cancer he was studying might be contagious. He is now curiously liberated from this madness to devote himself to something at which he stands a chance of being successful while leading a contented though conventional life as a general practitioner. Spain, in turn, loses an extreme longshot for a Nobel prize but gains a medical expert on the micro level.[1]

In the undecidability of Pedro's fate there is also a doorway to postmodern representations of the body. The interior monologue that narrates his train ride rambles among many descriptions of the way Pedro perceives his body to have been acted upon. In addition to comparing himself to castrated Turkish prisoners of yore left half-buried on the beach to scream, he declares that the organs have been washed out of the inside of his body (290). He laughs silently at his defeat and exhorts his imaginary tormentors to "flip me over; I'm done on this side," referring to St. Lorenzo's martyrdom on the grill just as the train passes by the Monastery of San Lorenzo del Escorial (295). The movement between a painful castration metaphor and a body-without-organs accepted with sarcasm strikes a chord present in the thinking of Gilles Deleuze and Félix Guattari. They see the body-without-organs in a positive light, unlike the castration image that emanates from the Oedipus complex, which for them has distorted models of mind-body interaction. The body-without-organs implies deterritorialization of desires, a freeing up of libidinal drives, in the sense that the lost organs were bound to the organizations of the molar organism, understood as a regime of social repression. With no organs to lose, Pedro is free from the social restraints of the polis, which he had referred to earlier as a body that wears its organs on the outside. The body-without-organs as the figure of the survivor (neither winner nor loser) cut loose from the machines of the state also has the potential for putting male and female expression on more even footing. It neutralizes the unequal charges of the Oedipus/ Electra complex, in which fear of castration and penis envy pertain to male and female subjects, respectively. It places them on the same line of desire, that of escape or flight.

The master narrative of the Oedipus complex, with its omnipotent father figure and object mother, begins to fade at the conclusion of this novel, making way for a postmodern diversity in physical representation that becomes more pronounced after Spain's transition to democracy.[2] Similarly, the architectural control over bodies in *Entre visillos,* associated with the father and hence with the tyrant, gives way to Martín Gaite's introduction into her apartment of an ambiguous, fantastical body-and-text in *El cuarto de atrás* (1978). In Spain the fading of master narratives or metadiscourses—Freudianism, Marxism, classical feminism, and other emancipation narratives—coincides with the passage from a hybrid despotic-capitalist system (in Deleuzian terms) to the global system Fredric Jameson calls late capitalism. The abruptness of Spain's convergence with the rest of Europe on the macro level, along with the persistence of semidevelopment (an educated elite that belongs to a "developed" society coexisting with social structures and caste prejudices that correspond to an "underdeveloped" one)[3] on the micro level, gives Spanish postmodernism an intensity and vigor that may account in part for the "boom" of the Spanish novel in the 1980s.

As Andrés Soria Olmedo has noted, the expected surge in literary production did not occur when the Francoist dictatorship ended in 1975. It had been predicted that writers would take hidden manuscripts out of their desks and publish them as soon as the regime that silenced them had vanished; some writers had propagated this belief themselves with a wait-and-see attitude.[4] The years of the transition to democracy (colloquially known as the unplugging, or *destape*) brought more mannerist versions of the experimental mode initiated by Martín-Santos, as well as a distinct predilection for the memoir, historical revisionism through fictionalized testimony, and metafiction. Exiles returned to Spain accounted for some of the outstanding titles, such as two novels already examined, Chacel's *Barrio de maravillas* and Rodoreda's *Mirall trencat*. Nonetheless, this was not the sudden explosion anticipated by the reading public.

Here I will focus attention on novels of post-transitional Spain, because they were written under approximately the same conditions that continue to prevail, which I would summarize as the "cultural dominant" of postmodernism. My view is consonant with that of Randolph Pope, who concludes his study of Antonio Muñoz Molina with the assertion that the latter's novels, published in the late 1980s, mark Spain's full entry, "for better or for worse, into international postmodernism." Gonzalo Navajas, on the other hand, maintains that this period goes beyond postmodernism into something new, which he hesitates to name. The differentiating characteristics he lists (e.g., nostalgia), while they represent astute observations of the texts in question, show no outright discrepancy with the postmodern.[5] Furthermore, the fiction of previous decades has far more in common with high modernity than with postmodernism, which is understandable, since the sociopolitical conditions of postmodernity were not in place in Spain at the time.

Charles T. Powell asserts that the Spanish democratic system was not solidified until the elections of October 1982, won by the Socialist Party (PSOE). This consolidation was fully recognized in the international sphere by Spain's acceptance into the European Com-

munity in 1986.[6] Hence, I use *post-transitional* to describe the period
(which coincides with the onset of the postmodern) beginning in
1982, acquiring full strength in 1986, and extending into the present.
By coincidence, the last book I discuss in detail, *Beltenebros*, was
published in 1989, carving out a neat century that started with
Insolación.

In the following pages I will try to bring broad social phenomena
as well as gleanings from my favorite readings in postmodern theory
to bear on corporeality in a select group of novels. The intersection of
these three distinct fields of knowledge may lead to some discordant
connections and conclusions, but I think it is worthwhile to take the
risk in order to cover the nearly unexplored terrain. Fredric Jameson's collected writings on postmodernism as "the cultural logic of
late capitalism" have supplied me with the clearest criteria for separating the high modern from the postmodern; most helpful is his
intuitive and analytical foregrounding of structures of feeling and
cultural dominants rather than aesthetics or stylistics. Parody and
pastiche can be found in modern and postmodern works alike. What
gives the postmodern novel a different sensibility is its emergence
from the peculiar conflation of video as dominant medium (film with
no afterimage and hence no memory),[7] the concomitant mediation of
consciousness by a Consciousness Industry more far-reaching and
all-absorbing than any that has exited before, the loss of historicity,
and the colonization of the present by a "nostalgia mode,"[8] an "inter-
nationalization" of capitalism that replaces the old imperialism and
has far-reaching consequences for the division of labor, banking,
corporate structure, and bureaucracy. While I agree with Pope that
no binary opposition of characteristics can describe the difference
between modernity and the postmodern,[9] I find one analogy irresistible: modernity is to the postmodern as Gene Kelly is to Michael
Jackson.

Unfortunately, Jameson concludes along the way that the *nou-
veau roman* is the last significant innovation of literary high modernism and that postmodern image addiction results in a "postliteracy"
that renders the novel an insignificant form or marker. I believe,
however, that this should be contested as an exaggeration, like his
assertion that "Zola may be taken as the marker for the last coexistence of the art novel and the best-seller within a single text."[10] The

1980s "boomlet" narrative of Spain is in fact characterized by its critical and popular appeal, especially in comparison with the less accessible experimental novel of the previous two decades. What is more, there is plenty happening both inside and outside the texts to keep them vital as a genre. They need not cater exclusively to postmodern sensibilities by being "picture books" instead of portrayals of a subjectivity: they can accomplish both goals, and satisfy readers who want to rest on the surface of images as well as those who are looking for an identity behind it all, because the postmodern subject yields fragments that lend themselves to collage. In particular, Spanish narrative of the 1980s contains prismatic reflections of a society in rapid transformation. These reflections show up either as part of the fictional situation or as a conspicuous escape, a kind of reverse reflection.

Fragmentation replaces alienation as the guiding principle behind postmodern narrative. Women write or publish a much larger proportion of titles than ever before, but many of the most innovative of them see the female subject as divorced from a dialectical struggle against patriarchy. Soledad Puértolas believes it is easier to find a publisher as a woman in the 1980s—a certain curiosity abounds regarding the once-silenced female perspective—but encounters some prejudice in the critical evaluation of writing by women. She rejects the notion that her writing should reflect on "women's issues" as a stifling by-product of the renewed interest in female perspectives.[11] The abandonment of the metanarrative of women versus the patriarchy as an excessively totalizing force leaves in its wake atoms of desire that coalesce in novels written by women, sometimes into unions that resemble homoerotism. However, consummation is usually absent, as is a radical, utopian rejection of heterosexuality. The fragmented female subjects of Soledad Puértolas and Adelaida García Morales unite on lines of escape or flight from society; feminism has passed through the filter of the micropolitics of desire.[12] To rely still more on the wonderful vocabulary of Deleuze and Guattari, these women are nomads who band together momentarily or schizos who include each other in their disjointed inner worlds.[13] The postmodern protagonist of novels written by men is also often a nomad or schizo fleeing the molar organism, but the mixture of erotism and comradeship does not appear, except in the works of authors dealing with explicit homosexuality; in Julio Llamazares's and Antonio Muñoz

Molina's works the female body is the object of desire found duplicated in a series of women. Lacan's epitome for what women want as opposed to what men want holds true for these two pairs of novelists: woman seeks an absolute Other that overwhelms the self (*l'Autre*), and man, the small object-other (*le petit objet a*).

The nomadic protagonist, who roams solo or in packs, and the schizo, who possesses "his own system of coordinates for situating himself at his disposal," represent creative responses to capitalist desiring-production.[14] More so than previous systems, capitalism encourages a proliferation of fluxes (rather like drives except that they are not fixed). It then sets about channeling and regulating them. Both the nomad and the schizo have disconnected their bodies from the machines of their society. As a consequence, they must constantly rethink what to do with their own machines. Deleuze and Guattari mention the more dysfunctional example of the anorectic's mouth: the proper use of this organ is no longer self-evident.[15] Anorexia, which strikes women almost exclusively, proves an unavoidable "diagnosis" for a main character in the García Morales novel. Addiction and/or substance abuse is another pitfall for the unplugged body: both Puértolas and Muñoz Molina, after the example of Martín-Santos, provide plots awash in alcohol or other drugs.

Between the disengaged body and the rest of the world there lies a medium, or several media. This is why pastiche becomes prevalent, even though it is not an exclusively postmodern practice. A palpable "atmosphere" can also intervene, through semiotic overload or an exotic, isolating landscape. Some combination of these characteristics unite the four novels we will discuss here: Adelaida García Morales's *El silencio de las sirenas* (1985), Julio Llamazares's *Luna de lobos* (1985), Soledad Puértolas's *Queda la noche* (1989), and Antonio Muñoz Molina's *Beltenebros* (1989). All of these works contain characters moving along lines of escape; the first two place a rapidly "mutating" subject in a wilderness setting, and the second two incorporate the frame of the espionage or *noir* novel—*Beltenebros* is more *noir* than *Queda la noche*, but both revolve around an international conspiracy—a pulp subgenre with strong roots in the cinema (Alfred Hitchcock's *The Man Who Knew Too Much*) but whose structural twists and turns go back as far as the Byzantine romance (*El Abencerraje*, 1565).

Fragmentation and interposed mediation of experience in these four novels suggest an array of changes in Spanish society. The loosening of the Catholic ideological hold over the government supports a relaxation of family structure, with divorce, postponement of marriage, and lower birth rates as the most apparent evidence. From the paternalism of dictatorship and male-headed households, influence crosses over into the domain of the Consciousness Industry, all the more effective for its subtlety. Censorship seems archaic compared with a bombardment of images and attitudes that succeeds in blocking out all else. Gender roles may blur, leading to a more dynamic Spanish womanhood, but a more thorough commodification of femininity ensures that gender distinctions and the encouragement to maintain them remain strong. Furthermore, we shall see how the disengaged or mutating body often winds up exaggerating one or more of the traits associated with its gender in prevailing discourses.

The first two novels, more purely atmospheric and lyrical, relate obliquely to the questions of new-found freedom from the older forms of restraint and connectedness to a social body and of what to do with one's paradoxical autonomy. The protagonist of Llamazares's *Luna de lobos* flees from the molar organism or Consciousness Industry with a historical pretense: he goes into hiding in the foothills of the Cordillera Cantábrica with three comrades after losing the final Civil War battle for his region in Asturias. The paucity of historical and even ideological references and the use of the present tense throughout the text indicate that only a vestige of modernist historicity is at work; the postmodern flattening of history and chronology holds sway in the concentration on the immediate surroundings and sensual stimuli. *Luna de lobos* may qualify as fictionalized testimony, but only in a general and existential sense. The novel reads as an inevitable companion piece to Adelaida García Morales's *El silencio de las sirenas,* which situates two isolated women in a mountain village of the Alpujarra, south of Granada. These college-educated women are not altogether alone; they are surrounded by traditional and superstitious village women, with whom communication is difficult. These imprisonment-in-the-wilderness narratives focus less on what the protagonists have left behind and more on what they cannot leave behind, much of which takes the form of physical clues written on their bodies. Disengaged from the social body and ensconced in their private worlds, their bodies undergo successive mutations that liken them to the beastly or monstrous. In each narrative the hero or heroine seeks refuge and, in the end, a more authentic way of life through a return to nature in a mountain range that should have the power to keep the molar organism at bay. But the mutations of their back-to-nature bodies echo Jameson's declaration that "postmodernism is what you have when the modernization process is complete and nature is gone for good."[16]

Llamazares's Angel (whose name anticipates his nonhuman status) hides out from Nationalist troops and then from the Guardia Civil for nine years following the Civil War. In the wilds, Angel's consciousness is as free-roaming as a wolf, while physically his movements are restricted because he must remain unseen by other human beings. Had he remained in human society, he reflects, he surely would have been interrogated and killed for having fought on the Republican side. Elsewhere he reflects that he surely would have married his girlfriend and raised a family with her. As it is, he watches her from behind trees at a village festival and calls himself, in a metaphor that insistently recurs, "a wolf in the middle of a flock."[17] The fantasy has an inescapable flip side: in his imprisonment-in-the-wilderness Angel is free not only of the persecution of his political enemies but of the behavior pattern, or lifestyle, into which he otherwise would have found himself channeled. Undomesticated and free from any social entanglements other than comradery with the other wolves or nomads in his pack, whose number dwindles until he is left completely alone by the end, he finds isolated moments of intimacy with the opposite sex. In keeping with Angel's gradual metamorphosis, his encounters are described in terms of animalistic passion; his most long-term lover, María (who appears only once in the fragmentary narrative), notes that he smells "like the wilds . . . like the wolves" (57). This brand of aftershave seems peculiarly effective, since women have only to look at him and get a whiff before letting themselves be dragged off to bed. Secrecy and immediate flight afterwards are required for their protection as well as for his, and even so, he tends to bring disaster down upon all the women with whom he has contact.

Each erotic interlude is followed by the death of one of Angel's fellow wolves or an act of violence: after the encounter with María, he finds that his sister has been savagely beaten by the Guardia Civil;

after making love to the wife of an anti-Francoist who is trying to smuggle them safely out of the country, Angel sees the husband's horse return riderless from a meeting with co-conspirators. Peter Brooks has commented that the erotic body is the most sentient kind and that the female body tends to hold the key to mystery in a patriarchal context;[18] Llamazares uses the heightened awareness of erotism as a prelude to danger. Each successive other who first meets his gaze and then bodily interlocks with him brings him closer to the ultimate mystery of death. As individuals, however, these female characters are barely distinguishable from each other, like interchangeable pieces of a puzzle.

One can imagine how *Luna de lobos* would have ended if Llamazares were a practitioner of magical realism or the neofantastic. Angel would have found himself sprouting hairs in inappropriate places and felt his teeth growing longer and sharper until the day when he could express himself only by howling at the moon. Llamazares, however, remains within the bounds of what is humanly possible (like Pedro of *Tiempo de silencio*, Angel slips away quietly by train) and for the most part neglects any static description of Angel's body during this gradual transformation from man to figurative wolf. It is mainly through movement that Angel is characterized as a wild animal: in countless similes in this narrative, which at times resembles a prose poem because of its lyricism, Angel resembles a beast crouching, pouncing, and running for his life. The stealthy movements of Angel and his pack are constantly contrasted with the terrified gestures and expressions of the few human beings they stumble upon. These people, living within the bounds of society, become textually aligned with the dogs that bark in fear each time the wolf pack approaches a settled area. Although wracked by guilt for getting others into trouble and dehumanized by constant fear himself, Angel is at least accorded the nobility of the wild as opposed to the domesticated animal, in line with a romanticization of the wolf common in the Western tradition (Jack London and Ernest Thompson Seton make a protagonist of the animal itself). The nomadic wolf-man of *Luna de lobos* gives a creative response, written in part through his mutating *intracuerpo*, to manipulation by a Consciousness Industry at the same time that he recovers lost testimony of a fate that befell some Spanish Republicans at the end of the Civil War.

However, even in the forest escape cannot be complete, especially since Angel carries with him the memories and paradigms of patriarchy. In particular, the masculine ideals of self-reliance and autonomy carried to the extreme are the forces that transform him from a man into a figurative beast; the body can never be constructed at total liberty from social norms.

In Adelaida García Morales's *El silencio de las sirenas* the mountains are the Sierra Nevada south of Granada, and the beast that one of the heroines is in danger of becoming is the mythical mermaid. This novel contains an interesting choice of narrator, not unlike that of Muñoz Molina's *El invierno en Lisboa* (1987), in which the narrator is a character and friend of the true focus of attention (like F. Scott Fitzgerald's Nick) and seems to have no life independent of this friendship.

Living vicariously through someone else's story is a prominent characteristic of Spanish new narrative, beginning with the inconspicuous Javier Miranda (whose name derives from the present participle of *mirar*, to look at) of Eduardo Mendoza's pivotal *La verdad sobre el caso Savolta* (1975). Being a spectator of one's own life, like being caught up in someone else's plot (the conspiracy motif of the last two novels), is an unmistakable response to the primacy of spectacle in the postmodern world. While it is true that all human experience has been mediated on some level by culture and by language, along with most postmodern theorists I believe that this mediation is quantitatively and qualitatively different in our time and that art on all levels must react to this in some way. Guy Debord phrases it well before going off on some improbable tangents: "In societies where modern conditions of production prevail [keeping in mind that postmodernism may be seen as the completion of the modernization process], all of life presents itself as an immense accumulation of spectacles. Everything that was directly lived has moved away into a representation."[19] María's narratorial spectatorship exhibits this tendency, although as she becomes more deeply involved she cannot resist making strategic inroads into the plot to change its outcome. Because of the novel's multilayered intertextuality, including both specific allusions (to Goethe and to Homer by way of Kafka) and implicit ones (an entire tradition of courtly and idealized love, especially in epistolary form), none of it can be taken at face value: the reader must take the reworking of references as an inversion, and finally as a subversion, of existing discourses. As Biruté Ciplijauskaité observes in a thorough study of this intertextuality, the text ultimately offers up the tradition to which it affixes itself as a spectacle.[20]

María, the Everywomanly narrator, has ostensibly been appointed to the obscure Alpujarran village as schoolteacher; Elsa, the extraordinary focus of her attention, has more obviously escaped from urban life and an unhappy love affair. Both women embark on an unsettling journey into Elsa's subconscious using hypnosis. Gradually a story of obsessive love is revealed on both planes, for Elsa writes letters and endlessly awaits replies from a philosophy professor in Barcelona whom she has met only twice. In her trances she is in love with the same man, but in the past century, and they are involved in a political conspiracy that eventually costs this previous incarnation of Elsa her life. Elsa escapes into the infinite space of women's desire; her love for Agustín Valdés (Eduardo in the past) is fed by small coincidences that she reads in Goethe, and her love grows beyond reasonable limits. María intervenes to tell Agustín the extent of Elsa's obsession, whereupon he cuts off all contact with her. A romantic triangle with definite shades of homerotism emerges in this intervention and in María's detailed descriptions of the ethereal Elsa while under hypnosis. Elsa's trance states apparently represent a desire to insert herself as a female subject into history, but the attempt fails, as she is only half-aware of what is going on in the complex web of intrigue constructed by men vying for power. Elsa's death on both planes also suggests, as Elizabeth Ordóñez notes, that she has been abandoned by the Symbolic Order, which traditionally presumes to speak for women rather than to regard them as subjects.[21]

In her waking life Elsa is intent on nurturing her immense love in her own writings, which appear in the novel as fragments from her diary and letters written to Agustín. Textual fragmentation such as this intensifies the fragmentation of Elsa's personality. The lyricism of Elsa's writings contrasts sharply with María's more matter-of-fact narration.[22] Love of Agustín/Eduardo's spectral body gradually leads Elsa away from physical vitality, represented by the fading away of her body. In fact, she desires the image of a man rather than a concrete union, which is why María's commonsensical advice fails to rouse her. Elsa seems to suffer almost clinically from anorexia, neglecting to eat and growing thinner and paler with each chapter until she dies, presumably of exposure, on a snowy hillside where she had been in the habit of taking walks by herself. In Elsa's syndrome we get a close look at the postmodern tendency to turn alienation into fragmentation: she splits up into several selves, including the dreaded siren she fears Agustín sees in her. She self-destructs rather than face the difficulty of putting the pieces back together; this will be María's task. María begins and ends her story with the objects and texts that compose the fragments of Elsa's two lives assembled in front of her on the table. The reader is left wondering how María will fill her life in Elsa's absence. *Luna de lobos* bears a similar textual fragmentation in that it covers a few months, in four sections, out of the total of nine years Angel spends in the wilds, and the reader finds out important plot developments that are thus in ellipsis after they occur, imitative of the way Angel is missing the "normal" life he might have led.

On the surface, Elsa as schizo assembles her identity independently of most social cues. Her personality emerges as fragmentary as a collage; its pieces she pulls from within the ever-changing system of fluxes inside of her body. Eventually, her raging desires transform her outward shape as well in the form of a mutation more literal than Angel's activities as a wolf. When she is still in contact with Agustín, she struggles against difference from the norm, screaming at him over the phone, "I am normal! . . . I am not a monster! I am not a monster!"[23] She seems to protest too much, and soon she slips into a desiring state in which she believes she recognizes her reflection everywhere, in paintings, novels, and history. They're me, she responds, much like Deleuze and Guattari's figure: "No one has ever been as deeply involved in history as the schizo, or dealt with it in this way. He consumes all of universal history in one fell swoop."[24] In her attempt to preserve the otherworldly image she wishes Agustín to have of her, she begins to exhibit the classic symptoms of anorexia: she barely eats, spends a long time examining herself in the mirror, and consumes plenty of caffeine. Meanwhile, she loses track of her *intracuerpo* and feels herself to exist only as a "sanctuary" of Agustín's memory (134). In Elsa we see the schizo combined with the female masochist, a figure redefined by Janet Benjamin, not as a woman who gets pleasure from pain (Freud's misinterpretation), but as a woman who "loses herself in the identification with the powerful other who embodies the missing desire and agency."²⁵ From this perspective, a whole investment of oneself is worthwhile even if one gets in return only a small fraction of the idealized other.

Eventually Elsa gives up her body entirely to allow it to blend in with the "inhuman peaks" of the Sierra Nevada (165). María lies down next to her where she finds her in the snow, but her *intracuerpo* is still engaged; the growing numbness in her extremities tells her insistently to arise. Elsa's sacrifice of her body so that it may attain some transcendent significance turns out to be fruitless, for Matilde, the witchlike leader of the village women, has her buried in the cemetery niche she had bought for herself, thereby subsuming her once again into the age-old category of silenced women.

Another kind of radical escape is inherent in Elsa's actions and María's fixation on them, a female version of Angel's flight from the Consciousness Industry of postmodern Spain. Angel finds a space in which he can roam invisibly and sporadically search for the *petit objet a,* Lacan's phrasing for the other sought by men in successive temporary incarnations. Elsa and María find a somewhat more mystical place where they can cultivate the feminine quest for the Absolute Other, the singular and unique figure capable of overwhelming the female self. In both instances they seek a space that is free from all hints of technology and hence of the media that most blatantly represent the Consciousness Industry. María describes the attraction of the wilderness as follows:

> Pensé que, al margen de los motivos que ella tuviera para rechazar la ciudad, era difícil marcharse de estas montañas. Pues aquí, para nosotras, la vida parecía hacer un alto y detenerse, con el fin de permitirnos descansar, escapar, jugar. Nada nos parecía necesario aquí arriba.

> [I thought of how, alongside the reasons she might have for staying away from the city, it was difficult to leave these mountains. Because here, for us, life seemed to call a truce and pause, in order to let us rest, escape, play. Nothing seemed necessary to us up here.] (163)

Apparently disengaged from the desiring-production of the capitalist molar organism, both Angel's and Elsa's bodies—and, one infers, María's—are bodies that refuse to remain harnessed and productive. As atoms of desire running along lines of escape, they are relatively free to develop their own coordinates for defining themselves in relation to others. Their affinity with beasts, mythical or real, turns their alienation into physical mutation, mirrored on the textual level in fragmentation that suggests a series of prose poems. Their escapes also suggest a new form of asceticism or mysticism—perhaps *postmysticism* best describes this trend. Like Angel, however, Elsa in the end turns a few conventional gender traits—passivity, adoration of the idealized Other, and an obsession with thinness—into the whole of her existence, allowing the cultural paradigm to take over her body and block any productive escape in life.

Angel and Elsa evidently react against the dominant of postmodernism and seek to recuperate the nature lost to them forever at any cost. The next pair of novels exhibit a more cooperative attitude toward their cultural situation; they are willing to take on some of its media and structures on their own terms and put them at the service of the micropolitics of individual desire. *Tiempo de silencio* once again contains a doorway to this postmodern strategy. On arriving at the train station, Pedro decides to buy a detective novel, implying a desire to lose himself in a momentarily absorbing plot while he flees the organ-clad city of Madrid.

Soledad Puértolas's *Queda la noche* draws on an image of international conspiracy that follows the heroine from one continent to another, unknown to her until the end. Local and, to some extent, international conspiracy plots have been a staple of fiction through the ages, but what differentiates the postmodern obsession with them is the degree of insidiousness with which they penetrate all aspects of a character's life and the rapidity with which the tables can turn, thanks to communications technology and the information explosion of the computer age. For the first time, humanity has the impression that it has created institutions that are truly inescapable and yet difficult to track, like the power blocks Oliver Stone causes to move sinisterly behind the scenes in *JFK*. As Pope elaborates, this does not necessarily entail an end to the "myth of privacy," but a rethinking of the relation of public to private life along more unpredictable and more intricate lines.[26] In Puértolas's fast-paced escape-and-quest narrative an affluent, unmarried thirty-two-year-old significantly named Aurora travels to the Far East to avoid the usual *veraneo* with her clinging parents and to break the habit of waiting by the phone for her lover, a married politician, to call. In Delhi she meets Ishwar, the first of four lovers she will encounter during the summer recounted in the narrative. The attraction of an ethnically different other in the midst of a barely understood Hindu ritual of purification provides Aurora with the needed liberation from her usual routine and affective life. Hashish and alcohol, and a series of disappearances on the part of Ishwar, also intervene in her experience of the affair. While all this is going on she is unaware of sliding into a web of connections between KGB agents and British counterspies. It is this espionage ring, and not the repercussions of her romance with Ishwar, that follows her back to Spain, where strange figures from the Indian sojourn continue to turn up, and her most persistent admirer turns out to be a female spy who fell in love with her at the hotel in Delhi and sacrificed her career to follow Aurora. By the end of the novel Aurora's current lover confronts her with, "You are not a spy, I am not a spy. We are not living in a film."[27] She realizes, however, that on the Asian trip she became everyone's mark because of her accessibility, that in the future she must avoid the insistent gaze of strangers.

Puértolas's novel expresses a new-found liberty for the female character within certain limits. Her body is her own, and she does not feel that she belongs to any of her lovers. She makes love, for example, to two men on the same afternoon. While she knows that she carries traces of the first when she goes to meet the second, she is, above all, convinced that "it was my body, and it served again to express love, desire, passion, trust, or insecurity, a bit of fear and recklessness and fleetingness" (199). Her sister Raquel, who remains in a loveless marriage out of inertia and fear of loneliness, provides a counterpoint to Aurora's self-governing sexuality. Like Pardo Bazán, Puértolas's narrator embellishes the ellipsis of sexual interludes, but the embellishments read as off-limits signs guarding Aurora's most intimate space rather than as ironic concessions to patriarchal decorum: "What happened next is something that concerns only Ishwar and myself, and anything that could be said would be inadequate or insufficient" (54). Aurora's body is the one hard kernel of privacy that remains intact amid the creeping tendrils of conspiracy, and her tone of voice brings home her will to keep it that way.

The most intense and most enduring attachment holding the

story together is the female spy Gudrun Holdein's infatuation with Aurora. The latter does not suspect anything when Gudrun photographs her with friends and even takes a video of her swimming in the hotel pool. But Gudrun cannot be content with the images of her desired object, so she travels to Spain to propose a trip to Toledo to Aurora. Gudrun is eventually undone by another of Aurora's lovers, a British agent who had been posing as a film director. In earlier writings Puértolas has taken on the objectification of women by the male gaze, as Akiko Tsuchiya illustrates regarding a short story from a 1982 collection.[28] *Queda la noche* offers a postmodern twist on the topic that blends well with the unpredictable nature of the espionage thriller and complicates the women-versus-the-patriarchy opposition of classical feminism. No one can tell from what source the objectifying gaze might issue.

The wry first-person voice that narrates these fragmentary episodes has adopted the spy genre for the sake of parody but also to ironically comment on the female subject, who "left herself open" to potentially dangerous involvement. The nomadic female subject chastises herself, not for testing the bounds of her new freedom, but for being vulnerable in a traditionally feminine way. As a result of the splitting up of feminism into the micropolitics of postmodernism, the objectifying gaze that traps women can come from any direction, including from other women. In addition, the rights and privileges won by women as a group now demand ingenuity and intelligence from the individual woman who wishes to take full advantage of them. Much of what needs to be learned has to do with the proper use and care of the female body.

Antonio Muñoz Molina avails himself of the spy-novel format to write a more blatant and more sordid pastiche, compared with the gentle self-irony of *Queda la noche,* of a species that has roots in Juan Marsé's *Si te dicen que caí.* The very excess of spy and detective-novel conventions strikes the reader of *Beltenebros*: the story is replete with sound-proof rooms, cars with fogged-up windows that drive in circles to disorient the passenger, suspicious characters who read upside-down newspapers in cafés, and a train-station locker-room key hidden in the toilet tank of a seedy bar. Parodying the spy novel in the texture of its language, *Beltenebros* contains bountiful examples of what I call divergent comparisons, similes that lead off into a detour, such as when the narrator states, "But I knew he wasn't there. I knew it like a blind man knows that it's nighttime and he's been left alone in the middle of a plaza."[29] Just as in the pulpier detective novels and David Mamet's screen parodies of them, the dialogue crackles with rapid-fire clichés like "Forgetting is a luxury, Darman" and "Some luxuries are necessities." Combined with these overflowing plot conventions and narrative strategies are images of semiotic overload coming from several directions: the protagonist, Captain Darman, an unwilling hitman for a fascist resistance operation, recalls his last victim, Walter, and Walter's wife Rebeca Osorio, who transmitted intelligence messages in their own peculiar ways. He planted them in the movies he projected in the always empty Universal Cinema (all the world's a cinema), she in the romance novels she published for that purpose only. Rebeca never went back to revise what she had already written, out of fear of dying of laughter or shame. At the present moment of the novel she has gone insane and now only uses the typewriter because the noise keeps her company.

The semiotic overload of subliminal messages encased in these films and mass-market paperbacks but not visible to the untrained eye calls to mind the excessive bombardment of the Consciousness Industry. Furthermore, the primacy of the spectacle makes its way into amorous relations in this novel in several steamy episodes in which the object of desire seems to have emerged from a *noir* film: an Italian woman with "excessive lines" wrapped in a shoulderless gown and the younger Rebeca Osorio, who is both parody and double of her mother, like the remake of a classic film. Tellingly, the two generations of Rebecas blend into each other and are indistinguishable in the mind of the protagonist until he has a chance to see the mother again and notice that she wears her age like a mask over unchanged features (216).

Alongside the celluloid quality of these heroines are their fluctuation between availability and distance, whether physical or attitudinal. The old Rebeca Osorio seemed to be made of flesh and blood only when she was angry; he imagines the new Rebeca Osorio as "warm and imaginary at once, nonexistent and hostile like the women in obscene postcards" (154). Unlike her mother, the hack novelist who produced objects of cultural consumption, this Rebeca is a commodity herself, a call girl who is involved with the protagonist's next scheduled victim, Andrade. His involvement with her is thus a business transaction, making him at once the inferior romantic rival of his intended victim, who does not have to pay, his accomplice, and his executioner, in short, his double. The real enemy turns out to be someone different and unexpected: the commissioner Ugarte, alias Beltenebros or Prince of Darkness, who has been framing the innocent men marked for execution by Darman.

Up to the last episode, Darman relives his earlier execution of the old Rebeca's lover Walter in flashbacks. The combination of solitude and guilt prevent Darman from putting these events in the past, and they often overtake him like sliding panels that block out the present in his interior monologue. Hence, past and present intermingle in this novel: chronological time is flattened out into an eternity of guilt and uncertainty for the protagonist. The process Jameson calls the erasure or evaporation of history into the present moment, with a consequent nostalgia for a present that never was, appears in the persistent time frames of *Beltenebros* and in Darman's "neutral nostalgia for some place where I have never been" (22).

Like Puértolas, Muñoz Molina avails himself of the postmodern structure of feeling for epistemological questioning. Darman is a hitman for the "good guys," selected especially for his acute vision and masterful aim with a gun. His nemesis Beltenebros/Ugarte/Valdivia has colorless eyes that are too sensitive for daylight but capable of seeing in the dark (the reverse of night blindness). Lying just below the surface of the plot are the issues of male gaze and accompanying phallic power, along with a broader exploration of the uncertainty and relativity of perception itself. Violence and sex are linked in the hero's mind: his possession of the gaze (desire) and the weapon (phallus) apparently leads him to unknowingly kill an innocent man and to brutalize the younger Rebeca Osorio in a scene that borders on rape (it is like the incited rape committed by Pascual Duarte). In both cases his guilt makes it unbearable for him to look at this victim's face afterwards. Tellingly, Darman refuses to accept another assignment until an unknown woman he glimpses on the dance floor awakens his mind and his body:

Me di cuenta entonces, con melancolía y asombro, casi con estupor, de que habían pasado muchos años desde la última vez que fui ver-

daderamente traspasado por la violencia pura del deseo, por esa
ciega necesidad de perderme y morir o estar vivo durante una fugaz
eternidad en los brazos de alguien. Yo era nadie, un muerto pre-
maturo que todavía no sabe que lo es, una sombra que cruzaba
ciudades y ocupaba en los hoteles habitaciones desiertas, leyendo,
cuando se desvelaba, las instrucciones a seguir en el caso de un
incendio.

[I realized then, melancholic and shocked and almost stupefied, that
many years had gone by since the last time I was really run through
by the pure violence of desire, by that blind necessity to lose myself
and expire or to be alive for a fleeting eternity in someone's arms. I
was nobody, a premature dead man who doesn't know it, a shadow
who crossed cities and occupied deserted hotel rooms, reading,
when unable to sleep, the instructions to follow in case of a fire.]
(54)

The heightened awareness of the erotic body leads him again
toward the fulfillment of a task that deals with danger and someone's
death, perhaps his own this time. Physical transformation in *Beltenebros* takes several forms: the erotic epiphany noted above, the rep-
licating bodies of women (Rebeca and her remake/daughter), the
genetic mutation of Ugarte's noctoscopic eyes. Regarding the hero,
vulnerability becomes associated with what are traditionally considered masculine powers: desire makes him tremble, and his predatory
skill backfires when he is apparently duped into killing the wrong
man. In a feminist twist of an ending that illustrates as well as any
other example could the rapprochement of male and female body
writing by the end of the twentieth century, Darman is rescued from
Ugarte's grasp by a naked Rebeca Osorio the younger. In the pitch-
dark cinema where Ugarte has trapped them both, she shines a
flashlight into his eyes and sends him over the balcony banister. With
the help of batteries and a bulb, women can possess the deadly gaze
as well. Whereas the filmic paradigm would require hero and heroine
to embrace with a sigh of relief after such a finale, *Beltenebros* ends
with Ugarte's plunge into the only darkness impenetrable to his gaze,
that of death.

Both Puértolas and Muñoz Molina elevate the *noir* to a postmodern version of the *nocturne* ("a painting of a night scene . . . a

romantic composition intended to embody sentiments appropriate to the evening or night"). The creation of a nocturnal mood, as much as the telling of a story, lie behind their narrative strategies. The nomadic character is then set loose in this dimly perceived setting, in much the same way that Llamazares's and García Morales's protagonists are sent off on tangents toward an irretrievable natural state. The private, mutating, and mystical bodies inscribed into all four novels battle against the banalization of the human body that we confront in the society of spectacle. Men and women actively write to reclaim that territory, to deterritorialize bodily desires, and to express the body as *vivencia* in never-ending flux.

Conclusion

When Virginia Woolf was questioned about a specifically women's writing, she was appalled at the idea of
writing "as a woman." Rather, writing should produce a becoming-woman as atoms of womanhood
capable of crossing and impregnating an entire social
field, and of contaminating men, of sweeping them up
in that becoming.

—Gilles Deleuze and Félix Guattari

THE ONE HUNDRED YEARS OF PHYSICAL DISCOURSE leaves several
clear, retraceable paths. The bolt of recognition that hit me when
I first read *Insolación* continues to strike every time. This is a historic
text for body writing in Spanish, when a woman's body speaks for
desire and makes demands of its possessor. On the way to protagonization, the body must pass through filters that have much in common with the situation of the woman who wishes to write. The body-
turned-against-itself puts into words the discomfort, confinement,
and simmering, pent-up desires of the woman who, like Asís, decides
to use her body's capacity for sexual expression, as well as of the
woman who, like Pardo Bazán, decides to use it for the act of writing.

The circumstances of writing will change, changing the situation
of the body in the twentieth century, but the body-as-text and the
body-as-process, both distinct divergences in Pardo Bazán's writing
from the male-oriented norm, will spread out and eventually cross
over into writing by men. The movement toward preserving a textually alive body, or body as *vivencia,* cannot fail to interest both
sexes as a means of transferring the vital flux of desire from mind to
page. Rosa Chacel puts the body to work for a variety of purposes,
most of them subversive. The gestation and maternal envelopment of
Estación. Ida y vuelta defy the suppression of the female form from
the virile new art. Teresa Mancha may prove difficult to rescue from

beneath the debris that cover her story, but through Leticia Valle, Chacel creates a heroine after her own heart: a diminutive intellectual who turns the tables on her tutor in hand-to-hand sexual combat. Telekinesis becomes the metaphor for male hubris in *La sinrazón*. The power of mind over matter mimics the privilege culturally accorded the mind as opposed to the body, and here the abuse of that power becomes the basis for moral and psychological estrangement from reality. Never ceasing to look backward to understand the body as *vivencia* in childhood and adolescence, Chacel has her heroines of *Barrio de Maravillas* ponder their image in art as they struggle to become artists themselves. Her retrospection across menopause and the reproductive years back to the onset of adolescence underlines the discreteness of female physical stages: the body's diversity is united by one consciousness.

Among the themes, figures, and concerns that emerge as primary in the intersections of physicality, textuality, and the feminine is the doorway. Whether it is the paraliptical frame that Pardo Bazán and Puértolas place around scenes of sexual consummation, or the accentuated passages from interiors to exteriors in the works of Martín Gaite, or the door to a former home, and hence a previous chapter in life, upon which Natàlia carves her former name Colometa, or the anthropomorphized entryway to Chacel's engulfing house-woman, the doorway is frequently present in these novels as an extension of feminine bodily space.

While the doorway and house prevail as static markers of the female form, the figure of the dancer often signifies the body in movement and as such exercises a distinct fascination over both male and female authors. The dance, as an expression of "man's physical being-with-others," inscribes the body in art in a way similar to these novelists' inscription of it into the text. As Terry Eagleton says in *The Body as Language*, "Within this formal space, the body assumes the expressiveness and spontaneity of a language, it becomes transformed into a symbol of real personal presence" (9). The training of the dancer comes to stand for the precise, subtle code of feminine behavior by combining discipline that comes from without (the artistic replacing broader cultural discipline) and the harnessing of the body's energy in a seemingly harmonious and spontaneous response. The dance of cigarette girls is temporarily the focus of attention for

Pardo Bazán's lovers and a source of jealousy for the aristocratic narrator; Rodoreda, who remembers her own longing to dance as a girl when forbidden by her parents, has Natàlia and Quimet meet at a dance in a public square; in Chacel, above all, there is the tango dancer who incarnates Woman's "virility" and whose body is parceled off and adored fetishistically by the narrator, as well as the ubiquitous ballet dancer, the female body subsumed into pure form and frozen in art. In the works of Muñoz Molina, viewing the female dancer from without is an energizing experience for the male spectator, who realizes he has not felt physically alive for a long time.

As Irigaray posited, the multiplicity and pluralism of feminine erotic drives, reflected in the diffusion of the erogenous over the female epidermis—its refusal to be confined or pinpointed—finds expression in these becoming-women novelists through sets of imagery that come to be associated with the inscribed body and prominently encode it, spreading it over the entire textual surface. Codes of heat and discomfort, of the sea and seasickness, of flowers and other vegetation, of jewelry and dolls, are used as means of naming, describing, and decorating this body and thereby reclaiming it as the inner space of women's *vivencia*. What these codes cover up is equally significant: there is little or no reference to specific parts of female genitalia (e.g., the clitoris) and to particular sexual occurrences (e.g., orgasm). In the works of male writers, we have seen sexuality bound up mainly in the phallus, which in turn is associated with the gaze (Pedro's "third eye" in *Tiempo de silencio*) and with aggression (Darman's problematic prowess with firearms in *Beltenebros*). Over time, bodily flexibility between the genders increases as rapprochement in writing continues. Failure to act the male role provokes intolerable feelings of castration in Pascual Duarte. Muñoz Molina's hero is saved by a woman with a mechanically enhanced "gaze."

The maternal potentiality has a privileged place in most of the novels by women. When romantic love is represented as a man's maternal nurturance of the heroine, we find a mirror image of a paradigm that was assumed until recently to be found only in writing by men. The primacy of the maternal also functions to transform the female body into a signifying, communicative organ in plots that involve actual motherhood. Instead of presenting an objectified vessel that subsumes motherhood into the categories of the miraculous or the natural, the writing of these women brings to life what Kristeva has called the "strangeness" or the "impossible syllogism" of mother-becoming. Would a male writer describe an infant as "an insatiable vampire," as Chacel has her (male) narrator do? As in other aspects of physical discourse, the becoming-woman writer constructs the maternal body as inseparable from the mind and culture and hence subject to constant change.

Pardo Bazán and Chacel exhibit a discrepancy in their treatment of bodies of the feminine masses, often presented as repulsive (except in the Pardo Bazán novels like *La tribuna,* which focus explicitly upon the lower classes), and the portrayal of the individual female body—inhabited, empathized with, and empowered. In this way their physical discourse retains a social privilege—that of class—that saves them from the total marginalization of the woman of the underclasses. There is a certain affinity with the horror of crowds described in writings by men, most saliently represented by Ortega in *La rebelión de las masas,* except that the dominant culture, the *mejores* above the *masas,* must be male, in order to usher in the new Age of Masculinity. The loss of individuation that occurs in a crowd setting has particular consequences from the point of view of the Spanish woman writer of past generations, who loses not only her role as artist in society but the status that has enabled her to be educated and literate in the first place.

In Rodoreda's writings, on the other hand, no such caste prejudice or fear of the masses seems to occur. It may be no coincidence that of the three, she came from the least privileged socio-economic background. In addition, her speaking from exile on behalf of an oppressed regional culture may better ally her voice with that of her Catalonian community in general. Whatever the reasons, her novels plainly champion the most economically disadvantaged women. Their physical vitality is often viewed as the condition that enables them to ascend the socioeconomic scale.

The body of the marginalized woman exemplified by Florita has grave implications for the destiny of Pedro in *Tiempo de silencio.* Her situation of powerlessness—sexually abused by her father and then subjected to the crudest of abortions—reaches across class boundaries to change the fate of the educated medical researcher duped into a futile attempt at saving her. Martín-Santos makes the fate of one inseparable from that of the other in a parallel that makes women's subjugation, and hence the reconquest of the female body from all outside forms of territorialization, an area of vital concern for men as well.

Despite the limited number of novelists explored at length here, some periodization is possible. Race, or racial mythology, is more heavily relied upon by the late-nineteenth-century, aristocratic novelist. In fact, it enters the narrative as the source of attraction for a love affair, the slight racial difference (meridional features) of the hero complementing the sexual otherness of the heroine in her overwhelmingly man-made urban environment. Blood ceases to be the locus of instinct or desire for the twentieth-century novelists; their social debates and novelistic experiments have less to do with the unraveling of naturalist oppositions. However, examples of women who are doubly different for being foreign, and who are either dangerous or ill-fated for this reason, are common. Furthermore, Chacel and Rodoreda are not presented with the same difficulty of having to feign ignorance of "normal" sexual matters; their writing exhibits more tension and fascination involving what is considered "perverse," rather than merely extramarital sexuality: obsessions (fetishes, sadomasochism, nymphomania, and narcissism in Rodoreda), sexual precocity, and homoerotism (in Leticia Valle's triangle). Chacel's avant-garde period evidenced the unleashing of hostility against traditional notions of femininity. Unlike her male peers, Chacel empowered most of her heroines with feminine forms of virility, indicating that a revalorization of the masculine need not be the only alternative to the exalted Woman of the nineteenth-century pedestal. On a textual level, the permeation of Chacelian narrative voices seems to play upon the expansive possibilities of motherhood. Rodoreda also formed part of a pre–Civil War avant-garde circle in Barcelona but has repudiated the novels she produced at that time. Her later writing turned more toward the fantastic to confound the border between matter and mind, perhaps sparked by Latin American "boom" fiction. Underlying her marvelous realism is a *vivencia* of the female body that leads to remythification, as well as a reconquest of the terrain of Catalan experience. Whatever the particular parameters in the case of each novelist, their development has been linked inextricably to the literary politics of their time, in which gender played as important a part as it did in the arenas of economic and familial structures.

The confession emerges as a frequent discursive strategy for allowing the body to voice its desire. At first glance this would seem an inhibition, but as happens in the confessional mode from St. Teresa onward in Spanish literature, the confession functions as a foothold for the subject's defense in the face of a more powerful configuration of knowledge and power, such as the Church. Thus, Asís confesses mentally to Father Urdax, and Leticia confesses to no one but herself, and both are starting points on the road to self-justification. Carmen Martín Gaite transposes the confessional mode into the context of architectural (symbolizing patriarchal) confinement in *Entre visillos* by representing the claustrophobic confessional booth itself and a heroine with few transgressions and much guilt. Camilo José Cela finds the confessional mode useful for eliciting the physical frustrations of Pascual Duarte. His protest of masculine difference is issued from a subordinate position that illustrates the source of his masculine vulnerability, but no sequence of words can assure him of the manhood constantly called into question by others. We even hear echoes of the confessional mode in the interior monologues of *Tiempo de silencio* and *Beltenebros*. In the last three cases, the protagonist confesses involvement in someone else's death, in contrast to the women writers's characters, who confess for using their own bodies in transgressive ways that do not directly harm others.

As the last link in the matrilineal chapters devoted to precontemporary writers, Mercè Rodoreda may seem an isolated example of Catalan writing in exile. However, her empowerment of the female body joins her with the preceding two novelists. Like Pardo Bazán, Rodoreda delves into *donjuanismo* in an unconventional way; the former places the will to Don Juan's power in the female subject, and the latter undercuts the legendary power of Don Juan by incarnating him as a weak and flighty *señorito* enslaved by his own fetishization of the female body. Rodoreda also reroutes other figures and conventions of patriarchal literature, giving new vitality to the feminine by representing the sea as maternal reservoir of semiotic drives and adopting the doll and the dollhouse as models of the nurturing relationship between novelist and her novelistic creations. Rodoreda has recycled these and other traditional *topoi* associated with essentialist femininity—flowers and other plants, dresses and jewelry—in order to create a gynocentric iconography around the body, a magical feminism that she substitutes for the feminine mystique of patriarchal Western culture.

The body as a slate for signifiers achieves prominence in the doll bodies of Rodoreda's novels; the plasticity of the doll body dissociates it from all functions other than that of signifying. Her foundling Cecília has only physical clues, all ambiguous, to indicate her lost origin. Writing on the body produces meaning in nearly all the texts considered, starting with the "letters of shame" that appear on Asís's skin, presumably decipherable only to her. Teresa Mancha's drawn-out toilette must result in a body indistinguishable from its packaging; this feminine text production is the only kind accorded Teresa in place of Espronceda's literary career. The young women of *Barrio de Maravillas* discover that much of literature has been written on the bodies of women and that much of art has envisioned the female form for them ahead of time. It is understandable that in becoming authors, women should adopt bodily writing for their purposes after a history of being no more than the slate. Cela also incorporates the figure of writing on the body, through the tattoos that adorn the bodies of the unfortunate; to be written upon rather than doing the writing befalls marginalized men as well as women. This is the situation Pascual endeavors to write himself out of, but the other texts that frame his narrative testify to his bodily ambiguity up to the very last moment.

The body as a site of discovery makes many appearances. In general, there is a constant contrast between "fake" or "object" bodies and real or somehow "vitalized" bodies (Rodoreda's dolls would be in the second category). Pardo Bazán's originality lies in part in her placing the female body, which is normally seen from without, commodified and fetishized in realism, in the category of lived-in significant bodies. What is more, its activity will not let the heroine follow her learned moral precepts or heed her acquired shame. Chacel makes physical means of knowing more problematic by having an adult man seduced by a child. Leticia's body falls into a textual gap and gives way to more than one interpretation. For Rodoreda, the body undoes social hypocrisy by pointing to origins and kinship and keeping the powerful erotic memory alive. The textual gap into which Pascual's body falls makes him prey to the reflections he finds of himself in others; the *intracuerpo* has nothing concrete to stabilize it. Martín Gaite's bodies speak only of suffocation from within their close quarters and preordained pathways.

For Martín-Santos, the body is in some ways a target of demystification: Pedro muses about the two women who have died, now two dead bodies not so different from each other. Their secrets have died with them. The medical perspective of Martín-Santos finds that no amount of dissection can uncover the mystery of a human being. But in other ways Martín-Santos imbues female bodies with the engulfing power of the amorphous mother, associated with the castrating authoritarian state. It is left to postmodern novelists to once more separate the female body from the myth of the Oedipus complex and at the same time to liberate the male body from the threat of castration. As the examples of Adelaida García Morales, Julio Llamazares, Soledad Puértolas, and Antonio Muñoz Molina show, the body is territory to be reconquered by both men and women from the banalization of the Consciousness Industry. The body-without-organs of the nomad or the schizo achieves the aim of freeing up desires that the late capitalist system would have attached to specific "machines." The danger inherent in disengagement is the negative side of postmodern fragmentation: the *intracuerpo* may not function reliably to mediate between mind and body. Indeed, Elsa's anorexia and Angel's male lonerism are symptomatic of the impossibility of reconstructing one's own body in pure isolation from society and culture.

Simulacra and popular media intercept the signals passing from one body to the next; there is also the buffer zone of drug-induced subjective states. As gender roles blur, bodies migrate over greater distances (a tendency seen already in the shifting between capital and provinces of *Entre visillos* and *Tiempo de silencio*), and older forms of repression loosen their grip on the desires of the body. Homoerotism, especially among women, reflects the fact that Cupid's arrow is no longer aimed by an outside authority; this would have been impossible in *Insolación,* where women are compartmentalized into their routines and can find the power they lack socially only in a male partner. Hence, we find these characters of postmodernity running along lines of flight into an irretrievable wilderness (anticipated by Pascual's nostalgia for absolutes) or into the *noir* of night. In the 1990s we may find out whether a possibility of postmysticism awaits them there.

Each chapter of political anatomy expressed in these novels constitutes a reconstruction of the body under evolving social conditions. The battle for the release of physical drives is fought on shifting fields against a variety of competing forces. The main constant is the compromise that all writers must reach in freeing individual energies, for constructing the body in literature depends on the raw materials at hand—language, paradigms, memory, vital circumstances—which guide the imagination and allow the fictional body to take shape in the mind's eye.

Notes

Novels Available
in English Translation

Works Cited

Index

Notes

Introduction

1. Beauvoir, *The Second Sex,* 34.

2. Rubio, "A la busca de un cuerpo (femenino) perdido (esbozo)," 69. Translations in the text are my own unless otherwise credited.

3. Gordon, interview.

4. Brooks, *Body Work,* 25.

5. For an exceptionally thorough and concise overview of points of contact between Hispanism and feminist critical currents, see Nichols's introductory chapter, "Mujeres escritoras y críticas feministas," in *Des/cifrar la diferencia,* 1–26. Also useful is a survey of women writers with detailed plot summaries in Pérez, *Contemporary Women Writers of Spain.*

6. Eagleton, *The Body as Language,* 12.

7. Spacks, *The Female Imagination,* 319.

8. Tony Tanner gives an exemplary analysis of the tendency of male authors to parcel off and fetishize the female form when she discusses Flaubert's "morselization" of Emma Bovary in the eyes of other characters, the narrator, and, ultimately, readers in *Adultery in the Novel,* 351.

9. Foucault, *The History of Sexuality,* 1:24–25, 36.

10. Diego, "Prototipos y antiprototipos de comportamiento femenino a través de las escritoras españolas del último tercio del siglo XIX," 239.

11. Ibid.

12. Tanner, *Adultery in the Novel,* 377.

13. Joyce Tolliver explores the relation between this dichotomy and the dynamic of active and passive syntactic modes in a Pardo Bazán short story in "Knowledge, Desire, and Syntactic Empathy in Pardo Bazán's 'La novia fiel,'" 910.

14. Irigaray, *Ce sexe qui n'en est pas un.*

Notes

Chapter 1: The Body-as-Text in Emilia Pardo Bazán's *Insolación*

1. Scanlon, *La polémica feminista en la España contemporánea.*
2. Herrero, *Fernán Caballero.*
3. Scanlon, *La polémica feminista en la España contemporánea,* 6.
4. Pattison, *Emilia Pardo Bazán,* 61.
5. I am indebted to the outlines of the work of Jacques Lacan and post-Freudian French feminism provided by Gossy, *The Untold Story,* 130; Smith, *The Body Hispanic;* and Grosz, *Sexual Subversions.* In addition, the first two are invaluable in tracing the intersections of these bodies of knowledge with Hispanism.
6. Ordóñez, "Inscribing Difference," 45.
7. González-Arias, "A Voice, Not an Echo," 49.
8. Hemingway, *Emilia Pardo Bazán,* 42–56; Shaw, *Historia de la literatura española,* 243.
9. The details of this alternating explicit audience, as well as the fluctuating sense of guilt displayed by Asís in her confession and the narrator's equivocally (dis)claimed responsibility for writing down what Asís *would have* confessed if she had chosen to do so, are perceptively analyzed by Joyce Tolliver in "Narrative Accountability and Ambivalence." The present study is an attempt to build upon this gender-based narratological study, adding a *corporeísta* focus.
10. Foucault, *The History of Sexuality,* 1:59–62.
11. Pardo Bazán, *Insolación,* 39; subsequent page references will be cited in the text.
12. Hemingway, *Emilia Pardo Bazán,* 42–56.
13. Ibid., 50.
14. Tolliver, "Narrative Accountability and Ambivalence," 103–18.
15. Scari, "La sátira y otros efectos humorísticos en *Insolación*," 12.
16. Miller, "Sensation and Gender in *The Woman in White.*"
17. Santiáñez-Tió, "Una marquesita 'sandunguera,'" 121.
18. The litany of bodily parts, synecdoche, and fetishization of the female form in contemporaneous English novels is thoroughly treated by Helena Michie in *The Flesh Made Word.*
19. Gilbert and Gubar, *The Madwoman in the Attic,* 45–92.
20. Bloom, *The Anxiety of Influence.*
21. Salcedo, *La Codorniz,* 86.
22. Tolliver, "Narrative Accountability and Ambivalence," 110.
23. González-Arias, "A Voice, Not an Echo," 37. The affair took place in 1888.
24. Gilbert and Gubar, *The Madwoman in the Attic,* 58.
25. Hilton, "Pardo-Bazán and Literary Polemics about Feminism," 41.
26. As part of a Jungian archetypal analysis, Mary E. Giles presents the sun and the sea as poles symbolizing ego and primal unconsciousness, respectively, demonstrating the interpretive resonance of this short novel, in "Feminism and the Feminine in Emilia Pardo Bazán's Novels."

27. The sun god also shows up anomalously as a nude statuette of Apollo among the furnishings of the heroine's prudish aunts (Hemingway, *Emilia Pardo Bazán,* 48).

28. Irigaray treats the relation of Woman and mysticism in "La mystérique," in *Speculum: De l'autre femme,* 238–52, and in "Femmes divines" and "Les femmes, le sacré, l'argent," in *Sexes et parentés,* 67–102.

29. Smith, *The Body Hispanic,* 75.

30. Osborne, *Emilia Pardo Bazán y sus obras,* 72.

31. Ibid., 76.

32. Zola, *L'Assommoir,* 310.

33. Just as the contents of Poe's *Purloined Letter* would be potentially incriminating to its aristocratic female addressee. The letter and Woman are conjoined in this passage, and it is interesting to note that these two terms are Lacan's "irreducibles," or remainders in literature, constituting what, according to Lacan, calls Poe's text into being (Smith, *The Body Hispanic,* 70).

34. The "good lady with her lions" is the goddess Cybeles, an unobtrusive way of introducing an element of aquatic "feminine fecundity," according to Alfred Rodríguez and Saúl Roll, "*Pepita Jiménez* y la creatividad de Pardo Bazán en *Insolación,*" 30. It also establishes the presence of a female deity in Madrid.

35. Smith, *The Body Hispanic,* 71.

36. Charnon-Deutsch, *Gender and Representation,* 2. For Blanca Andreu, the concept of feminine virtue exemplified in literature of mass consumption bears a resemblance to the ideology behind some of Galdós's "fallen" heroines—the overly ambitious Amparo of *Tormento* (1884), for example (*Galdós y la literatura popular,* 149).

37. Santiáñez-Tió, "Una marquesita 'sandunguera,'" 126.

38. Gossy, *The Untold Story,* 2.

39. Smith, *The Body Hispanic,* 42.

40. Ibid., 41.

41. Barthes, *The Pleasure of the Text,* 9.

42. Pérez Galdós, *Tristana,* 75.

43. José Maria de Pereda, cited in López-Sanz, *Naturalismo y espiritualismo en Galdós y Pardo-Bazán,* 98.

44. Sobejano, introduction to *La Regenta* by Leopoldo Alas; Gilman, *Galdós and the Art of the European Novel.*

45. Smith, *The Body Hispanic,* 95.

46. Tolliver, "Narrative Accountability and Ambivalence," 116.

47. Hemingway, *Emilia Pardo Bazán,* 49.

48. Foucault, *The History of Sexuality,* 1:124.

49. Barthes, *The Pleasure of the Text,* 9.

50. Foucault, *The History of Sexuality,* 1:39.

51. Kristeva, *Histoires d'amour,* 245.

52. Ibid., 244.

53. Ibid., 249.

54. Tolliver, "Narrative Accountability and Ambivalence," 114; Spacks, *The Female Imagination*, 317.

55. González-Arias, "A Voice, Not an Echo," 3.

56. Gilman, *Galdós and the Art of the European Novel*, 322–23, 320.

57. Tanner, *Adultery in the Novel*, 273.

58. Gilman, *Galdós and the Art of the European Novel*, 352.

69. Alas, *La Regenta*, 736.

60. My views are consonant with those of Fanny Rubio on the female body in Galdós and Clarín. She deems the treatment in the former "unrealized" and that of the latter both a "desired body" and a totality of sensory references. She has studied the "mutilation" of the female body in some of Pardo Bazán's other novels, but to my knowledge she has not discussed the topic with reference to *Insolación* (77–78).

61. The others Foucault lists are the sexualization of children, the specification of perversions, and the regulation of populations (*The History of Sexuality*, 1:114).

62. Santiáñez-Tió, "Una marquesita 'sandunguera,'" 127.

63. From *Discipline and Punish*, in *The Foucault Reader*, 173.

64. Gallop, *Thinking through the Body*, 4.

65. Teresa A. Cook has attempted this in *El feminismo en la novela de la condesa de Pardo Bazán*.

66. If only because of one of his surnames, Gabriel Pardo de la Lage would be a likely candidate for authorial spokesperson; yet we have seen that his opinions are espoused or discarded according to his vital situation.

Chapter 2: Rosa Chacel

1. Ríos-Font, "'Horrenda adoración,'" 224.

2. Although she relies mainly on texts of mass consumption, Susan Faludi demonstrates the paradox of real women wielding power while images of women express nostalgia for past subjugation in *Backlash*. It is unfortunate that in the section she devotes to academic writing, Faludi groups feminist gender-based techniques with the more traditional essentialist positions on femininity. This flaw in her otherwise perceptive book appears to be an instance of prevalent anti-intellectualism seducing nonacademic writers.

3. Chacel, "Conversación con Rosa Chacel." The first two diaries are *Alcancía* (*Ida*) and *Alcancía* (*Vuelta*), published in 1982 but covering Chacel's years of exile in South America. The work in progress counts, however, as the fourth in a series of autobiographies, since this category would include *Desde el amanecer* (1972), a remembrance of childhood written, unlike the two diaries, with the intention of publication. It was in fact thought unusual and daring for Chacel to publish the first two diaries, obviously written for personal rather than "literary" uses. As we shall see, Chacel often blurs the personal and the literary, exposing the division between them as artifice.

4. Kronik, "Of Nations, Generations, and Canon Formations."

Notes

5. Chacel does speak of attending a few of her contemporaries' *tertulias* but complains that she felt extremely uncomfortable and out of place. This is interestingly related in physical terms: feeling ill-dressed, chubby, looking like a hick. Yet Chacel customarily insists that her being female had nothing to do with her feeling marginalized (Mangini, "Introducción" to *Estación. Ida y vuelta,* 18–20).

6. Cano, *La poesía de la generación del 27,* 14–15.

7. Although Jiménez includes a sketch of her from 1931 in his *Españoles de tres mundos,* unlike the sketches of male authors, the piece does not refer to her work or mention that she is a writer, focusing instead on her appearance and calling her a *niña mayor* (grown-up little girl) (262).

8. Gil-Albert, "In promptu," 26.

9. Pérez Firmat, *Idle Fictions;* Spires, *Transparent Simulacra.*

10. Fernández Cifuentes, *Teoría y mercado de la novela en España,* 310–48.

11. Chacel also recalls having been Valle-Inclán's favorite pupil when she was a student at San Bernardo and he a professor of aesthetics there ("Conversación con Rosa Chacel," 12).

12. Mangini "Introduction to *Estación. Ida y vuelta,* 39; Pérez, *Contemporary Women Writers of Spain,* 62.

13. As early as 1923, Freud's major works had been translated into Spanish and were among the most talked-about phenomena in Spanish literary circles (Fernández Cifuentes, *Teoría y mercado de la novela en España,* 285). Chacel probably read the Biblioteca Nueva edition while living in Rome in 1921–22 (Rodríguez Fischer, "El tiempo abarcado," 14).

14. Chacel "La escritura femenina es una estupidez," interview by Mariano Aguirre, *El País,* 30 Jan. 1983, cited in Mangini, Introduction to *Estación. Ida y vuelta,* 51.

15. My viewpoint has already been admirably put into words by Elizabeth Ordóñez: "*L'Écriture féminine* in recent Spanish narrative by women cannot be found in a particular style or form of discourse. Rather, it should be considered an impulse, an energizing myth which impels today's woman writer to create with a confidence and authority unimagined by her foremothers. It may mean subjecting traditional myths to scrutiny and even, at times, turning them on their head. . . . Or it may mean exposing the female body, shaking off layers of suppression to reveal reverberations of erotic and textual desire" ("Inscribing Difference," 56). Ordóñez refers to contemporary novelists; as we shall see, Chacel's attitudes toward the body are not so unequivocally liberating, since her milieu was more male-dominated.

16. Chacel, "Conversación con Rosa Chacel," 26.

17. Simone Bosveuil criticizes Chacel for seeming to write for herself instead of for others in "Proust y la novela española de los años 30," 130–31.

18. By Gerald G. Brown, for example, in *Historia de la literatura española,* 231.

19. It is true that some anthologists and critics—Jaime Brihuega among them (*Las vanguardias artísticas en España, 1909–1936*)—classify some of the later Noventayochistas and even Felipe Trigo as *vanguardistas.* But I am inclined

in writing this not to include them as bona fide vanguardists, however modern they may be, but rather to render the avant-garde a subset of, rather than a synonym for, Spanish modernism. Those who bristle at such a definition of the early-twentieth-century Spanish avant-garde movement may prefer to believe that I am speaking of the uniqueness of Chacel's novel among the second, or younger, wave of 1920s vanguardists.

20. Chacel, cited in Pérez, *Contemporary Women Writers of Spain*, 61–62. Nonetheless, except for this germinal function the work still stands alone, for Chacel would never write in such an avant-garde vein again.

21. This view is shared by Ruiz-Malo Soria, "Reencuentro con una novela de Rosa Chacel"; Myers, "*Estación, ida y vuelta*"; Mangini, "Women and Spanish Modernism"; Johnson, "*Estación. Ida y vuelta*"; Rodríguez Fischer, "Tras la senda de Ortega y Gasset"; and Gil Casado, "El experimento narrativo de Rosa Chacel."

22. Even the publication history of this novel reveals underlying stress in the mentorship of Chacel and Ortega. Although he encouraged her often throughout her career, Ortega refused to publish her first novel in its entirety, accepting only the first chapter. According to Chacel, he claimed that the rest of the manuscript "got lost among some other papers" (Chacel, "Conversación con Rosa Chacel," 14–15).

23. "Ortega," *Revista de Occidente* 4, nos. 24–25 (1983): 79, cited in Rodríguez Fischer, "Tras la senda de Ortega y Gasset," 51.

24. Pérez Firmat, *Idle Fictions*, 25.

25. Mangini, "Women and Spanish Modernism," 19–22. I would qualify this fusion of the "I" and the *novia*. The protagonist does not, for example, "fall in love with itself" (21); there is enough representation of the first lover to indicate that she is at the same time a separate character. The narrator is able to leave her, to fall in love with another woman, yet when he returns to her he returns to himself. It would be most accurate to call these characters separated and fused at once.

26. Gil Casado, "El experimento narrativo de Rosa Chacel," 165.

27. Myers, "*Estación, ida y vuelta*," 79–80. Janet Pérez's assertion that Chacel extrapolates on some tendencies in Unamuno's *novelas existenciales* is also well taken and hints at the rift between Ortega's theory and Chacel's praxis ("Vanguardism, Modernism, and Spanish Women Writers in the Years between the Wars," 40).

28. Rodríguez Fischer, "Tras la senda de Ortega y Gasset," 54.

29. Mangini, "Women and Spanish Modernism," 23.

30. Ortega y Gasset, "Juventud," in *Dinámica del tiempo*, 471. His conviction that the current generation must break with the past is presented in *El tema de nuestro tiempo*, 151.

31. Guemárez, "Juan Ramón Jiménez y el grupo de escritores de 1927."

32. Ortega y Gasset, "Juventud," 473.

33. This matter is examined more fully by Robert Wohl in *The Generation of 1914*.

Notes

34. Poggioli, *The Theory of the Avant-Garde,* 178–79.
35. Mangini, Introduction to *Estación. Ida y vuelta,* 51.
36. Fernández Cifuentes, "Unamuno y Ortega," 48.
37. Ibid., 49.
38. Julián Marías dubbed her an *autor/auctor* in "Azar, destino, y carácter de Rosa Chacel," 13.
39. Ortega y Gasset, *La deshumanización del arte e Ideas sobre la novela,* 416.
40. Among them Virginia Woolf and Patricia Meyer Spacks, as noted by Mangini, "Women and Spanish Modernism," 24.
41. Sieburth, "Interpreting *La Regenta,*" 274.
42. Susan Suleiman sets the parameters of avant-garde creation this way before examining them more closely in *Subversive Intent,* 36.
43. Ortega y Gasset, "¿Masculino o femenino?" in *Dinámica del tiempo,* 471–75.
44. Chacel, *Estación. Ida y vuelta,* 162–63; subsequent page references will be cited in the text.
45. Myers, "*Estación, ida y vuelta,*" 81–82.
46. Suleiman, *Subversive Intent,* 179.
47. Ibid., 15.
48. Even in praising her decades later, Julián Marías is careful to specify that she is a *rara avis* among women: "No hay muchos escritores; el número de escritoras es exiguo, aunque las mujeres que escriben hoy sean legión" (There are not many [male] writers; the number of women writers is minute, although the women who are writing these days may be multitudinous) ("Azar, destino, y carácter de Rosa Chacel," 9). This sort of thinking, which cast her as an exception to the rule, or as a good writer despite being female, surely was even more prevalent at the beginning of her career and probably contributed to the shifting attitude she adopted textually toward the figure of Woman and her tendency to disown gender as an important factor in her own development.
49. Not altogether germane to the present study but worthy of discussion is Chacel's subtextual commentary on the cinema as art form, which begins in this novel with the momentary conversion of the text into a screenplay (or with the protagonist wondering how his story would sound as a film) and is developed throughout her *oeuvre.*
50. Acceptance of Ortega's literary theory is predicated upon a fixed human nature, or soul, one of the least antitraditional aspects of his aesthetics. The soul must be taken into account by writers; it becomes a restraint on the free play of the imagination. To co-opt Foucault's phrase, "the soul is the prison of the body (of the text)."
51. Chacel, "Conversación con Rosa Chacel," 14–15.
52. Of course the use of bodily imagery in Ortega's work as a whole deserves a study of its own; it is one of the figures through which he helps make the essay a personal and literary genre.
53. Ortega y Gasset, "Vitalidad, alma, espíritu," 447.

54. About this inner-body image Ortega has interesting things to say: "When this matter is studied well, it would probably be discovered that the image each individual has of the interior of his or her own body is quite different. Herein lies one of the roots of our personalities" (ibid., 449).

55. Not only does this section end rather abruptly but the majority of the essay is devoted to the more abstract zones of spirit and soul.

56. Ortega y Gasset, "Vitalidad, alma, espíritu," 450, 462.

57. His "confession" is not without irony, and he defers giving away the secrets of seduction so as not to incur the wrath of fellow Don Juans the world over, in ibid., 456. In *Memorias de Leticia Valle* Chacel gives her young female character the chance to do the overwhelming instead, subverting the Don Juan myth.

58. Ortega y Gasset, "Juventud," 464.

59. Ortega y Gasset, "¿Masculino o femenino?" 474.

60. Ibid., 476.

61. Nietzsche, *The Joyful Wisdom*.

62. Ortega y Gasset, "¿Masculino o femenino?" 477, 480.

63. Fuentes, "La narrativa española de vanguardia (1923–1931)," 158.

64. This is to be expected when we consider the omnipresence of industrial, technological, and modern urban discourse in avant-garde literature of the period, a predominant current analyzed by Juan Cano Ballesta in *Literatura y tecnología*. A salient title in this vein of writing is José Díaz Fernández's *La Venus Mecánica* (1929).

65. Read, *Visions in Exile*, 66.

66. Suleiman, *Subversive Intent*, 87.

67. This mode, conspicuously absent from Chacel's fiction, is alluded to in her diary *Alcancía (Ida)*, when she reflects that her friend Elisabeth has equated the joy of writing with sexual pleasure. Chacel favors a more complete form of sublimation through art: "Of all the elements that make up the human being, sex is the one I am least interested in preserving" (25 July 1946, 20).

68. The wordplay of *Estación* also unravels clichés turning around the body that are not clearly gender-motivated. For example, the narrator says of "having one's arm twisted" that he prefers gentle orthopedics to dislocation (105) and contemplates the possibility of "losing one's arm" as if it were a misplaced object (147). This literal transformation of figurative language that takes the physical for granted also has the function of restoring the original physical meaning to these clichés.

69. Salinas, *Víspera del gozo*, 11.

70. The house made woman lends itself also to expression in the visual arts, such as Salvador Dalí's *Mae West* (*La cabeza de Mae West, usable como un apartamento surrealista*), ca. 1934 (Art Institute of Chicago).

71. Chacel, "Advertencia," *Teresa*, 6. This prologue probably dates from the 1963 edition, the first Spanish one. Subsequent page references will be cited in the text.

72. Chacel also points out that the most flawed of her books is *Acrópolis*.

She is the most obliging of any novelist when it comes to labeling her least effective books and what makes them so (Chacel, "Conversación con Rosa Chacel," 17).

73. Fernández Cifuentes, *Teoría y mercado de la novela en España*, 342–51.

74. *Enciclopedia universal ilustrada europeo-americana*, 1924, s.v. "Espronceda, José de."

75. Chacel does not fail to mention Emilia Pardo Bazán as precursor, alongside Leopoldo Alas and Benito Pérez Galdós.

76. Fernández Cifuentes, *Teoría y mercado de la novela en España*, 349.

77. Since it was substantially revised between the time of its completion and the time of its original publication, I cannot say her technique in the first version might have been closer to that in her first novel. Chacel claims that during the revision she eliminated the imposition of a romantic prose style.

78. I am much indebted to Susan Kirkpatrick for her excellent analysis of this paradigm and its relation to Espronceda's poetry in "Gómez de Avellaneda's *Sab*," 115–30.

79. The encyclopedia lends credence to this point of view, focusing on Espronceda's illness after the affair and glossing over the fact that it was Teresa who died in poverty and oblivion: "He was so madly in love with her that, despite common opinion, instead of her being a victim of Espronceda, he was a victim of hers" (*Enciclopedia universal ilustrada europeo-americana*, 1924, s.v. "Espronceda, José de"). To cite one of many instances of subsequent critical partiality, Jaime Gil de Biedma, while admitting that little is known about Teresa Mancha as an independent historical personage, does not fail to call her "strong-willed and devilish in character" ("Prologue," 10).

80. As Kirkpatrick comments, "The Spanish liberals who sought freedom for individual rights and the pursuit of self-interest left no place for women in their concept of political expression. Political equality for women simply was not conceived as a possibility in early nineteenth-century Spain" ("Gómez de Avellaneda's *Sab*," 120).

81. Chacel, "Conversación con Rosa Chacel," 17.

82. The narrator specifies that for men the after-effects of love are different:

Acaso, en resumen, era esto el sino de su sexo: arder un momento en la hora arrebatada del deseo y después caer, rodar en la monotonía, flotar sin fuerzas ni gobierno en la grosera masa de lo cotidiano. ¡No así los hombres! Ni siquiera aquellos que más pudieran parecer íntegramente arraigados en el amor: sabían salir de él, dejarlo sin desgarramiento, como se deja un sueño delicioso al saltar de la cama para emprender las mil actividades, llenas también de estímulo.

[Perhaps, in sum, this was the fate of her sex: to burn for a moment in the thrall of desire and then fall, wallow in monotony, float lifelessly and helplessly in the vulgar stuff of daily life. Not so with men! Not even those who might seem most entrenched in it: they knew how to emerge from it, shed it without getting torn, as one leaves behind a delightful dream upon jumping out of bed to undertake a thousand tasks, also full of excitement.] (148)

Something of Chacel's distaste (since decorum did not exercise the power it held over Pardo Bazán) for representing explicit sex may be explained here. The passage specifies that it is social inequality that is repeated in the physical aspect of heterosexual relations, making female lovers appear the losers in the exchange.

83. Chacel insisted that St. Teresa's narratives were motivated by "el deber de rendir cuentas" (the need to account for one's actions). That her story was elicited by powerful male figures and hence turned out to be more of a defense than a confession of guilt is a point made by Alison Weber in *Teresa of Avila and the Rhetoric of Femininity*. This is where the similarities between their points of view end, however, as Chacel makes no effort to reconstruct politics of the age and hints that beneath the mystic's well-known obfuscations lie only "puerile anxieties." It should be noted that Chacel was writing before the recent literary rediscovery of St. Teresa, at a time when she was still associated mainly with the Spain of Franco and hence was a symbol for much of what Chacel detested (Chacel, *La confesión*, 20).

The disagreement between Chacel and myself regarding what constitutes confession probably has to do with discrepancy between the recently evolved concept of literary confessionalism, toward which I gravitate, and the religious definition of the confession, with its sacramental and sacrosanct paradigm.

84. Chacel, "Conversación con Rosa Chacel," 20.

85. Ibid., 14.

86. Not germaine to the present study but worth noting is that around the time of writing this book Chacel had added another author to her list of those who made an impression on her: Edgar Allan Poe (Mangini, Introduction to *Estación. Ida y vuelta*, 23).

87. Chacel, *Memorias de Leticia Valle*, 7; subsequent page references will be cited in the text.

88. Villena, "*Memorias de Leticia Valle*," 42.

89. As Fernández Cifuentes notes, the 1930s already saw a turn toward the *novela social* (*Teoría y mercado de la novela en España*, 357). In this sense there is a general precedent for the abandonment of "dehumanized" practices.

90. St. Teresa's "Dedication" alternates between the singular and the plural in what has been called a *lapsus* (Chicharro, Prologue, in Teresa de Jesús, *Libro de la vida*, 117–18). It may indeed be a *lapsus,* but it looks like an overdetermined one, indicative of the male confessor who stands for the world of men, in which St. Teresa is set adrift by the act of picking up pen and paper.

91. Villena, "*Memorias de Leticia Valle*," 42. Villena also mentions a Dostoyevsky novel (which he erroneously refers to as "Diary of a Madman," a short story by Gogol, but which is more likely to be *The Dead*) that Chacel has read in which, she claimed, a gentleman is seduced by a young girl and must hang himself.

92. Ibid., 41.

93. This pattern of escape from social norms or opprobrium by crossing national boundaries can be found in each of Chacel's novels, a parallel to the

frequency of her own border crossings. In fact, I do not think that it is extrapolating too much to see her early and numerous escapes from Spain as enabling her to become one of the few Spanish women of her generation to break the traditional silence.

94. Suleiman, *Subversive Intent,* 144.

95. Here, as in *Estación,* the masses of women (in an Orteguian sense) are represented in a negative light, as frivolous, bourgeois, superficial, and so on. The individual women represented by and surrounding the heroine, however, are of a different sort in that they form an elite, not so much in socioeconomic terms, but in intellectual or spiritual ones. Hence, they feel reviled by the physical evidence that associates them with the feminine masses.

96. As Susan Suleiman asserts, the playful manipulation of boundaries of self in which women avant-garde writers often engage incorporates the experience of motherhood into writing and makes possible a more expansive form of literary creativity (*Subversive Intent,* 179). Chacel's first novel partakes of this as well, albeit under the cloak of a masculine narrator.

97. Dámaso Alonso's translation appeared in 1922; Chacel read it in Rome. Of all other authors, it is Joyce with whom she claims to feel the greatest affinity (Mangini, Introduction to *Estación. Ida y vuelta,* 16–17).

98. Erikson, *Identity,* Gilligan, *In a Different Voice.*

99. Joyce, *A Portrait of the Artist as a Young Man,* 14–15.

100. This despite Chacel's version of the local anecdote that inspired the plot, in which she said that she suspected that the young girl had done the seducing because the gentleman in question was very handsome (Pérez, *Contemporary Women Writers of Spain,* 63).

101. She read all of Freud's works that were available in translation while she was in Italy, and from the first *Dora* was regarded as central to the psychoanalytic corpus.

102. A plethora of Dora-inspired commentary has emerged; some outstanding pieces are to be found in Bernheimer and Kahane's collection *In Dora's Case.*

103. Martín Gaite, *Desde la ventana,* 99.

104. Freud, *Dora,* 131.

105. Ibid., 65.

106. Suleiman, *Subversive Intent,* 96.

107. Freud, *Dora,* 56.

108. "Ortega is the teacher one follows and Unamuno the teacher who pursues us" (Chacel, "Conversación con Rosa Chacel," 23).

109. "Reason has its passions, which the heart cannot comprehend" (Chacel, *La sinrazón,* 362); subsequent page references will be cited in the text.

110. Chacel muses that its narrative style is too "un-Spanish," too dissimilar to that of popular novelists like Torrente Ballester ("Conversación con Rosa Chacel," 21).

111. Chacel, *Barrio de Maravillas,* 35; subsequent page references will be cited in the text.

Notes

Chapter 3: Mercè Rodoreda

1. This is the position of Randolph Pope in "Mercè Rodoreda's Subtle Greatness." The volume of criticism *The Garden across the Border,* ed. Kathleen McNerny and Nancy Vosburg, provides further evidence of scholarly interest in this Catalan author. In addition to her novels, the focus of this chapter, her short stories have received more attention of late (see Altisent, "Intertextualidad y fetichismo en un relato de Mercè Rodoreda").

2. Martí-Olivella, "The Witches' Touch," 159–69.

3. Patricia Hart coined the term *magical feminism* with reference to Isabel Allende's fiction; this is closely related to the gynocentric remythification of Woman arising from Rodoreda's use of marvelous realism, to be described in the following sections. Hart understands *magical feminism* as "magical realism employed in a femino-centric work, or one that is especially insightful into the status or condition of women described in the work" (*Magic in the Fiction of Isabel Allende*).

4. These include Dolors Monserdá, Víctor Català (Caterina Alpert), Felip Palma (Palmira Ventós), Josep Miralles (Maria Domènech), and L'Escardot (Carme Karr) (Segura i Soriano, "La literatura de mujeres como fuente de documentación").

5. My analysis is limited to her post–Civil War novels, as she has disavowed her earlier avant-garde efforts. From this group I have also excluded *Aloma* (1938, 1969), a work dating from her pre-exile years but difficult to situate in either period, since its later edition was substantially rewritten. In passing, I have drawn a few examples from *Quanta, quanta guerra* (1980) and *La mort i la primavera* (1986), but I have chosen not to dwell upon them, since I feel that they do not display Rodoreda's talents to best advantage. I will cite all works as I read them—in Castilian translation.

6. Ortega writes of the cultivation of *ingenuísmo* in "Mujer, guerra, y neurosis en dos novelas de M. Rodoreda."

7. Martí-Olivella, "Foreword."

8. Resina, "The Link in Consciousness."

9. Ibid., 236.

10. See Arnau, *Introducció a la narrativa de Mercè Rodoreda.*

11. Castellanos, *Mujer que sabe latín . . . ,* 7.

12. Arnau chronicles the development of Rodoredan fiction from a realist to a "mythic" mode, with *El carrer de les Camèlies* as turning point, in the prologue to the first volume of Mercè Rodoreda, *Obres completes,* 22–27. Since Arnau's terminology here is somewhat problematic, I hope to define the transition more precisely and relate how it takes place in physical discourse.

13. Salinas, "Defensa de la carta misiva y de la correspondencia epistolar," 43.

14. Kristeva, "Motherhood according to Giovanni Bellini," 237.

15. Beauvoir, *The Second Sex,* 36–37.

16. Many of the problems female authorship confronts regarding motherhood, aggravated by psychoanalytic theory, are examined by Susan Suleiman in "Writing and Motherhood."

17. Martí-Olivella, "The Witches' Touch," 166.

18. Chodorow, *The Reproduction of Mothering*, 157.

19. Biruté Ciplijauskaité cites rhythmic repetition as one of Rodoreda's main stylistic techniques, along with parataxis, insinuation, and unexpected reversals at the ends of chapters (*La novela femenina contemporánea*, 47–48).

20. Rodoreda, *La Plaza del Diamante*, 8; subsequent page references will be cited in the text.

21. McNerny, "A Feminist Literary Renaissance in Catalonia," 127.

22. Radway, *Reading the Romance*, 156.

23. Ibid., 211.

24. Todorov, *The Fantastic*, 6.

25. Martín Gaite, *Desde la ventana*, 91.

26. Kristeva, "Motherhood according to Giovanni Bellini," 237.

27. María Silvina Persino has perceptively analyzed Marsé's "dis-membering" of the body and its relation to feminist "re-membering" in "*Si te dicen que caí.*"

28. The word used, *contrahecho,* is interchangeable with *hunchbacked.* This draws together the fact of Cecília's thwarted motherhood and her fascination for the humpbacked character in *Rigoletto,* who carries his dead daughter in a sack (Rodoreda, *La calle de las Camelias,* 209; subsequent page references will be cited in the text.

29. Poch, *Dona i psicoanalisi a l'obra de Mercè Rodoreda.*

30. A comparison with *Nada* (1944), another work with tinges of *tremendismo,* is revealing. This is something of a reverse *Nada* in social terms, for although both young women are raised in Barcelona by families other than their original ones, Laforet's heroine enjoys the advantage of a university education and is already assimilated into society at large, even if it is by means of a monstrous family. In Rodoreda, the narrator represents a woman less similar to the author herself whose marginalization is complete and inescapable. Without even a rudimentary formal education in sight for her, Cecília's only valuable commodity is her body.

31. Frye, *Anatomy of Criticism* (1957), cited in Todorov, *The Fantastic,* 11.

32. Todorov, *The Fantastic,* 25.

33. Ibid., 89.

34. Chiampi, *O realismo maravilhoso,* 59.

35. Alejo Carpentier and Isabel Allende have sought to geographically limit the application of marvelous or magical realism, Carpentier to Latin America, Allende to the Third World as a whole ("The Magical Stories of Isabel Allende"). It is more likely that the condition of superimposed cultural strata, especially that of postcolonial former territories of Spain (a definition that can conceivably be stretched to include Catalonia), favors the eruption of this literary technique.

However, in the last analysis, as Chiampi makes clear, it is not on the level of external reality but on the level of the text itself and the way it functions that marvelous realism comes into play (*O realismo maravilhoso*, 47).

36. Arnau's view of this novel as a turning point in Rodoreda's style, which will tend ever more toward the oneiric, was most perceptive at the time, since the two works that manifest this tendency most, *Quanta, quanta guerra* and the posthumously published *La mort i la primavera*, had yet to appear in print.

37. Kristeva, cited in Grosz, *Sexual Subversions*, 74.

38. One is reminded above all of *Quanta, quanta guerra*. The narrator, a young boy who inadvertently becomes a soldier, is jeered at because of a lentil-shaped birthmark on his forehead, which supposedly marks him as a nephew of the devil. Most other characters are introduced with some "key" physical detail, such as a pointed nose or pointed ears. The uses of such physical markers in the narrative are shown to tie in here with folklore that invests a magical value in writing on the body.

39. In these pages I deal with the floral motif in passing as it relates to the totality of bodily codes. I deal more extensively with it and with its relation to Catalan folklore, in "*Vinculada a les flors.*"

40. Rodoreda, *Jardín junto al mar*, 91, 261.

41. Arnau, "La obra de Mercè Rodoreda," 249.

42. Romer et al., "Feminismo y literatura," 348.

43. On account of its structure, which places considerable distance between plot and discourse, and on account of its cross-generational sweep, Arnau has compared it to *Cien años de soledad* (1967) (see Arnau, Prologue to vol. 1 of *Obres completes*, 36).

44. Spacks, *The Female Imagination*, 319.

45. García Márquez, "Recuerdo de una mujer invisible," 6.

46. Rodoreda, *Espejo roto*, 311; subsequent page references will be cited in the text.

47. Arnau, "La obra de Mercè Rodoreda," 251.

48. Scarry, *Literature and the Body*, 9.

49. Gallagher and Laqueur, *The Making of the Modern Body*, 14.

50. Erikson, *Identity*.

51. Life-sized dolls called *ninyots* play an important role in Catalonian and Valencian festivals. The Fallas Festival in Valencia each February witnesses the ritualistic destruction of groups of papier-maché *ninyots* that represent perceived social ills. As with the floral motif, there is an intersection of significant objects in the material life of Rodoreda's Catalonian community and codes that come to represent the feminine.

52. Fernández Cifuentes, *García Lorca en el teatro*, 30–81. The ultimate consequence of this in the world of García Lorca is a liberation of language itself from the restrictions of the physical body (83). It is important to keep in mind that the difference between the novel and the drama leaves room for differences in the meanings produced in each by plasticity of the body. The theater is of necessity an arena for the physical body, while fiction cannot contain either

carnal or plastic bodies but only representations thereof. In the context of Rodoreda's novels, I find that the centering of discourse on the body achieved by the plasticity of the woman-doll or doll-woman is indeed common ground.

53. Arnau, *Introducció a la narrativa de Mercè Rodoreda,* 294.

54. Arnau, Prologue to vol. 1 of *Obres completes,* 37.

55. Resina, "The Link in Consciousness," 230.

56. Arnau, "La obra de Mercè Rodoreda," 254.

57. Colometa/Natàlia's friend Julieta enjoys one night of embracing her boyfriend and feeling like a rich woman at the outbreak of war, in a mansion with mirrors that sounds very similar to that of *Mirall trencat.* But for most of the novelist's marginalized heroines before the novel in question, physical *jouissance* is a luxury, like writing, lying outside of their reach. The most they hope for is the recovery of a maternal figure.

58. Freud, *Dora,* 90.

Chapter 4: Body Politics in Novels in Franco's Spain

1. Brooks, *Body Work.*

2. Spacks, *The Female Imagination.*

3. Ilie, *La novelística de Camilo José Cela,* 72.

4. Ibid., 48.

5. The label probably originates in Gregorio Marañón's prologue to the 1946 edition.

6. Matías Montes-Huidobro underlines the affection for inanimate and therefore safe objects in "Dinámica de la correlación existencial en *La familia de Pascual Duarte.*"

7. Jerez-Farrán, "Pascual Duarte y la susceptibilidad viril."

8. Foucault, *The History of Sexuality,* 1:59.

9. Cela, *La familia de Pascual Duarte,* 28; subsequent page references will be cited in the text.

10. Gullón, "Contexto ideológico y forma narrativa en *La familia de Pascual Duarte,*" 2.

11. Livingstone, "Ambivalence and Ambiguity in *La familia de Pascual Duarte.*"

12. Barry Jordan makes this point convincingly in *Writing and Politics in Franco's Spain.* Inexplicably, he does not mention *Entre visillos.*

13. Martín Gaite, *Entre visillos,* 18; subsequent page references will be cited in the text.

14. While I disagree with Joan L. Brown's characterization of the perspective as "camera-eye objectivity," I agree with her finding of a claustrophobic sense in the spatial constructions (see Brown, *Secrets from the Back Room,* 66–70).

15. Another way that background descriptions take on poetic meaning in this novel is as metaphors for the discursive mode itself. John Kronik points out, for example, that the beveled mirror with multiple reflections of heads that

appears in one scene ties in with the proliferation of narrative points of view: unlike the typical social novelist, Martín Gaite calls into doubt the possibility of a single authoritative narratorial voice encompassing reality. She does this by including the voices of Pablo (the foreign intruder) and Tali (through her diary) (see Kronik, "A Splice of Life," 52).

16. In her essay *Usos amorosos de la postguerra española,* Martín Gaite discusses the perplexity of growing up at a time when isolation from pernicious foreign influences was viewed as the ideal but a world of growing communications was making this isolation increasingly impossible.

17. Benjamin not only critiques extant psychoanalytical schema but proposes new and more dynamic paradigms for development in *The Bonds of Love.*

18. Alfonso Rey expounds upon these formal and ideological challenges in *Construcción y sentido de "Tiempo de silencio,"* 11.

19. I say "half-veiled subversion" mainly in comparison with the more blatant variety that Juan Goytisolo would soon perpetrate against the same targets, using the parody and demythification begun here by Martín-Santos.

20. Labanyi, *Myth and History in the Contemporary Spanish Novel,* 66.

21. The novelist was himself imprisoned on four occasions between 1957 and 1962 for political activities. José-Carlos Mainer gives a brief biographical sketch in his prologue to Martín-Santos's *Tiempo de destrucción,* 9–12.

22. Martín-Santos, *Tiempo de silencio,* 94; subsequent page references will be cited in the text.

23. In an engaging piece of pop sociology, *The Hearts of Men,* Barbara Ehrenreich charts male disillusionment with the "breadwinner" role.

Chapter 5. Nomads and Schizos: Postmodern Trends in Body Writing

1. Schraibman, *"Tiempo de silencio y la cura psiquiátrica de un pueblo,"* 3.

2. If I appear to neglect other important writers of the "new novel" after Martín-Santos, such as Juan Benet, the Goytisolos, and Juan Marsé, it is because they have been studied from so many perspectives elsewhere and because what they offer in the evolution of body writing is not so different from what has been seen before Martín-Santos (e.g., the avant-garde release of hostilities against the female body). I am eager to proceed to the recent past, which offers a different structure of feeling vis-à-vis the body.

3. The provocative concept of semidevelopment was formulated by Fernando Morán in *Novela y semidesarrollo,* 197–99.

4. Soria Olmedo, "Fervor y sabiduría," 107.

5. Pope, "Postmodernismo en España," 120; Navajas, "Una estética para después del posmodernismo," 129–51.

6. Powell, "La transición política hacia un régimen democrático," *España hoy,* 74.

7. Jameson elaborates: "Memory seems to play no role in television, commercial or otherwise (or, I am tempted to say, in postmodernism generally):

nothing here haunts the mind or leaves its afterimages in the manner of the great moments of film (which do not necessarily happen, of course, in the 'great' films). A description of the structural exclusion of memory, then, and of critical distance, might well lead on into the impossible, namely, a theory of video itself—how the thing blocks its own theorization becoming a theory in its own right" (*Postmodernism,* 70–71).

8. Ibid., 20.

9. Pope, "Postmodernismo en España," 111–12.

10. Jameson, *Postmodernism,* xv, 63.

11. Puértolas, interview.

12. Jaume Martí-Olivella convincingly unites the quest for the mother with homoerotism in the works of Martín Gaite, Esther Tusquets, and Carme Riera. The narratives he treats date from the transition (late 1970s) and exhibit more obvious political overtones of solidarity with other women against patriarchy than do the 1980s novels about which I write ("Homoeroticism and Specular Transgression in Peninsular Feminine Narrative," 17–25).

13. Ponder as I may, I can find no better definition for these figures than the one already formulated by Steven Best and Douglas Kellner: "Schizos withdraw from repressive social reality into disjointed desiring states, nomads roam freely across open planes in small bands, and rhizomes are deterritorialized lines of desire linking bodies with one another and the field of partial objects" (*Postmodern Theory,* 103).

14. Deleuze and Guattari, *Anti-Oedipus,* 15.

15. Ibid., 38.

16. Jameson, *Postmodernism,* ix.

17. Llamazares, *Luna de lobos,* 129; subsequent page references will be cited in the text.

18. Brooks, *Body Work,* 12.

19. Debord, *Society of the Spectacle.*

20. Ciplijauskaité, "Intertextualidad y subversión en *El silencio de las sirenas,*" 171.

21. Ordóñez, *Voices of Their Own,* 189–90.

22. Ciplijauskaité, "Intertextualidad y subversión en *El silencio de las sirenas,*" 169.

23. García Morales, *El silencio de las sirenas,* 63; subsequent page references will be cited in the text.

24. Deleuze and Guattari, *Anti-Oedipus,* 21.

25. Benjamin, *The Bonds of Love,* 116.

26. Pope, "Postmodernismo en España," 114.

27. Puértolas, *Queda la noche,* 181; subsequent page references will be cited in the text.

28. Tsuchiya, "Language, Desire, and the Feminine Riddle," 69–80.

29. Muñoz Molina, *Beltenebros,* 66; subsequent page references will be cited in the text.

Novels Available in
English Translation

Cela, Camilo José. *Pascual Duarte's Family*. Translated by John Marks. London: Eyer & Spottiswoode, 1946. Originally published as *La familia de Pascual Duarte*.

———. *The Family of Pascual Duarte*. Translated by Anthony Kerrigan. Boston: Little, Brown, 1964. Originally published as *La familia de Pascual Duarte*.

Chacel, Rosa. *Maravillas District*. Translated by Susan Kirkpatrick. Lincoln: Univ. of Nebraska Press, 1992. Originally published as *Barrios de Maravillas*.

———. *Memoirs of Leticia Valle*. Translated by Carol Maier. Lincoln: Univ. of Nebraska Press, 1994. Originally published as *Memorias de Leticia Valle*.

García Morales, Adelaida. *The Silence of the Sirens*. Translated by Concilia Hayter. London: Collins, 1988. Originally published as *El silencio de las sirenas*.

Martín Gaite, Carmen. *Behind the Curtains*. Translated by Frances López-Morillas. New York: Columbia Univ. Press, 1990. Originally published as *Entre visillos*.

Martín-Santos, Luis. *Time of Silence*. Translated by George Leeson. New York: Harcourt, Brace, & World, 1964. Originally published as *Tiempo de silencio*.

Muñoz Molina, Antonio. *Prince of Darkness*. Translated by Peter Bush. London: Quartet, 1993. Originally published as *Beltenebros*.

Rodoreda, Mercè. *The Pigeon Girl*. Translated by Eda O'Shield. London: Deutsch, 1967. Originally published as *La Plaça del Diamant*.

———. *The Time of the Doves*. Translated by David Rosenthal. New York: Taplinger, 1980. Originally published as *La Plaça del Diamant*.

———. *Camellia Street*. Translated by Davie Rosenthal. St. Paul, Minn.: Graywolf, 1993. Originally published as *El carrer de les Camèlies*.

Works Cited

Alas, Leopoldo [Clarín, pseud.]. *La Regenta.* 1884. Edited by Gonzalo Sobejano. Barcelona: Noguer, 1976.

Allende, Isabel. "The Magical Stories of Isabel Allende." Interview by William A. Davis. *Boston Sunday Globe,* 4 Apr. 1991.

Altisent, Marta. "Intertextualidad y fetichismo en un relato de Mercè Rodoreda." *Revista Hispánica Moderna* 43, no. 1 (1990): 58–67.

Andreu, Alicia. *Galdós y la literatura popular.* Madrid: Sociedad General Española de Librería, 1982.

Arnau, Carme. Prologue to *Obres completes,* by Mercè Rodoreda, 1:5–45. Barcelona: Edicions 62, 1976.

———. *Introducció a la narrativa de Mercè Rodoreda: El mite de la infantesa.* Barcelona: Edicions 62, 1979.

———. "La obra de Mercè Rodoreda." *Cuadernos Hispanoamericanos* 383 (May 1982): 239–57.

Barthes, Roland. *The Pleasure of the Text.* 1973. Translated by Richard Miller. New York: Farrar, Straus & Giroux, 1975.

Beauvoir, Simone de. *The Second Sex,* 1949. Translated and edited by H. M. Parshley. New York: Vintage, 1989.

Benjamin, Janet. *The Bonds of Love: Psychoanalysis, Feminism, and the Problem of Domination.* New York: Pantheon, 1988.

Bernheimer, Charles, and Claire Kahane, eds. *In Dora's Case: Freud-Hysteria-Feminism.* New York: Columbia Univ. Press, 1985.

Best, Steven, and Douglas Kellner. *Postmodern Theory: Critical Interrogations.* New York: Guilford, 1991.

Bloom, Harold. *The Anxiety of Influence.* New York: Oxford Univ. Press, 1973.

Bosveuil, Simone. "Proust y la novela española de los años 30: Ensayo de interpretación." In Villanueva, *La novela lírica,* 121–35.

Works Cited

Brihuega, Jaime. *Las vanguardias artísticas en España, 1909–1936*. Madrid: Ediciones Istmo, 1981.

Brooks, Peter. *Body Work: Objects of Desire in Modern Narrative*. Cambridge: Harvard Univ. Press, 1993.

Brown, Gerald G. *Historia de la literatura española: El siglo XX*. Translated by Carlos Pujol. Barcelona: Ariel, 1985.

Brown, Joan L. *Secrets from the Back Room: The Fiction of Carmen Martín Gaite*. University, Mo.: Romance Monographs, 1987.

Busquets, Loreto. "The Unconscious in the Novels of Mercè Rodoreda." *Catalan Review* 2, no. 2 (1987): 101–17.

Cano, José Luis. *La poesía de la generación del 27*. Madrid: Guadarrama, 1973.

Cano Ballesta, Juan. *Literatura y technología (las letras españolas ante la revolución industrial: 1900–1933)*. Madrid: Orígenes, 1981.

Castellanos, Rosario. *Mujer que sabe latín . . .* Mexico City: Secretaría de Educación Pública, 1973.

Cela, Camilo José. *La familia de Pascual Duarte*. 1942. Reprint. Madrid: Destino, 1990.

Chacel, Rosa. *Estación. Ida y vuelta*. Madrid: Ediciones Ulises, 1930.

——. *Teresa*. Buenos Aires: Nuevo Romance, 1941; Barcelona: Bruguera, 1983.

——. *Memorias de Leticia Valle*. Buenos Aires: Emecé, 1945; Barcelona: Lumen, 1985.

——. *La sinrazón*. Buenos Aires: Losada, 1960; Andorra la Vella: Andorra, 1970.

——. *La confesión*. Barcelona: Edhasa, 1971.

——. *Barrio de Maravillas*. Barcelona: Seix Barral, 1976.

——. *Alcancía (Ida)*. Barcelona: Seix Barral, 1982.

——. "Conversación con Rosa Chacel." Interview by Kathleen Glenn. *Letras Peninsulares* 3, no. 1 (1990): 11–26.

Charnon-Deutsch, Lou. *Gender and Representation: Women in Spanish Realist Fiction*. Amsterdam: J. Benjamins, 1990.

Chiampi, Irlemar. *O realismo maravilhoso: Forma e ideologia no romance hispano-americano*. São Paulo: Editora Perspectiva, 1980.

Chodorow, Nancy. *The Reproduction of Mothering: Psychoanalysis and the Sociology of Gender*. Berkeley and Los Angeles: Univ. of California Press, 1978.

Ciplijauskaité, Biruté. "Intertextualidad y subversión en *El silencio de las sirenas* de Adelaida García Morales." *Revista Hispánica Moderna* 41, no. 2 (1988): 167–74.

——. *La novela femenina contemporánea (1970–1985); Hacia una tipología de la narración en primera persona*. Barcelona: Anthropos, 1988.

Cook, Teresa A. *El feminismo en la novela de la condesa de Pardo Bazán*. La Coruña, Spain: Diputación Principal, 1976.

Debord, Guy. *Society of the Spectacle*. Detroit: Black & Red, 1983. Unpaginated.

Deleuze, Gilles. *The Deleuze Reader*. Edited by Constantin V. Boundas. New York: Columbia Univ. Press, 1993.

Works Cited

Deleuze, Gilles, and Félix Guattari. *Anti-Oedipus: Capitalism and Schizophrenia.* 1972. Translated by Robert Hurley, Mark Seem, and Helen R. Lane. Minneapolis: Univ. of Minnesota Press, 1983.

Diego, Estrella de. "Prototipos y antiprototipos de comportamiento femenino a través de las escritoras españolas del último tercio del siglo XIX." In Durán and Rey, *Literatura y vida cotidiana,* 233–50.

Durán, María Angeles, and José Antonio Rey, eds. *Literatura y vida cotidiana: Actas de las cuartas jornadas de investigación interdisciplinaria, Seminario de estudios de la mujer, Universidad Autónoma de Madrid.* Zaragoza: Universidad de Zaragoza; Madrid: Universidad Autónoma de Madrid, 1987.

Eagleton, Terry. *The Body as Language: Outline of a "New Left" Theology.* London: Sheed & Ward, 1970.

Ehrenreich, Barbara. *The Hearts of Men: American Dreams and the Flight from Commitment.* New York: Doubleday, Anchor Books, 1983.

Erikson, Erik. *Identity: Youth and Crisis.* New York: Norton, 1968.

"Espronceda, José de." *Enciclopedia universal ilustrada europeo-americana.* Barcelona: Hijos de J. Espasa, 1924.

Faludi, Susan. *Backlash: The Undeclared War against American Women.* New York: Crown, 1991.

Fernández Cifuentes, Luis. *Teoría y mercado de la novela en España: Del 98 a la República.* Madrid: Gredos, 1982.

———. "Unamuno y Ortega: Leer una novela / Hacer una novela." In *Essays on Hispanic Literature in Honor of Edmund L. King,* edited by Sylvia Molloy and L. F. Cifuentes, 45–59. London: Tamesis, 1983.

———. *García Lorca en el teatro: La norma y la diferencia.* Zaragoza: Prensas Universitarias de Zaragoza, 1986.

Foucault, Michel. *The Foucault Reader.* Translated and edited by Paul Rabinow. New York: Pantheon, 1984.

———. *The History of Sexuality.* Vol. 1, *An Introduction.* 1976. Translated by Robert Hurley. New York: Vintage, 1990.

Freud, Sigmund. *Dora: An Analysis of a Case of Hysteria.* 1905. Edited by Philip Rieff. New York: Collier, 1963.

Fuentes, Victor. "La narrativa española de vanguardia (1923–1931): Un ensayo de interpretación." In Villanueva, *La novela lírica,* 155–66.

Gallagher, Catherine, and Thomas Laqueur, eds. *The Making of the Modern Body: Sexuality and Society in the North Century.* Berkeley and Los Angeles: Univ. of California Press, 1987.

Gallop, Jane. *Thinking through the Body.* New York: Columbia Univ. Press, 1988.

García Márquez, Gabriel. "Recuerdo de una mujer invisible: Mercè Rodoreda." *Clarín, Cultura y Nación,* June 30, 1983.

García Morales, Adelaida. *El silencio de las sirenas.* Barcelona: Anagrama, 1985.

Gil Casado, Pablo. "El experimento narrativo de Rosa Chacel." *Nuevo Hispanismo* 2 (spring 1982): 163–71.

Works Cited

Gil de Biedma, Jaime. Prologue to *El diablo mundo, El estudiante de Salamanca, Poesías,* by José de Espronceda. Madrid: Alianza, 1966.

Gil-Albert, Juan. "In promptu." In Revenga, *Rosa Chacel,* 26.

Gilbert, Susan, and Sandra Gubar. *The Madwoman in the Attic: The Woman Writer and the Nineteenth-Century Literary Imagination.* New Haven: Yale Univ. Press, 1979.

Giles, Mary E. "Feminism and the Feminine in Emilia Pardo Bazán's Novels." *Hispania* 63, no. 2 (1980): 357–67.

Gilligan, Carol. *In a Different Voice: Psychological Theory and Women's Development.* Cambridge: Harvard Univ. Press, 1982.

Gilman, Stephen. *Galdós and the Art of the European Novel: 1867–1887.* Princeton: Princeton Univ. Press, 1981.

González-Arias, Francisca. "A Voice, Not an Echo: Emilia Pardo Bazán and the Novel in Spain and France." Ph. D. diss., Harvard University, 1985.

Gordon, Mary. Interview by Susannah Hunnewell. *New York Times Book Review,* Aug. 8, 1993, 25.

Gossy, Mary. *The Untold Story: Women and Theory in Golden Age Texts.* Ann Arbor: Univ. of Michigan Press, 1989.

Goytisolo, Juan. "Quevedo: la obsesión excremental." In *Desidencias,* 117–36. Barcelona: Seix Barral, 1977.

Grosz, Elizabeth. *Sexual Subversions: Three French Feminists.* Sydney: Allen & Unwin, 1989.

Guemárez, Diana. "Juan Ramón Jiménez y el grupo de escritores de 1927: Historia de una polémica." Dissertation in progress, Harvard University.

Gullón, Germán. "Contexto ideológico y forma narrativa en *La familia de Pascual Duarte.*" *Hispania* 68, no. 1 (1985): 1–8.

Hart, Patricia. *Magic in the Fiction of Isabel Allende.* Madison, N.J.: Fairleigh Dickinson Univ. Press, 1989.

Hemingway, Maurice. *Emilia Pardo Bazán: The Making of a Novelist.* Cambridge: Cambridge Univ. Press, 1983.

Herrero, Javier. *Fernán Caballero: Un nuevo planteamiento.* Madrid: Gredos, 1963.

Hilton, Ronald. "Pardo-Bazán and Literary Polemics about Feminism." *Romantic Review* 44 (1953): 40–46.

Ilie, Paul. *La novelística de Camilo José Cela.* Madrid: Gredos, 1963.

Irigaray, Luce. *Speculum: De l'autre femme.* Paris: Minuit, 1974.

——. *Ce sexe qui n'en est pas un.* Paris: Minuit, 1977.

——. *Sexes et parentés.* Paris: Minuit, 1987.

Jameson, Fredric. *Postmodernism, or the Cultural Logic of Late Capitalism.* Durham, N.C.: Duke Univ. Press, 1992.

Jerez-Farrán, Carlos. "Pascual Duarte y la susceptibilidad viril." *Hispanófila* 32, no. 2 (1989): 47–63.

Jiménez, Juan Ramón. *Españoles de tres mundos: Viejo Mundo, Nuevo Mundo, Otro Mundo.* Edited by Ricardo Gullón. Madrid: Afrodisio Aguado, 1960.

Johnson, Roberta. "*Estación. Ida y vuelta:* Un nuevo tiempo en la novela." In

Works Cited

Prosa hispánica de vanguardia, edited by Fernando Burgos, 201–8. Madrid: Orígenes, 1986.

Jordan, Barry. *Writing and Politics in Franco's Spain.* London: Routledge, 1990.

Joyce, James. *A Portrait of the Artist as a Young Man.* 1915. Rev. ed. Edited by Richard Ellman. New York: Viking, 1972.

Kirkpatrick, Susan. "Gómez de Avellaneda's *Sab:* Gendering the Liberal Romantic Subject." In Valis and Maier, *In the Feminine Mode,* 115–30.

Kristeva, Julia. "Motherhood according to Giovanni Bellini." In *Desire in Language: A Semiotic Approach to Literature and Art,* edited by Leon S. Roudiez, translated by Thomas Gora, Alice Jardine, and Leon S. Roudiez, 237–70. New York: Columbia Univ. Press, 1980.

———. *Histoires d'amour.* Paris: Denoël, 1983.

Kronik, John W. "A Splice of Life: Carmen Martín Gaite's *Entre visillos.*" In *From Fiction to Metafiction: Essays in Honor of Carmen Martín Gaite,* edited by Mirella Servodidio and Marcia K. Welles, 49–60. Lincoln, Nebr.: Society of Spanish and Spanish-American Studies, 1983.

———. "Of Nations, Generations, and Canon Formations." Paper presented at the annual meeting of the Modern Language Association, Washington, D.C., 29 Dec. 1989.

Labanyi, Jo. *Myth and History in the Contemporary Spanish Novel.* Cambridge: Cambridge Univ. Press, 1989.

Livingstone, Leon. "Ambivalence and Ambiguity in *La familia de Pascual Duarte.*" In *Studies in Honor of José Rubia Barcia,* edited by Roberta Johnson and Paul Clarence Smith, 95–108. Lincoln, Nebr.: Society of Spanish and Spanish-American Studies, 1982.

Llamazares, Julio. *Luna de lobos.* Barcelona: Seix Barral, 1985.

López-Sanz, Mariano. *Naturalismo y espiritualismo en Galdós y Pardo-Bazán.* Madrid: Pliegos, 1985.

Mainer, José Carlos. Prologue to *Tiempo de destrucción,* by Luis Martín-Santos, 1–27. Barcelona: Seix Barral, 1975.

Mangini, Shirley. "Women and Spanish Modernism: The Case of Rosa Chacel." *Anales de la Literatura Española Contemporánea* 12, nos. 1–2 (1987): 17–28.

———. Introduction to *Estación. Ida y vuelta,* by Rosa Chacel, edited by Shirley Mangini, 11–65. Madrid: Cátedra, 1989.

Marías, Julián. "Azar, destino, y carácter de Rosa Chacel." Prologue to *La sinrazón,* by Rosa Chacel, 1–15. Buenos Aires: Losada, 1960; Andorra la Vella: Andorra, 1970.

Martí-Olivella, Jaume. "Foreword." *Catalan Review* 2, no. 2 (1987): 9–15.

———. "The Witches' Touch: Towards a Poetics of Double Articulation in Rodoreda." *Catalan Review* 2, no. 2 (1987): 159–69.

———. "Homoeroticism and Specular Transgression in Peninsular Feminine Narrative." *España Contemporánea* 5, no. 2 (1992): 17–26.

Martín Gaite, Carmen. *Entre visillos.* 1958. Reprint, Madrid: Destinolibro, 1989.

Works Cited

———. *Desde la ventana: Enfoque femenino de la literatura española.* Madrid: Espasa-Calpe, 1987.

———. *Usos amorosos de la postguerra española.* Barcelona: Anagrama, 1987.

Martín-Santos, Luis. *Tiempo de silencio.* Barcelona: Seix Barral, 1962.

McNerny, Kathleen. "A Feminist Literary Renaissance in Catalonia." In *Feminine Concerns in Contemporary Spanish Fiction by Women,* edited by Carolyn Galerstein, Roberto C. Manteiga, and Kathleen McNerny, 124–33. Potomac, Md.: Scripta Humanistica, 1988.

McNerny, Kathleen, and Nancy Vosburg, eds. *The Garden across the Border: Mercè Rodoreda's Fiction.* Cranbury, N.J.: Susquehannah Univ. Press, 1994.

Michie, Helena. *The Flesh Made Word: Female Figures and Women's Bodies.* New York: Oxford Univ. Press, 1987.

Miller, D. A. "Sensation and Gender in *The Woman in White.*" Gallagher and Laqueur, *Making of the Modern Body,* 107–36.

Montes-Huidobro, Matías. "Dinámica de la correlación existencial en *La familia de Pascual Duarte.*" *Revista de Estudios Hispánicos* 16, no. 2 (1982): 213–22.

Morán, Fernando. *Novela y semidesarrollo: Una interpretación de la novela hispanoamericana y española.* Madrid: Taurus, 1971.

Myers, Eunice. "*Estación, ida y vuelta:* Rosa Chacel's Apprenticeship Novel." *Hispanic Journal* 4, no. 2 (1983): 77–84.

Muñoz Molina, Antonio. *Beltenebros.* Barcelona: Seix Barral, 1989.

Navajas, Gonzalo. "Una estética para después del posmodernismo: La nostalgia asertiva y la reciente novela española." *Revista de Estudios Hispánicos* 25, no. 3 (1991): 129–51.

Nichols, Geraldine C. *Des/cifrar la diferencia: Narrativa femenina de la España contemporánea.* Madrid: Siglo Veintiuno, 1992.

Nietzsche, Friedrich. *The Joyful Wisdom.* 1882. Translated by Thomas Common. New York: Frederick Ungar, 1960.

Ordóñez, Elizabeth J. "Inscribing Difference: 'L'Écriture Féminine' and New Narrative by Women." *Anales de la literatura española contemporánea* 12, nos. 1–2 (1987): 45–58.

———. *Voices of Their Own: Contemporary Spanish Narrative by Women.* Lewisburg, Pa.: Bucknell Univ. Press; London: Associated Univ. Presses, 1991.

Ortega, José. "Mujer, guerra, y neurosis en dos novelas de M. Rodoreda (*La plaza del Diamante y La calle de las Camelias*)." In *Novelistas femeninas de la postguerra española,* edited by Janet W. Pérez, 71–83. Madrid: Porrúa Turanzas; Potomac, Md.: Studia Humanitatis, 1983.

Ortega y Gasset, José. *El tema de nuestro tiempo.* 1923. In *Obras completas,* 3:143–206. Madrid: Revista de Occidente, 1957.

———. "Vitalidad, alma, espíritu." 1924. In *Obras completas,* 2:443–71. Madrid: Revista de Occidente, 1947.

———. *La deshumanización del arte e Ideas sobre la novela.* 1925. In *Obras completas,* 3:353–420, 1957.

Works Cited

——. *Dinámica del tiempo*. 1927. In *Obras completas*, 3:459–80, 1957.

Osborne, Robert E. *Emilia Pardo Bazán y sus obras*. Mexico City: De Andrea, 1964.

Pardo Bazán, Emilia. *Insolación*. 1889. Reprint, Madrid: Taurus, 1980.

Pattison, Walter. *Emilia Pardo Bazán*. New York: Twayne, 1971.

Pérez, Janet W. *Contemporary Women Writers of Spain*. Boston: Twayne, 1988.

——. "Vanguardism, Modernism, and Spanish Women Writers in the Years between the Wars." *Siglo XX/20th Century* 6, nos. 1–2 (1988–89): 40–43.

——. "Plant Imagery, Subversion, and Feminine Dependency: Josefina Aldecoa, Carmen Martín Gaite, and Maria Antònia Oliver." In Valis and Maier, *In the Feminine Mode*, 78–100.

Pérez Firmat, Gustavo, *Idle Fictions: The Hispanic Vanguard Novel, 1926–1934*. Durham, N.C.: Duke Univ. Press, 1982.

Pérez Galdós, Benito. *Tristana*. 1892. Reprint, Madrid: Alianza, 1992.

Persino, María Silvina. "*Si te dicen que caí*: Una lectura de los cuerpos." *Revista de Estudios Hispánicos* 25, no. 3 (1991): 57–71.

Poch, Joaquim. *Dona i psicoanàlisi a l'obra de Mercè Rodoreda (un estudi del narcisisme femení)*. Barcelona: Publicacions Universitàries, 1987.

Poggioli, Renato. *The Theory of the Avant-Garde*. Translated by Gerald Fitzgerald. Cambridge: Harvard Univ. Press, Belknap Press, 1968.

Pope, Randolph. "Mercè Rodoreda's Subtle Greatness." In *Women Writers of Contemporary Spain: Exiles in the Homeland*, edited by Joan L. Brown, 116–35. Newark: Univ. of Delaware Press; London: Associated Univ. Presses, 1991.

——. "Postmodernismo en España: El caso de Antonio Muñoz Molina." *España Contemporánea* 5, no. 2 (1992): 111–20.

Powell, Charles. "La transición política hacia un régimen democrático." In *España hoy*, edited by Antonio Ramos Gascón, 2 vols., 1:71–107. Madrid: Cátedra, 1991.

Puértolas, Soledad. Interview by Lynn K. Talbot. *Hispania* 71, no. 4 (1988): 882–83.

——. *Queda la noche*. Barcelona: Planeta, 1989.

Radway, Janice A. *Reading the Romance: Women, Patriarchy, and Popular Literature*. Chapel Hill: Univ. of North Carolina Press, 1984.

Read, Malcolm K. *Visions in Exile: The Body in Spanish Literature and Linguistics, 1500–1800*. Amsterdam: J. Benjamins, 1990.

Resina, Joan Ramon. "The Link in Consciousness: Time and Community in Rodoreda's *La Plaça del Diamant*." *Catalan Review* 2, no. 2 (1987): 225–46.

Revenga, Luis, ed. *Rosa Chacel: Premio Nacional de las Letras Españolas (1987)*. Madrid: Ministerio de Cultura, 1988.

Rey, Alfonso. *Construcción y sentido de "Tiempo de silencio."* Madrid: Porrúa Turanzas, 1977.

Ríos-Font, Wadda. "'*Horrenda Adoración*': The 'Feminism' of Felipe Trigo." *Hispania* 76, no. 2 (1993): 224–34.

Rodoreda, Mercè. *La Plaza del Diamante.* Translated by Enrique Sordo. 1965. Barcelona: Edhasa, 1982. Originally published as *La Plaça del Diamant* (Barcelona: Club dels Novel·listes, 1962).

———. *La calle de las Camelias.* Translated by José Batlló. Barcelona: Edhasa, 1982. Originally published as *El carrer de les Camèlies* (Barcelona: Club dels Novel·listes, 1966).

———. *Jardín junto al mar.* Translated by J. F. Vidal Jové. Barcelona: Planeta, 1975. Originally published as *Jardí vora el mar* (Barcelona: Club dels Novel·listes, 1967).

———. *Espejo roto.* Translated by Pere Gimferrer. Barcelona: Seix Barral, 1986. Originally published as *Mirall trencat* (Barcelona: Club dels Novel·listes, 1974).

———. *Cuánta, cuánta guerra.* Translated by Ana María Moix. Barcelona: Edhasa, 1982. Originally published as *Quanta, quanta guerra* (Barcelona: Club dels Novel·listes, 1980).

———. *La muerte y la primavera.* Translated by Enrique Sordo. Barcelona: Seix Barral, 1986. Originally published as *La Mort i la Primavera* (Barcelona: Club dels Novel·listes, 1986.

Rodríguez, Alfred, and Saúl Roll. "*Pepita Jiménez* y la creatividad de Pardo Bazán en *Insolación*." *Revista Hispánica Moderna* 44, no. 1 (1991): 29–34.

Rodríguez Fischer, Ana. "El tiempo abarcado." In Revenga, *Rosa Chacel*, 9–24.

———. "Tras la senda de Ortega y Gasset." In Revenga, *Rosa Chacel*, 49–56.

Romero, Isabel, Isabel Alberdi, Isabel Martínez, and Ruth Zauner. "Feminismo y literatura: La narrativa de los años 70." In Durán and Rey, *Literatura y vida cotidiana*, 337–58.

Rubio, Fanny. "A la busca de un cuerpo (femenino) perdido (esbozo)." In Durán and Rey, *Literatura y vida cotidiana*, 67–90.

Ruiz-Malo Soria, Manuela. "Reencuentro con una novela de Rosa Chacel: *Estación, ida y vuelta*." *Nueva Estafeta* 17 (Apr. 1980): 67–71.

Salcedo, José Manuel, ed. *La Codorniz: Antología, 1941–1944.* Madrid: Arnao, 1987.

Salinas, Pedro. *Víspera del gozo.* 1926. Madrid: Alianza, 1974.

———. "Defensa de la carta misiva y de la correspondencia epistolar." *El Defensor*, 19–114. 1954. Reprint, with a foreword by Juan Marichal, Madrid: Alianza, 1986.

Santiáñez-Tió, Nil. "Una marquesita 'sandunguera,' o el mito del naturalismo en *Insolación*." *Revista de Estudios Hispánicos* 23, no. 2 (1989): 119–34.

Scanlon, Geraldine. *La polémica feminista en la España contemporánea (1868–1974).* Translated by Rafael Mazarrasa. Mexico City: Siglo Veintiuno, 1976.

Scari, Robert M. "La sátira y otros efectos humorísticos en *Insolación*." *Duquesne Hispanic Review* 11, no. 1 (1972): 1–14.

Scarlett, Elizabeth. "*Vinculada a les flors:* Flowers and the Body in *Jardí vora el mar* and *Mirall trencat*." In McNerny and Vosburg, *The Garden across the Border*. Cranbury, N.J., Susquehannah Univ. Press, in press.

Works Cited

Scarry, Elaine, ed. *Literature and the Body: Essays on Populations and Persons.* Baltimore: Johns Hopkins Univ. Press, 1988.

Schraibman, Joseph. "*Tiempo de silencio* y la cura psiquiátrica de un pueblo: España." *Insula* 32, no. 365 (1977): 3.

Segura i Soriano, Isabel. "La literatura de mujeres como fuente de documentación para la recuperación de la experiencia histórica de las mujeres (la literatura escrita en catalán)." In Durán and Rey, *Literatura y vida cotidiana,* 251–60.

Shaw, Donald L. *Historia de la literatura española: El siglo XIX.* 1973. Translated by Helena Casamiglia. Rev. ed. Barcelona: Ariel, 1983.

Sieburth, Stephanie. "Interpreting *La Regenta:* Coherence vs. Entropy." *Modern Language Notes* 102, no. 2 (1987): 274–91.

Smith, Paul Julian. *The Body Hispanic: Gender and Sexuality in Spanish and Spanish American Literature.* Oxford: Clarendon, 1989.

Sobejano, Gonzalo. Introduction to *La Regenta,* by Leopoldo Alas, 9–52. 1884. Edited by Gonzalo Sobejano. Barcelona: Noguer, 1976.

Soria Olmedo, Andrés. "Fervor y sabiduría: La obra narrativa de Antonio Muñoz Molina." *Cuadernos Hispanoamericanos* 458 (Aug. 1988): 107–11.

Spacks, Patricia Meyer. *The Female Imagination.* New York: Alfred A. Knopf, 1975.

Spires, Robert C. *Transparent Simulacra: Spanish Fiction from 1902–1926.* Columbia: Univ. of Missouri Press, 1988.

Suleiman, Susan Rubin. "Writing and Motherhood." In *The (M)other Tongue: Essays in Feminist Psychoanalytic Interpretation,* edited by Shirley Nelson Garner, Claire Kahane, and Madelon Sprengnether, 353–77. Ithaca: Cornell Univ. Press, 1984.

———. *Subversive Intent: Gender, Politics, and the Avant-garde.* Cambridge: Harvard Univ. Press, 1990.

Tanner, Tony. *Adultery in the Novel: Contract and Transgression.* Baltimore: Johns Hopkins Univ. Press, 1979.

Teresa de Jesús. *Libro de su vida.* 1562. Edited by Dámaso Chicharro. Madrid: Cátedra, 1982.

Todorov, Tzvetan. *The Fantastic: A Structural Approach to a Literary Genre.* 1970. Translated by Richard Howard. Cleveland: Press of Case Western Reserve Univ., 1973.

Tolliver, Joyce. "Knowledge, Desire, and Syntactic Empathy in Pardo Bazán's *La novia fiel.*" *Hispania* 72, no. 4 (1989): 909–18.

———. "Narrative Accountability and Ambivalence: Feminine Desire in *Insolación.*" *Revista de Estudios Hispánicos* 23, no. 2 (1989): 103–18.

Tsuchiya, Akiko. "Language, Desire, and the Feminine Riddle in Soledad Puértolas's 'La indiferencia de Eva.'" *Revista de Estudios Hispánicos* 25, no. 1 (1991): 69–80.

Valis, Noël, and Carol Maier, eds. *In the Feminine Mode: Essays on Hispanic Women Writers.* Lewisburg, Pa.: Bucknell Univ. Press; London: Associated Univ. Presses, 1990.

Works Cited

Villanueva, Darío, ed. *La novela lírica*. Vol. 2. Madrid: Taurus, 1983.

Villena, Luis Antonio de. "*Memorias de Leticia Valle:* La seducción inversa." In Revenga, *Rosa Chacel*, 41–44.

Weber, Alison. *Teresa of Avila and the Rhetoric of Femininity*. Princeton: Princeton Univ. Press, 1990.

Wohl, Robert. *The Generation of 1914*. Cambridge: Harvard Univ. Press, 1979.

Zola, Émile. *L'Assommoir*. 1877. Reprint, Paris: Presse Pocket, 1978.

Index

Index

Index

Femininity, 17, 77, 89, 101, 147–48, 190–92; disgust with, 50–51, 72, 80; as cultural dominant, 62–63; commodification of, 172; *see also* Mystification; Remythification

Fernández Cifuentes, Luis, 56

Fernández Santos, Jesús: *Los bravos*, 149

Fetishization, 50–51, 131–32, 191; by male writers, 8, 17; "commodity fetishism," 27, 35; ironic, 64–66

Fitzgerald, F. Scott, 175

Floral imagery, 121, 123, 188

Foucault, Michel, 1, 37, 39; strategies of sexualization, 8–9, 44; on confession, 13, 144

Fragmentation, 8, 170–72, 176–79

Franco, Francisco, 140, 154

Francoism, 108, 141, 158, 164, 168, 206 n. 83

French feminism, 12, 17, 61

Freud, Sigmund, 59, 61, 78, 85–86, 137, 177; *Dora*, 50, 79, 90–91, 155; *see also* Freudianism; Oedipus complex; Psychoanalysis

Freudianism, 17, 49, 84, 106, 112, 167; *see also* Freud, Oedipus complex; Psychoanalysis

Fromm, Erich: *Escape from Freedom*, 158

Frye, Northrop, 116

Fuentes, Victor, 63–64

Galdiano, José Lázaro, 19, 42

Gallop, Jane, 45

García Lorca, Federico, 128–29

García Márquez, Gabriel, 70, 124; *Cien años de soledad*, 138

García Morales, Adelaida, 6, 170, 193; *El silencio de las sirenas*, 7, 171–72, 175–79, 185

Gender, 50–51, 54, 56, 86; male pseudonyms, 10, 101; gender-crossing, 58–60; *see also* Anxiety of (female) authorship; Body; Femininity; Feminism; Masculinity; Maternity; Sexuality

Generación del '27, 47, 54

Gil-Albert, Juan, 48

Gil-Casado, Pablo, 53

Gilbert, Sandra, 11–12, 17–18

Gilligan, Carol, 86

Gilman, Stephen, 34, 42–43

Goethe, Wolfgang von, 175–76

Gómez de Avellaneda, Gertrudis, 18

Gómez de la Serna, Julio, 52–53

Gómez de la Serna, Ramón, 49, 52, 54

González-Arias, Francisca, 39

Gordon, Mary, 3

Gossy, Mary, 4

Goya y Lucientes, Francisco de, 157

Goytisolo, Juan: *Señas de identidad*, 77, 81, 92

Grignan, Madame de, 104

Guattari, Félix, 7, 167, 170–71, 177, 186

Gubar, Susan, 11–12, 17–18

Gullón, Germán, 145

Heat imagery, 43, 188; as code for desire, 12, 23–24, 137–38; as lure for male, 158–60, 163

Hemingway, Maurice, 13–15

Herrero, Javier, 10

Hitchcock, Alfred, 171

Homoeroticism, 145–46, 170, 176, 180–81, 190, 193; in adolescence, 75, 87, 89–91

Homosexuality, 63

Humor, 11, 15–16, 18, 21–22

Hysteria, 44, 90

Ilie, Paul, 141–42

Incest, 23–24, 38, 135, 138, 159

Ingenuísmo, 101

Interior monologue, 53–54, 60

Intoxication, 27, 82, 153, 160, 171, 193

Irigaray, Luce, 9, 32, 45, 188, 199 n. 28

Jackson, Michael, 169

Jameson, Fredric, 167, 169, 173; *see also* Consciousness Industry

Janés, Clara, 47

Jarnés, Benjamín, 49, 63–64, 69–70

Jerez-Farrán, Carlos, 143, 145

Jewel imagery, 129–30, 188

Jiménez, Juan Ramón, 48, 55, 154

Joyce, James: *Portrait of the Artist as a Young Man*, 50, 78–79, 86–88

Jung, C. G., 62

Kelly, Gene, 169

Kristeva, Julia, 32, 39–40, 105, 118, 188–89

Labanyi, Jo, 5, 157–58

Lacan, Jacques, 12, 24, 41, 171

Index

Index

Feminist Issues: Practice, Politics, Theory
Alison Booth and Ann Lane, Editors

Carol Siegel
*Lawrence among the Women: Wavering Boundaries
in Women's Literary Traditions*

Harriet Blodgett, ed.
*Capacious Hold-All: An Anthology of
Englishwomen's Diary Writings*

Joy Wiltenburg
*Disorderly Women and Female Power in the Street
Literature of Early Modern England and Germany*

Diane P. Freedman
*An Alchemy of Genres: Cross-Genre Writing
by American Feminist Poet-Critics*

Jean O'Barr and Mary Wyer, eds.
Engaging Feminism: Students Speak Up and Speak Out

Kari Weil
Androgyny and the Denial of Difference

Anne Firor Scott, ed.
Unheard Voices: The First Historians of Southern Women